England's Debt to India

England's Debt to India

A Historical Narrative of Britain's Fiscal Policy in India

By

LAJPAT RAI

GYAN

Published by

GYAN

Gyan Publishing House
5, Ansari Road
Daryaganj, New Delhi-110002
Phone: 011-47034999, 9811692060
E-mail: books@gyanbooks.com

Distribution Network
gyanbooks.com
India, USA, Canada, UK, Australia, France

ISBN: 978-81-212-7997-0 (PB)
First Published, 1917

2nd Impression 2023

Printed at: Gyan Press, Delhi.

ENGLAND'S DEBT TO INDIA
Author: LAJPAT RAI

ENGLAND'S DEBT TO INDIA

ENGLAND'S DEBT TO INDIA

A Historical Narrative of Britain's Fiscal Policy in India

By

LAJPAT RAI

Author of "Young India."

" The toad beneath the harrow knows
Exactly where each tooth-point goes.
The butterfly upon the road
Preaches contentment to the toad."

NEW YORK

B. W. HUEBSCH

1917

AS A MARK OF THE AUTHOR'S DEEP RESPECT

AND

INDIA'S GRATITUDE,
THIS BOOK IS DEDICATED

TO

THOSE BRAVE, HIGHMINDED, AND HONEST ENGLISHMEN AND ENGLISHWOMEN WHO HAVE NOT HESITATED TO SPEAK THE TRUTH ABOUT THE EFFECTS OF BRITISH RULE IN INDIA THOUGH BY DOING SO THEY EARNED THE DISLIKE OF THEIR COUNTRYMEN,

AND

ON WHOSE TESTIMONY, PRINCIPALLY, THIS BOOK IS BASED.

LAJPAT RAI.

"India will not remain, and ought not to remain content to be a hewer of wood and a drawer of water for the rest of the Empire."

—J. Austen Chamberlain,

Secretary of State for India, in the *London Times,* March 30, 1917.

PREFACE

THIS book is a kind of companion volume to my other book, "Young India." In "Young India," I have discussed British rule in India, from the political standpoint. In this volume, I have discussed its economic effects. There is not a single statement in this volume which is not supported by the best available British testimony, official and non-official. My own opinions and personal knowledge have been mentioned only incidentally if at all. Similarly the opinions of other Indian publicists have been kept in the background. It is a sad commentary on the prevailing moral code of the world that those who succeed in imposing their rule upon less powerful nations should also brand the latter as unworthy of credit. Thus every Britisher believes that an Indian critic of British rule is necessarily affected by the "inevitable racial and political bias" of his position, while he in his turn is entirely free from it!

In the ordinary course of nature, the man whom the shoe pinches is the best person to know about it but in politics the laws of nature are reversed. In judging of governments and rulers, it is they whose word is to be accepted and not that of the governed and the ruled.

Consequently to avoid that charge I have chosen to speak from the mouths of the English themselves.

Looked at from that point of view the volume lays no claim to originality. It is more or less a compilation from British publications, government and private. The case for India has before this been most eloquently put forth by Mr. Digby in his monumental work ironically called "Prosperous British India." Particular phases have been dealt with by Messrs. Hyndman, Wilson and others from whom I have profusely quoted. My own countrymen, Messrs. R. C. Dutt and Naoroji, have done valuable work in this line. The works of the former,—"Early History of British Rule," "India in the Victorian Age," "Famines in India," and "England and India," published by Messrs. Kegan Paul, Trench, Trübner and Co., of London, are monuments of his industry, research and moderation. Mr. Naoroji's "Poverty of India" is a collection of the economic writings of that veteran Indian nationalist during half a century of his active political life. These works of Messrs. Digby, Dutt and Naoroji must for a long time continue to be the classics of Indian economics and no student of the latter can afford to neglect them. My obligations to them are unlimited.

I have made free use of the books of Messrs. Digby and Dutt, though I have refrained from quoting Mr. Dutt's own language. At one time I thought of taking up the subject, from where they had left it in 1901; but in developing my ideas I decided that a change of arrangement also was needed to bring the matter within the grasp of the lay reader. Mr. Dutt has arranged his books chronologically, dealing with the same matter in several chapters, scattered all over the two volumes of his "Economic History of British Rule." I have tried to include everything relating to one subject in one place, thus avoiding repetitions otherwise unavoidable. For example, I have given a complete history of the cotton industry from the earliest times to date in one chapter and so also with shipping and shipbuilding. Similarly everything relating to drain has been included in one chapter and so on. The book is thus, in my judgment, an improvement on those referred to above. It brings the whole subject up to date and makes it easily understandable by the ordinary lay reader. I would like to have added chapters dealing with finance and currency, famine insurance, banking, railway rates, etc., but the size which I fixed for this volume having already been exceeded, I must reserve these subjects for another volume, if needed.

There is talk of great adjustments being made in the British Empire, after the war. India also is on the tiptoe of expectations. The Jingo Imperialists in England and India are already making proposals which if accepted, are sure to cause further economic loss to India. Some want India to take over a part of the British war debt; others are looking with jealous eyes at India's "hoarded wealth"—the existence of which is known only to them. What will happen no one can foretell; but one of the reasons which have impelled the writer to publish this volume at this juncture is to remind the Anglo-Saxon public how India has so far fared economically under British rule. Any fresh burden might tend to break the proverbial camel's back. We know that the English will do what they please; yet we have dared to say: perchance it may fall on fruitful ground. The book is not written in a spirit of hostility to British rule. It is not my object to irritate or to excite. What I aim at is to give matter for thought and reflection and to supply a reason for the exercise of restraint in the determination of the fiscal policy which British statesmen may decide to follow towards India after the war. Great Britain has suffered huge losses in the war. As soon as war is ended, there will be a cry to make them up. No other part of the Empire offers such a field as India. She has the largest area and the largest population. She has no voice in her government and is helpless to make herself heard. She can neither check nor retaliate. What can be easier than to make her pay for the war? What this is likely to mean to India may be gathered from this volume. What feeling it will create in India may be imagined. The world is anxious to know how Great Britain is going to reward India's loyalty and devotion. If the decision rests with men of the type of Lord Sydenham it is already given. He recommends the immediate and final rejection of all the demands made by India for post-war reforms as embodied in the memorandum of the elected members of the Viceroy's council. These demands are extremely moderate. They fall far short of even home rule. Their rejection will be very distressing to India. We hope that wiser counsels will prevail and the statesmanship of England will prove that India did not pin her faith to British justice in vain. India has stood by England magnificently and some of the nationalist leaders have had a hard time in resisting the advances made by the enemies of Great Britain. Let us hope that they were not labouring under vain illusions and that Great Britain was sincere when she professed to stand for right and justice in international dealings. In the meantime British statesmen are very assiduously engaged in impressing on the neutral world that India is happy, prosperous, and the most lightly taxed country on earth.

For the benefit of the reader I reproduce the following interview which the Finance Minister of India is said to have given to a correspondent of the Associated Press:

"FINANCE MINISTER DENIES THAT INDIA GROANS UNDER TAX. TOTAL REVENUE, DISTRIBUTED AMONG 244,000,000 PEOPLE, SEVEN SHILLINGS PER CAPITA

"Simla, India, Dec. 20. (Mail correspondence to the Associated Press.)—So far from the people of India groaning under an enormous burden of taxation, India is one of the most lightly taxed countries on the face of the earth, according to Sir William Meyer, minister of finance for India, in response to the charges of over-taxation preferred by so-called extremists.

"The total revenues, imperial and provincial, for the current year, during which some additional taxation was imposed, amounted to £86,500,000, Sir William said, and this sum distributed among the 244,000,000 people of British India gave a resultant contribution per capita of only seven shillings. He pointed out that in three other Asiatic countries, Japan, Siam, and the Dutch Indies, the rate per head was much higher, being 23 shillings in Japan, 13 shillings 4 pence in Siam and 11 shillings 3 pence in the Dutch Indies.

"The finance minister said the land revenue has been

one of the points upon which opponents of the government have been most bitter, it being claimed that the farmer was kept in poverty by taxation. Sir William stated that of the total revenue of £86,500,000 for this year, about £22,000,000 was derived from the land, India being mainly an agricultural country.

STATE TAKES UNEARNED INCREMENT

"According to immemorial traditions in India the state has always claimed a share in the produce of the soil, he continued. At the close of the eighteenth century the state share was commuted for a fixed money payment in various tracts, mostly in Bengal, but over the greater part of India we revise the money value of that share every 30 years or so with reference to the increase, or possible decrease, if that should occur, in the value of the agricultural produce. The state thus takes to itself a share of what is known to economists as the unearned increment, a policy that ought to find favour with enlightened socialists. Theoretically, after making liberal allowance for cultivation expenses, the state share is one-half of the resultant net profit, but as a matter of fact our recent settlements have been in practice much more lenient than this, and the amount we take is much less than was exacted by previous native rulers. Liberal remissions are also given when crops suffer from drought, flood or other calamities."

Let the reader study this pronouncement in the light of the facts disclosed in this volume. We will not forestall his judgment nor point out to him the misstatements with which the interview bristles. Let him only, judge of a statesman, giving the incidence of taxation without stating the figure of income. The burden of taxation always goes with the capacity to pay. If a man earning $10 a year pays about $2 (7s.)

in taxes can he be said to be the most lightly taxed person in the world? Yet it was only last year that this finance minister added to the burden of taxation and raised the tax on one of the great necessities of life — salt. This he did in spite of the universal opposition of the country and the results as reported by the press are most disheartening. The price of salt has risen considerably beyond the means of the people to pay, and there is a general cry of pain.

Will the people of England, with whom the ultimate responsibility for the government of India rests, look up and compel their statesmen to put into practice the principles for which they say they have been fighting this war? We will wait and see.

I tender my acknowledgments to the numerous writers whom I have quoted as also to the publishers of books and magazines referred to by me. The manuscript has been very kindly read for me by Professors E. R. A. Seligman and H. R. Mussey of Columbia University, New York, as also by my friend Dr. Sunderland. Professor H. R. Mussey has also read the proofs. My acknowledgments are due to them for valuable suggestions. The writing of this book has been made possible only by the courtesy of the librarians of Columbia University, whose uniform kindness I cannot sufficiently admire.

LAJPAT RAI.

New York,
10th February, 1917.

A WORD ON REFERENCES

It will be observed that no uniformity has been maintained in the spelling of Indian names. The reason is that we have not altered the original spellings of the different quotations given. With regard to the following names, use of a single work is indicated when the author's name is used instead of the work by title.

Mill always means "The History of British India," by James Mill.
Torrens always means "Empire in Asia," by W. M. Torrens, M.P.
Thorborn always means "The Punjab in War and Peace," by S. S. Thorburn.
Blunt always means "India under Ripon," by Wilfred Scawen Blunt.
Loveday always means "The History and Economics of Indian Famines," by A. Loveday.
Morison always means "Economic Transition in India," by Sir Theodore Morison.
Baines always means "Baines' History of Cotton Manufacture."

It may be stated generally that italics in quotations from other authors are ours unless the context shows otherwise.

With regard to Indian currency, it must be kept in mind that a rupee consists of 16 annas, an anna being equivalent to an English penny or two cents in American money. Three rupees are thus approximately a dollar in American money, and fifteen rupees make one English pound sterling.

POST-SCRIPTUM

India's "Gift" of One Hundred Million Pounds to England. Since the above was put in type our worst fears have come to be true. The British Government of India has decided, with the sanction of the Secretary of State for India, to float a war loan in India of an unlimited amount. The idea is to make a "gift" of £100,000,000 (or $500,000,000) to the British Exchequer. The amount of the loan, or as much as is raised, will be made over to the Government of Great Britain and liability for the rest will be accepted by the Government of India. The British Cabinet have, with the sanction of the House of Commons, accepted this "gift" and in lieu thereof allowed the Indian Government to raise their customs duty on the imports of cotton goods by four per cent. ad valorem. This transaction involves an additional burden of £6,000,000 a year (or $30,000,000) on the Indian tax payer. It is expected that out of this some £1,000,000 will be recovered by the additional duty on cotton imports and the rest will be raised by additional taxation.

The British statesmen have called it "a free gift of the people of India" and have thanked the latter for their "generosity." The fact is that the people of India or their representatives in the Legislative Council were never consulted about it. The transaction was settled between the Government of India and the Secretary of State for India, at Whitehall and then announced to the Indian Legislature as a *decision*. The *Manchester Guardian* and the London *Nation* have exposed it in its true colours. The former says, in its issue of March 15th:

"The great services which Indian manhood and Indian production have rendered in this war we all gratefully acknowledge. But their very magnitude is an argument against the wisdom and justice of adding to them a contribution in money and in financing that contribution mainly at the expense of the poor who have already made the greatest sacrifices. Mr. Chamberlain [the Secretary of State for India] says that the assumption of the £100,000,000 loan was a free will offering coupled with the condition that the Indian cotton trade should be given protection. Mr. Chamberlain obscures one not unimportant circumstance. It is we who govern India and not the Indian people. The initiative in all financial proposals necessarily comes from the government we appoint in India and cannot reach the light of public discussion in the Legislative Council or elsewhere until they have received the sanction of the Secretary of State here. For Mr. Chamberlain to throw upon the people of India the responsibility for originating and devising the £100,000,000 contribution and the protective duties which have been coupled with it, is as unconvincing a rhetorical exercise as the House of Commons has witnessed for many a long day. The responsibility for the whole scheme from the first to the last is his and that of the Indian Government. We have said more than once and we repeat it, that in our opinion a wise statesmanship would both find better use in India for India's millions and employ India more advantageously for the common cause by using more of her manhood and less of her money."

In a previous issue of the same paper it was observed:

"Why was the matter of a financial contribution from India raised now? For our own part we have the gravest doubts as to the wisdom or justice of taking any financial contribution from India. We believe that this is not the best way for India and the Empire, in which India can serve the common cause and the loss it represents to an extremely poor population like that of India is very much greater than the gain it represents to England. If we really are seriously concerned that India should develop in every way the vast potentialities of her indigenous industries it would be better to spend that £100,000,000 on developing her resources than to take that money from India and in exchange give Bombay a tariff."

The London *Nation* in its issue of March 17th says: "The people of India have no voice in this or any other act of Government, and, if they had, they would be forced to think twice before contributing out of their *dire poverty* [the italics are ours] this huge sum of a hundred millions to the resources of their wealthy rulers. Nor ought a poor subject people already burdened with large increases of war taxation to be compelled by its Government to make this gift." Further on, the *Nation* characterises the whole transaction as one of "sheer dishonesty" and adds: "India is not self-governing and this particular action is not the action of a body justly claiming to represent the will or interests of the Indian people. It is the arbitrary action of a little group of officials conniving with a little group of prosperous business men and playing on the mistaken economic nationalism of a somewhat larger number of educated natives. It is a bad and a foolish game."

The writer of "a London Diary" column in the *Nation* described it as "merely a case of one official in India signalling to another in England."

The Viceroy of India, making his final speech on the Budget, remarked that the Budget will involve "a sacrifice in a large measure of the necessities of ordered Government" and that "one result must be the arrested progress in education, in sanitation, in public works and kindred subjects which are in other countries the touchstone of civilised life." What this means in the case of India, will be made clear in the following pages.

As to how much India has done for England during this war we beg to refer the reader to an article written by Mr. Yusaf Ali, a retired Indian civil servant in the *Nineteenth Century and After* for February 8, 1917, from which we give a few extracts in an appendix. Discussing the economic effect of the war on India Mr. Ali remarks: "In 1915, the prices broke famine records." And again:

"In India, unfortunately, on account of the war, the isolation of the country, and the local crop having been short by 17½%, the price was very high. . . . The question of high food prices in India affects very materially her further capacity for taxation or for having further financial burdens. The small average individual income of India is mainly spent on the barest necessities of life. When the necessities rise over 100%, it does not mean an inconvenience; it means loss of vitality and efficiency."

According to this writer, "The services of India are

estimated at a value of $240,000,000 for the two and a half years that the war will have lasted at the close of the present financial year." Calculating the pre-war insurance, afforded by India's expenditure on the army of £14,000,000 (or $70,000,000) a year, at fifteen years' purchase he fixes its value to the Empire at £210,000,000, or $1,050,000,000. He also explains how India has helped the Imperial authorities by various other financial measures and by a war loan of £4,500,000 and concludes: "The fact is that India, so far from having superfluous capital, was and is urgently in need of capital, and the launching of a more ambitious scheme must hinder, instead of helping, the cause which India is upholding with so much self-sacrifice."

Evidently the raising of this new loan of $500,000,000 was in the air when he wrote the article and Mr. Yusaf Ali, who is permanently settled in London, with his English wife, thought it was his duty to raise a voice of protest. The fact that the article was published in the *Nineteenth Century and After* shows the high esteem in which the writer is held in journalistic circles in England. Mr. Yusaf Ali has never identified himself with the Nationalistic party and his views are those of a loyalist whose loyalty does not necessarily mean his supporting everything, just or unjust, which the Government does. His protest, however, proved to be a cry in the wilderness.

In this connection it might be of interest to add the following extract from the Proceedings of the Government of India, in the Legislative Department: "Replying to the Hon. Maharaja Manindra Chandra

Nandi's question regarding contributions to the war by Indian Native States and Indian Provinces the Hon. Sir Reginald Craddock said: 'Complete or detailed figures of the amounts subscribed in all the Provinces of India towards the war and the charities connected with it, cannot be given. The statement given below gives such information as is immediately available.'" Then follow the details of sums given, aggregating £2,047,375. "In addition to the figures given in the statement, lavish contributions both in cash and kind have been made by the ruling Princes and Chiefs in India. It is regretted that details of these cannot conveniently be supplied."

All these "lavish" contributions, however, failed to satisfy the British and the Government did not scruple to load an additional burden of $500,000,000 on the already crushed shoulders of the Indian ryot.

Indian opinion, rather timidly expressed, may be gathered from the following report of a speech made by a Hindu member of the Viceroy's Legislative Council, on the occasion of the discussion, on the current year's Budget. Said the Hon. Mr. Rangaswami Iyengar: "My Lord, the provision of a hundred millions sterling together with its interest, which amounts nearly to double the gift towards the war expenditure of the Empire, is undoubtedly the most prominent feature of the budget of this year. Apart from the consideration, as has been pointed out by our esteemed colleague, the Hon. Pandit Madan Mohan Malaviya, of neglecting to take this Council into confidence before the contribution was made, the burdening to the breaking point of a country, whose poor people are already suffering owing to results of a peculiar economic policy of the Government of India, without leaving a margin for emergencies, should furnish an insoluble problem to the statesman. . . .

"In this connection it has to be pointed out, especially in view of the unmerited complaints brought against India in certain Anglo-Indian organs, that even without this huge contribution India has borne more than her own fair share as compared with other parts of the Empire from the services already rendered by her in her sacrifice of men and money.

"Here is a statement as regards the help in men alone until the end of 1916:

1: Four expeditionary forces...	300,000
2: Wastage and renewal.......	450,000
3: Transport, Marine, etc.	50,000
	800,000
Increase in units since war......	300,000
To end of 1916	1,100,000

"All these men have been trained in India and not in Salisbury as was the case with the Colonials.

"Again, coming to contributions in money till 1916:

Military stores, services, and supplies....	£50,000,000
Advanced to Britain from Reserves, etc..	27,000,000
Deduct loans from Britain............	*Nil*
Total	£77,000,000

"Whereas the help the Colonies rendered in this direction partook mostly of the nature of loans. I challenge if any Colonies peopled with richer classes have made a similar sacrifice. Is it fair to strain the resources further?"

How these financial exactions are likely to cripple India, where millions have died from famine within the last fifty years; where within the last twenty years, millions have died from plague, where even now thousands die every week from the same fell disease and where the vast bulk of the people are illiterate and so abjectly poor, as to excite pity even from the stone-hearted, may better be imagined than described.

For the latest testimony to this effect we may cite from an article that has appeared in *The Quarterly Review* (British) for April, 1917, over the signature of Mr. W. H. Moreland, C. S. I., C. I. E.

"It is a matter of common knowledge that the standard of life in India is undesirably low; that while the masses of the people are provided with the necessities of a bare existence they are in far too many cases badly housed and badly clothed, badly doctored and badly taught, often overworked and often underfed; and that the present income of the country, even if it were equitably distributed, would not suffice to provide the population with even the most indispensable elements of a reasonable life."

Finally it may be noted that the Indian Budget for military expenditure has, in the current year, been raised to £26,000,000 while before the war it was only £20,000,000. Besides troops fighting in the trenches, India has also supplied England with the following medical equipment:

40 Field Ambulances
6 Clearing Hospitals
35 Stationary Hospitals

18 General Hospitals
9 x-ray Sections
8 Sanitary Sections
7 Advanced Depots
1 General Medical Store Depot

About 2,327 doctors and nurses, and about 720 nursing orderlies.

These figures are taken from the speech which the Secretary of State for India made in the House of Commons in March, 1917. He also made mention of the fact that India had supplied about 20,000 camp followers. The Government of India is at the present moment engaged in raising a "labour" army in India for work in England and in other places. Let those, who have been talking so much of how England has protected India, take into consideration these facts as well as those given in the body of the book, and then say honestly, who has been the greater gainer by this connection. India can await patiently and securely the verdict of posterity on this point.

Recent Happenings in England. Rain of Words. In the meantime things have happened in England which we cannot omit noticing in connection with the main theme of this book. The meetings of the Imperial War Conference in March; the participation in it for the first time of delegates from India; the courtesies extended to the latter and the honours conferred on them by the various public bodies of the British Isles, including the conferring upon the delegates of the freedom of the cities of London, Manchester, Edinburgh and Cardiff, and the honourary degrees of some of the universities, have furnished opportunities for some pleasant talk on both sides which, judged by standards of sweetness, politeness and occasional frankness, is refreshing. For the first time since the British connection with India were the Indian delegates allowed to participate in the deliberations of an Imperial Conference; for the first time they were considered worthy of being honoured with the freedom of British cities. For the first time it was conceded that India might look forward to a day when she may be treated as a partner in the Empire, and not as a hewer of wood or drawer of water for the latter. Reading the speeches and assuming the honesty and sincerity of the speakers, an Indian may take comfort in the hope that a day of real freedom was dawning upon his unfortunate country, and that this time at least, the British meant what they said.

If words of sympathy, promises of a future state of autonomy, compliments and acknowledgments could bring happiness and prosperity to the millions of India, she has had a copious outburst of them within the last two months and a half, nay in fact, from the very beginning of the war. If, however, the value of words is to be judged by deeds, an Indian may still be pessimistic about actual realisations.

"Sweet words are now raining upon India," remarks the *Investor's Review*, London (April 28, 1917), "and we trust foreshadow generous deeds." Do they? is the question.

India would be content if even half of what has been said were realised in the near future. The actual behaviour of the Government in India and in England, however, is not at all encouraging. The restrictions on the freedom of speech and the freedom of meeting have not been relaxed in the least. In one province, alone, 800 young Indians are rotting in jails without ever having had a chance of being tried for their supposed offences. The inequalities in the public services, civil and military, have not been removed. The appointments to the executive offices both in India and in England are of the most reactionary type. The solicitations of the Indian Nationalists to get larger appropriations for education and sanitation are still unheeded. The only thing actually done is the increase in the cotton duties, of which we have spoken above.

The Speeches of the Maharaja of Bikanir. The Position of Indian Princes. The speeches of the Maharaja of Bikanir and of Sir S. P. Sinha, the Indian delegates to the Imperial War Conference, have done at least one good. They have cleared the atmosphere somewhat. The Maharaja has made it absolutely clear that the ruling princes of India are in full accord with the people of India in demanding self-government, and fiscal autonomy. In the words of the *Investor's Review,* "The Maharaja impressively pointed out that far from being alarmed at the political progress of India, the ruling princes of India rejoice in it. At least 10 per cent. of the more important states already have representative self-government, and every year the constitutional government is being extended. Though 'autocrats,' the princes of India are marching with the times. If they are of that mind," asks the *Investor's Review,* "why should we hesitate?"

Those who read the speeches made by the Indian delegates to the Imperial War Conference in London, should bear in mind that neither of them were the spokesmen of the Indian Nationalist Party. One of them, Sir S. P. Sinha, did, no doubt, preside at an annual meeting of the Indian National Congress in 1915, but that was his only connection (first and last) with the movement. Before his election to the office of president of that session, he was a government man, and soon after he again became a government man. He is an official of the Government of India and owes his prosperity, his rank and his wealth to the Government.

The Maharaja of Bikanir comes from an ancient royal family of India, though the state over which he rules is not a first-class principality. By heredity, instinct, and tradition he is an autocrat. For his elevation to the present position of prominence in Indian political life, he is under obligations to the British Government of India. He comes from a family which has, for the last four hundred years, kept well with the paramount authority, Mughal or British. Personally he is an enlightened and progressive ruler. Under these circumstances, he has rendered signal service to the cause of his country, worthy of the great ancestry from which he has sprung, in making some fairly bold and outspoken utterances about the aspirations of India. At last, in him, the princes of India have found a worthy representative, and the people of India a sincere, though by the limitations of his position, a rather halting champion of their rights. Speaking at the luncheon given by the Empire Parliamentary Association, he said that the unrest that exists in India is of two kinds:

"That which the seditionists attempt to spread, happily with small results, has to be faced and is being faced and suitably tackled by the authorities, and it is our earnest hope that it may be possible gradually to eradicate the evil, which is a cancerous growth, not, however, peculiar to India. The other kind of unrest is what has been happily described by a British statesman as 'legitimate.' It is in the minds of people who are as loyal as you or I. (Hear, hear.) I decline to believe that British statesmanship will not rise to the occasion, and it depends on whether Indian problems are or are not handled with sympathy, with imagination, with broad-minded perspicacity, that that legitimate unrest will die out or continue. It is the strong opinion of many who have given the subject thought that if the people of India were given a greater voice and power in directions in which they have shown their fitness we should hear much less of the unrest, agitation, and irresponsible criticism which is certainly gaining ground. Desperation would give way to patience, for India has confidence in the word and good faith of England, and the enemies of order and good government would be foiled. The 'unchanging East' is changing very rapidly and beyond conception." (Report in the *Daily Telegraph,* London.)

The speech has evoked some pertinent comments in the British press. The *Daily Telegraph* remarks (April 25, 1917):

"Every one is aware that at the conclusion of the war not only India expects, but the majority of us at home also look forward to a considerable development along the lines of political reform."

The Prime Minister's Pronouncement. The clearest pronouncement, however, is that of the Prime Minister, who in the speech delivered at the Guildhall on April 27, said with reference to India: "I think I am entitled to ask that these loyal myriads should feel, not as if they were a subject race in the Empire, but partners with us." "These are heartening words," says the London organ of the Indian Congress. "It remains to follow them by deeds." "Unhappily," remarks the same paper (April 27), "those who monopolise place and power in India have still to be converted. There is copious talk of the 'new angle of vision,' but precious little indication of any real intention to quicken the rate of progress. It is idle, and also insincere to profess anxiety to help Indians along the road to self-government if the whip hand is perpetually to be held over them."

Coming to the economic side of the question, we observe that there is a great deal of hazy talk of the future economic development of India. Most of the papers and the Under Secretary of State for India, still think of India as a supplier of raw materials to the Empire. In fact, one paper (*The Contract Journal*) holds out prospects of exploitation to the British investor; on the other hand, the *Stock Exchange Gazette* and *The Investor's Review* are happy over the prospects of the development of Indian powers of self-government. The most authoritative pronouncements, however, in the matter, are those of Mr. Austen Chamberlain, the Secretary of State for India. Speaking at a luncheon given by the chairman of the East India section of the London Chamber of Commerce, he said that the development of India was not only an economic, but a political necessity of the first consequence. Even more pronounced and significant is the speech which he delivered at the Savoy Hotel on March 29, in which he is reported to have said that India would not remain and ought not to remain content to be a hewer of wood and a drawer of water for the rest of the Empire. It was essential to her sound and healthy development that her own industries should progress! We hope Mr. Chamberlain is sincere and earnest.

It has since been given out that in future an Indian will represent India in the Imperial War Cabinet. An Indian nominated by the British Government, however, could not represent India in the same sense as the premiers of the dominions would represent the latter. The concessions, though important in appearance, are thus shadowy in effect. Similarly, the talk of Trade Preference within the Empire is not likely to benefit India.

Says *India,* the organ of the Indian Congress in London, " Mr. Bonar Law informed the House of Commons on Friday last that the Imperial War Cabinet had unanimously accepted the principle that each part of the Empire, having due regard to the interest of our Allies, shall give specially favourable treatment and facilities to the produce and manufactures of other parts of the Empire," that " there is no intention whatever of making any change during the war." Mr. Lloyd George made a similar announcement in his speech in the city on the same day, after the usual preliminary denunciation of the wickedness and folly of adherence to old party systems and policies.

" Nevertheless, the Prime Minister may rest assured that India intends to have something to say on this matter. If she is to embark upon the career of commercial development which is being so confidently marked out for her, she must have protection for her growing industries: and her most formidable competitor is the British manufacturer. The application of the policy of Imperial Preference, which is now foreshadowed, will simply mean that India must take Lancashire goods at Lancashire's prices, while shutting out Japan and the United States from her markets. What, then, was the object of the flourish of trumpets with which Mr. Chamberlain heralded the increase in the import duties on cotton goods? Here is a fiscal change made during the war defended on the ground that it is consonant with Indian opinion, and marked already for a place on the political dust heap when the war is over."

Are not the British past masters in the art of taking away with the left what they give by the right hand?

But India is now awake and will not be fooled as she has been in the past.

LAJPAT RAI.

May 25, 1917,
New York City.

CONTENTS

CONTENTS

CONTENTS

PART III

CONTENTS

CONTENTS

CONTENTS

APPENDICES

PART ONE

"We are accustomed to think of the British Empire as consisting mainly of men of Anglo-Saxon blood, and as being on the whole, well-governed, highly civilised and wealthy. As a matter of fact, the Empire consists of Asiatics, *it is more cursed by poverty than any other great state,* and the great majority of its adult population are unable to read or write. The first and the greatest of all the problems of Empire is the problem of India. Among the prominent facts with regard to India which are confessed in statistical abstracts, is that the average death-rate for the ten years ending in 1908, was between 34 and 35 per thousand; which represents an excess of unnecessary deaths, judging by the standards of a country like Japan, of some four millions per annum.

"*Poverty and ignorance are the obvious causes of this appalling death-rate.* The fundamental duty of the Government is to protect the people against devastating plagues and famines; and the obvious means of doing so is to train the most gifted of the Native population to lead the people in the fight against the evil that besets them. How little the British Government in India realises this duty may be judged by the statistics of graduates turned out in the year 1909–10, in the different professions. In Medicine there were but thirty,—in Engineering only seventeen,—in Agriculture not a single one; but in Arts there were 2116 and in Law, 576." "The Making of Modern England," by Gilbert Slater, 1915, page 276.[1]

[1] Italics are ours.

ENGLAND'S DEBT TO INDIA

A HISTORICAL NARRATIVE OF BRITAIN'S FISCAL POLICY IN INDIA

CHAPTER I

A HISTORICAL RETROSPECT

India Once Was Rich. It is almost universally acknowledged that India is a *poor* country, in the sense that the economic condition of the Indian people is not good,—their average income being (according to official calculation made in 1904, during the viceroyalty of Lord Curzon) only £2, or $10.00 a year. But such was not always their condition. There was a time when India was rich—immensely rich, rich in every thing which makes a country great. glorious and noble. Her sons and daughters were distinguished in every walk of life. She produced scholars, thinkers, divines, poets, and scientists, whose achievements in their respective spheres were unique in their own times. Some of them remain unique even to-day. Among her children were sculptors, architects, and painters whose work compels admiration and exacts the praise of the most exacting art-critics of the modern world. Her law-makers, jurists, and sociologists have left behind them codes and ideas of justice inferior to none produced under similar conditions. Under their own codes, the people of India were prosperous and happy.

Thornton's "Description of Ancient India."

"Ere yet the Pyramids looked down upon the valley of the Nile,—when Greece and Italy, those cradles of European civilisation, nursed only the tenants of a wilderness,—India was the seat of wealth and grandeur. A busy population had covered the land with the marks of its industry; rich crops of the most coveted productions of Nature annually rewarded the toil of husbandmen; skilful artisans converted the rude produce of the soil into fabrics of unrivalled delicacy and beauty; and architects and sculptors joined in constructing works, the solidity of which has not, in some instances, been overcome by the evolution of thousands of years. . . . The ancient state of India must have been one of extraordinary magnificence."

Such is the picture of ancient India drawn by a British historian, by no means partial to India, in the opening paragraphs of his "History of British India."

Sufficiency with Security and Independence—the Golden Age. This estimate of the magnificence of ancient India is not merely rhetorical. That the India of ancient times was wealthy and prosperous is amply borne out by incontestable testimony. Whether the "Golden Age" of India is a historical fact or a myth depends upon our individual conception of a golden age,—but we do know that the part of India included in the Empire of Darius (Afghanistan and the Northwestern Punjab) was the "richest" province of all his dominions.[1] We know also, that certain cities in Northern India, described in the Hindu Epics, and confirmed by accounts of the Greeks, were of great

[1] "Early History of India" by V. R. Smith, 3d ed. p. 33.

size and architectural magnificence. Lastly, as far back as the middle of the seventh century B. C., the villagers of India had "sufficiency for their simple needs." "There was security; there was independence,—there were no landlords and no paupers."[2] The mass of the people "held it degradation to which only dire misfortune would drive them, to work for hire."[3] Add to these facts, that "there was little, if any crime," and a picture of the Golden Age is completed.

So far as the conditions of international trade are concerned, we find that, except under British rule, India has always had more to sell and less to purchase, in manufactured goods,—that the balance of trade was always in her favour: that the Romans have left on record bitter complaints of the constant drain of gold and silver from their country into India,—a complaint repeated by Englishmen as late as the eighteenth century; and that, for more than a century and a half (1603–1757) the profits of the East India Company were made by the importation of Indian manufactures into England. During that time, England was the purchaser and India the vendor of manufactured goods, largely for cash.

General Condition of the People Under Hindu and Mohammedan Rule. As to the general condition of the people under Hindu and Mohammedan governments during the twenty-two centuries for which we have authentic historical data, beginning with the invasion of Alexander the Great, and ending with the British occupation of Indian provinces at different

[2] "Buddhist India" by Rhys Davids, London, 1903, p. 49.
[3] *Ibid.*, p. 51.

times from 1757 to 1858, ample testimony shows that the mass of the population had sufficient to satisfy their simple wants, except in periods of famine; that the country had prosperous bankers, who loaned money to prince and peasant, negotiated commercial paper, and held all kinds of securities; and that an extensive home and foreign trade was carried on continuously.

It has become the fashion for English publicists and historians to stress what they deem the superiority of British to native rule in India. Doubtless the former has its peculiar merits, but to assert that the country has never before known such "economic prosperity," or experienced the administration of such even-handed justice as under British rule, is to disclose unjustifiable mental bias or ignorance. A number of just and fair-minded Englishmen have deplored such utterances, and a service may be rendered to both England and India by transcribing a few opinions on that point:

India Reform Pamphlet. In a pamphlet on "India Reform" (No. IX), published in 1853 by the India Reform Society of London, which had thirty-seven members of Parliament on its committee, the subject was examined in the light of historical evidence.—

"We found the people of India, it is said, abject, degraded, false to the very core. . . . The most indolent and selfish of our own governors have been models of benevolence and beneficence when compared with the greatest of the native sovereigns. The luxurious selfishness of the Moghul Emperors depressed and enfeebled the people. Their predecessors were either unscrupulous tyrants or indolent debauchees. . . . Having the command of the public press in this country and the sympathy of the public mind with us, it is an easy task thus to exalt ourselves at the expense of our predecessors. We tell our own story and our testimony is unimpeachable; but if we find anything favourable related of those who have preceded us, the accounts we pronounce to be suspicious. We contrast the Moghul conquest of the fourteenth century with the 'victorious, mild and merciful progress of the British arms in the East in the nineteenth.' But if our object was a fair one, we should contrast the Mussalman invasion of Hindusthan with the contemporaneous Norman invasion of England — the characters of the Mussalman sovereigns with their contemporaries in the West — their Indian wars of the fourteenth century with our French wars or with the Crusades — the effect of the Mohammedan conquest upon the character of the Hindu with the effect of the Norman conquest upon the Anglo-Saxon when 'to be called an Englishman was considered as a reproach — when those who were appointed to administer justice were the fountain of all iniquity — when magistrates whose duty it was to pronounce righteous judgments were the most cruel tyrants and greater plunderers than common thieves and robbers'; when the great men were inflamed with such a rage of money that they cared not by what means it was acquired — when the licentiousness was so great that a princess of Scotland found 'it necessary to wear a religious habit in order to preserve her person from violation!' (Henry of Huntington, Anglo-Saxon Chronicle, and Eadmon.)

"The history of Mohammedan dynasty in India is full, it is said, of lamentable instances of cruelty and rapacity of the early conquerors, not without precedent in the contemporary Christian history; for when Jerusalem was taken by the first Crusaders, at the end of the eleventh century, the garrison, consisting of 40,000 men, 'was put to the sword without distinction; arms protected not the brave, nor submission the timid; no age or sex received mercy; infants perished by the same sword that pierced their mothers. The streets of Jerusalem were covered with heaps of slain, and the shrieks of agony and despair resounded from every house.' When Louis the Seventh of France, in the twelfth century, 'made himself master of the town of Vitri, he ordered it to be set on fire.' In England, at the same time, under our Stephen, war 'was carried on with so much fury, that the land was left uncultivated, and the instruments of husbandry were left or abandoned,'—and the result of our French wars in the fourteenth century, was a state of things 'more horrible and destructive than was ever experienced in any age or country.' The insatiable cruelty of the Mohammedan conquerors, it is said, stands recorded upon more undeniable authority than the insatiable benevolence of the Mohammedan conquerors. We have abundant testimony of cruelty of contemporary Christian conquerors,—have we any evidence of their benevolence?"

"As attempts are thus systematically made, in bulky volumes, to run down the character of Native governments and sovereigns, in order that we may have a fair pretext for seizing upon their possessions, it becomes necessary to show that we have a Christian Roland for every native Oliver; that if the Mohammedan conquerors of India were cruel and rapacious, they were matched by their Christian contemporaries. It is much our fashion to compare India in the fifteenth and sixteenth centuries with England in the nineteenth, and to pique ourselves upon the result. 'When we compare other countries with England,' said a sagacious observer,[4] 'we usually speak of England as she now is,—we scarcely ever think of going back beyond the Reformation, and we are apt to regard every foreign country as ignorant and uncivilised, whose state of improvement does not in some degree approximate to our own, even though it should be higher than our own was at no distant period.' It would be almost as

[4] Sir Thomas Munro.

fair to compare India in the sixteenth with England in the nineteenth century, as it would be to compare the two countries in the first centuries of the Christian era, when India was at the top of civilisation, and England at the bottom."

The Observations of Mr. Torrens, M. P., comparing India with Europe. The matter has been discussed lucidly, forcibly and fairly by Mr. Torrens, M.P., who points out that

"There never was an error more groundless than that which represented the ancient systems of Indian rule as decrepit or degrading despotisms, untempered by public opinion. It accords too well with the arrogance of national self-love and seems too easily to lull the conscience of aggression to pretend that those whom it has wronged were superstitious slaves, and that they must have so remained but for the disinterested violence of foreign civilisation introduced by it, sword in hand. This pretentious theory is confuted by the admissions of men whose knowledge cannot be disputed and whose authority cannot be denied."[5]

As to the so-called usurpations, infamies and fanaticism of Indian monarchs, he asks the reader to compare them with the deeds and practices of the Borgias, Louis XI., Philip II., Richard III., Mary Tudor and the last of the Stuarts, and to "look back at the family picture of misrule" in Europe, from Catherine de Medici to Louis le Grand,— from Philip the Cruel to Ferdinand the Fool,— from John the Faithless to Charles the False,— not forgetting the parricide Peter of Muscovy and the Neapolitan Bourbons! "It is no more true," he concludes, "of Southern Asia than

[5] Torrens, "Empire in Asia," London, p. 100.

of Western Europe to say that the everyday habits of supreme or subordinate rule were semi-barbarous, venal, sanguinary or rapacious."

It is generally assumed that Indian civilisation and prosperity attained its flood-mark during the period which intervenes between the invasion of Alexander (327 B.C.) and that of Mahmud of Ghazni (1000 A.D.). When Mahmud invaded India, the country was overflowing with wealth. To quote the language of Reform Pamphlet No. 9: "Writers, both Hindu and Mussulman, unite in bearing testimony to the state of prosperity in which India was found at the time of the first Mohammedan conquest. They dwell with admiration on the extent and magnificence of the capital of the Kingdom of Canauj, and of the inexhaustible riches of the Temple of Somnath." The wealth that Mahmud carried away from India was insignificant compared to what remained there. His raids were confined chiefly to the northwestern provinces; only for two brief periods did he penetrate into the Doab between Ganga and Jamna, and only once in Gujrat, Kattiawar. The whole of Central India, which had for so long remained the centre of great political activities under the *Nandas, the Mauryas* and *the Guptas;* the whole of Eastern India, covering the rich and fertile tracts which comprise the modern provinces of Bengal and Assam; the whole of the south had remained untouched.

India Under the Mohammedans. The first Mohammedan dynasty began its rule at Delhi in 1206 A.D., and from that time on, the Mohammedan rulers of India spent whatever they acquired from India within the country itself. From 1206 A. D. to the middle of the eighteenth century, when the British began to acquire rights of sovereignty in India, only twice was the country raided with any degree of success.

Raid of Tamerlane. The first of these two raiders was Tamerlane, who sacked Delhi in 1398 A. D., and is said to have carried off "very great" booty. Tamerlane's expedition also covered only a small part of the country invaded by him — he never went beyond Delhi.

In 1526 A. D. came the Mogul invasion by Baber. Baber, however, came to stay and die in India.

From 1206 to 1526 A.D. During the centuries from 1206 to 1526 A. D. the country was, no doubt, in a state of constant unrest on account of the frequent wars between the indigenous Hindu population and the "foreign Mohammedan rulers." Sometimes even the latter fought among themselves out of rivalry, as was not infrequently the case in the England of the same centuries. There was, however, no drain of wealth out of India, and the frequent wars did not materially interfere with the processes of production and the amassing of wealth. From the account of travellers who visited the country during these centuries, as well as from the histories of the period, we have enough material to judge of the general economic prosperity of the people. Elphinstone says:

"The condition of the people in ordinary times does not appear to have borne the marks of oppression. The historian of Feroz Shah (A. D. 1351–1394) expatiates on the happy state of the ryots, the goodness of their houses and furniture, and the general use of gold and silver ornaments by their women." Elphinstone adds that "although this writer is a panegyrist whose writings are not much to be trusted, still the mere mention of such details as that every ryot has a good bedstead and a neat garden shows a more minute attention to the comforts of the people than would be met with in a modern author."

Elphinstone on the General State of the Country.

The general state of the country must no doubt have been flourishing. Nicolo de Conti, who travelled about 1420 A. D. speaks highly of what he saw in Guzerat, and found the banks of the Ganges covered with towns amidst beautiful gardens and orchards, and passed four famous cities before he reached Maarazia, which he describes as a powerful city filled with gold, silver and precious stones. His accounts are corroborated by those of Barbora and Bartema, who travelled in the early part of the sixteenth century.[6]

Cæsar Frederic and Ibn Batuta.

Cæsar Frederic gives a similar account of Guzerat, and Ibn Batuta, who travelled during the anarchy and oppression of Mohammed Tuglak's reign, in the middle of the fifteenth century, when insurrections were raging in most parts of the country, enumerates the large and populous towns and cities, and gives a high impression of the state the country must have been in before it fell into disorder.[7]

Abdurizag.

"Abdurizag, an ambassador from the grandson of Tamerlane, visited the South of India in 1442, and concurs with other observers in giving the impression of a prosperous country. The Kingdom of Kandeish was at this time in a high state of prosperity under its own kings; the numerous stone embankments by which

[6] Elphinstone, Vol. II, p. 203.
[7] *Ibid.*, p. 206.

the streams were rendered applicable to irrigation are equal to anything in India as works of industry and ability."[8]

Baber.

"Baber, the first sovereign of the Moghul dynasty, although he regards Hindusthan with the same dislike that Europeans still feel, speaks of it as a rich and noble country, and expresses his astonishment at the swarming population and the innumerable workmen of every kind and description. Besides the ordinary business of his kingdom, he was constantly occupied with making aqueducts, reservoirs and other improvements, as well as introducing new fruits, and other productions of remote countries."[9]

Sher Shah.

Baber's son, "Humayun, whose character was free from vices and violent passions, was defeated, and obliged to flee from Hindusthan, by Sher Shah, who is described as a prince of consummate prudence and ability, 'whose measures were as wise as benevolent,' and who, notwithstanding his constant activity in the field, during a short reign had brought his territories in the highest order, and introduced many improvements into his civil government.

"He made a high road extending for four months' journey from Bengal to the Western Rhotas near the Indus, with caravanserais at every stage, and wells at every mile and a half. There was an Imam and Muezzin at every mosque, and provisions for the poor at every caravanserai, with attendants of proper caste for Hindus as well as for Mussulmen. The road was planted with rows of trees for shade, and in many places was in the state described when the author saw it, after it had stood for eighty-two years."[10]

[8] Elphinstone, Reform Pamphlet No. 9, p. 10.

[9] *Ibid.*

[10] Elphinstone, Vol. II, p. 151. Reform Pamphlet No. 9, pp. 10 and 11.

Akbar.

"It is almost superfluous to dwell upon the character of the celebrated Akbar, who was equally great in the cabinet and in the field, and renowned for his learning, toleration, liberality, clemency, courage, temperance, industry and largeness of mind. But it is to his internal policy that Akbar owes his place in that highest order of princes whose reigns have been a blessing to mankind. He forbade trials by ordeal, and marriages before the age of puberty, and the slaughter of animals for sacrifice. He employed his Hindu subjects equally with Mohammedans, abolished the capitation tax on infidels as well as all the taxes on pilgrims, and positively prohibited the making slaves of persons taken in war. He perfected the financial reforms which had been commenced in those provinces by Sher Shah. He remeasured all the lands capable of cultivation within the Empire; ascertained the produce of each *bigah;* determined the proportion to be paid to the public; and commuted it for a fixed money rent, giving the cultivator the option of paying in kind if he thought the money rate too high. He abolished, at the same time, a vast number of vexatious taxes and fees to officers. The result of these wise measures was to reduce the amount of public demand considerably." [11]

Pietro del Valle.

The Italian traveller, Pietro del Valle, wrote in 1623, "generally all live much after a genteel way and they do it securely; as well because the king does not persecute his subjects with false accusations, nor deprive them of anything when he sees them live splendidly and with the appearance of riches!" [12]

Shah Jehan.

"But the reign of Shah Jehan, the grandson of

[11] Reform Pamphlet No. 9, p. 11 on the authority of Elphinstone, Vol. II.

[12] Quoted by Reform Pamphlet, p. 12.

Akbar, was the most glorious ever known in India. His own dominions enjoyed almost uninterrupted tranquillity and good government; and although Sir Thomas Roe was struck with astonishment at the profusion of wealth which was displayed when he visited the Emperor in his camp in 1615, in which at least two acres were covered with silk, gold carpets and hangings, as rich as velvet, embossed with gold and precious stones could make them, yet we have the testimony of Tavernier that he who caused this celebrated peacock throne to be constructed, who, at the festival of his accession, scattered amongst the bystanders money and precious things equal to his own weight, 'reigned not so much as a king over his subjects, but rather as a father over his family.'

"After defraying the expenses of his great expedition to Candahar and wars in Balk, Shah Jehan left a treasure of about £24,000,000, in coins and vast accumulations of wrought gold, silver and jewels." [13]

Aurangzeb and His Successors.

Notwithstanding the misgovernment of Aurangzeb and the reign of a series of weak and wicked princes, together with the invasion of Nadir Shah, who carried away enormous wealth when he quitted Delhi in 1739, the country was still in a comparatively prosperous condition.[14]

The Raid by Nadir Shah. The raid by Nadir Shah was the second one which took place between 1206 A. D. and 1757 A. D. He carried off "enormous wealth," but how enormous could it have been when one considers that even he did not go beyond Delhi, leaving the rest of the north, the greater part of the west, and the en-

[13] Reform Pamphlet on the authority of Elphinstone, Vol. II, pp. 293–299.

[14] Reform Pamphlet No. 9, p. 16.

tire east and south of India unaffected and untouched? Throughout the Mohammedan dominance, large parts of India remained under Hindu rule, and the historians are agreed that in the territories of the Hindu princes general prosperity prevailed. Some of them are said to have attained to a pitch of power and splendour which had not been surpassed by their ancestors.

Pre-British Period. We are, however, more directly concerned with the economic condition of India in the period immediately preceding the establishment of British power. We have some vivid glimpses preserved for us in the accounts of the contemporary European travellers and Anglo-Indian administrators,—writers of the type of Malcolm, Elphinstone, Monroe, Orme, and Todd.

Principal Political Divisions of the Country. The country was then divided into several political divisions. The rulers were practically independent masters of their respective territories, though some acknowledged a nominal suzerainty of the Grand Mogul. In the north, Bengal, Behar, and Orissa were ruled by the Nawab of Bengal, with his seat in Murshidabad. Oude was administered by the Nawab Vizir who had several feudatories, including the Rajah of Benares. The Mahrattas were practically supreme in Delhi where the Grand Mogul still maintained the shadow of his glory,—also in Rajputana, Central India and the Western Ghauts. The South was divided between the Nawab of Hyderabad, with the Nawab of Arcot and the Rajah of Tanjore under him, and the principality of Mysore, with a Hindu prince as sovereign and a Mohammedan minister as ruler. The Northwest, comprising the land of the Five Rivers and the territory between the Sutlej and the Jamna, were still nominally under the Mogul. By the time, however, that the British established themselves at Delhi, it had completely passed into the hands of the Sikhs, and it was from them that the British finally took it. Scindh was under the Amirs.

We will now briefly narrate the means whereby Britain acquired these territories, with a statement of their economic condition before and after British occupation.

Tanjore and Arcot. Let us begin with the South. The small Hindu principality of Tanjore, off the coast of Coromandel, was the first victim of British aggression. For several centuries this state had enjoyed the rights of sovereignty; and in 1741, Pratap Singh succeeded to the throne as a result of a domestic revolution with which the English had nothing to do. The latter acknowledged him unhesitatingly as ruler, and established a kind of friendship with him against their rivals, the French. The brother of Pratap Singh, one Sahujee, subsequently approached the British with an offer of the fort and jagir of Devikotah as the price of their help to put him on the throne. The British "despatched an army to dethrone" Pratap Singh.[15] The expedition failed, and a second was resolved on. Devikotah was taken, and they "entered into negotiations with Pratap Singh — agreed to desist from further hostilities — to abandon him for whom they pretended to have fought, but engaged to secure his person and to receive a fixed sum for his maintenance, on con-

[15] Torrens, pp. 20-21; Mill, Bk. IV, p. 91.

dition of being suffered to remain undisputed masters of Devikotah and the circumjacent territory." This was the beginning of the conquest of Hindustan.

The principality of Tanjore was included in the dominions of the Nawab of Carnatic, who in his turn, was considered to be under the Subah of Deccan. The desire for the possession of Devikotah on the part of the British had its origin in their rivalry with the French. When, in 1754, the English and the French made peace, and signed a treaty, mutually renouncing any further designs of territorial aggression in India, and agreeing to interfere no more in the affairs of the local governments, it might have been expected that the troubles of the people of Carnatic were over.

Muhammad Ali, the friend of the English, had been acknowledged the Nawab of Carnatic. The ink on this compact was scarcely dry when the British entered into negotiations to reduce certain other Hindu principalities included in the Nawab's dominions which the latter asserted owed large sums of tribute-money to him. The French authorities at Pondicherry protested without result. Eventually they were drawn into hostilities and worsted. The first treaty with the Nawab of Carnatic was made in 1763, in which he acknowledged his liability to the East India Company for all the expenses they had incurred in the war with the French, and undertook to pay them off by annual instalments of 28 lacs of rupees, i.e., £280,000. In the course of time, the Nawab was asked to bestow a grant of lands, the rents and revenues of which should be credited to the debt. This had, of course, to be conceded. The *Jagirdar,* however, was soon to become the master.

Before the century was over, the Nawab of Carnatic, the first patron of the British, when they landed friendless and " shelterless " on the coast of Coromandel," later their ally in the war with the French, became reduced to the position of the mere creature of the honourable company, and wholly at the mercy of its servants. By the time Lord Wellesley came to make a fresh treaty with the Nawab, " The Carnatic had been inmeshed in the net of our friendship and the noose of our protection."[16] By the treaty made by Lord Wellesley, it was declared that four-fifths of the revenue of the principality, the management of which had already passed into the hands of the company, was forever vested in the company, and the remaining one-fifth appropriated for the support of the Nawab. These emoluments, along with the dignity and prestige of the nawabship, were enjoyed by the last scion of the family till 1853, when "Lord Dalhousie thought the time had arrived to let the curtain fall upon the farce of gratitude to Arcot. The cabinet of Lord Aberdeen, the Court of Directors assenting, he forbade Azimshah, the successor of the last nawab, to assume the title, and refused to pay him the stipulated fifth of the revenues, which he claimed as undisputed heir, " upon the ground that when treaties are made ' forever,' the suzerain is not bound longer than the sense of expediency lasts."[17] In commenting upon what took place in 1792, at the time of the death of the Nawab who

[16] Arnold, Dalhousie's "Administration of British India," London. Vol. II, p. 171.
[17] Torrens, pp. 378–79.

first entered into relations with the British, James Mill in his "History of British India" says:

"A fact is here forcibly urged upon our attention, of which it is important to find the true explanation. Under their dependence upon the British Government, it has been seen that the people of Oude and Karnatic, two of the noblest provinces of India, were, by misgovernment, plunged into a state of wretchedness with which no other part of India,—hardly any part of earth, had anything to compare. In what manner did the dependence of the native states upon the English, tend to produce these horrid effects?" [18]

This question may best be answered in the words of the Duke of Wellington, who as an historian of the administration of his brother, the Marquis of Wellesley, says, speaking of the treaty made with the Nawab in 1792:

"One of the great evils in this alliance, or in all those of this description formed in India, was that it provided that the Company should not interfere in the internal concerns of the Nawab's government. At the same time the interference of the Company in every possible case was absolutely necessary for the support of the Native Government, *and was practised on every occasion.*" Another evil which affected this, as well as every alliance of the same description, was . . . that the Nawab *was obliged to borrow money at large interest* in order to make his payment at the stipulated periods and . . . the laws were made by the Company's civil and military and the European inhabitants of Fort St. George and its dependencies. In this view of the evil, it was of enormous magnitude." [19]

[18] Book VI, pp. 51–52.
[19] Muir, "The Making of British India," p. 217.

From the time the operation of the treaty of 1792 was observed, every governor had endeavoured to prevail upon the Nawab to consent to an alteration of it whereby the Company's resources should be secured and the evils above described be prevented. The endeavours, however, failed to prevail upon the Nawab to hear to any modification of the treaty; when the war with Tipu broke out, the country was labouring under all the disadvantages of the system, its resources were depleted, and its inhabitants, from long oppression, disaffected. In these conditions the Marquis of Wellesley decided upon annexation. He found a pretence ready to hand in the correspondence which the Nawab and his son had been carrying on with the neighbouring Prince Tipu. The Marquis decided that "in consequence of this *breach of treaty,* the company had a right to act in the manner best suited to their own interest." That arrangement has been recorded above. The method whereby the signature of the Nawab was obtained is however most significant.

"When the orders from the Marquis of Wellesley reached Madras, the Nawab, *Omdat 'ul Omra,* was in such a state of health as to be incapable of attending to business, and soon afterwards he died. His supposed son was then apprised of the discoveries (i.e., the correspondence) and the sentiments of the British Government in consequence, together with the measures about to be adopted in Carnatic. He refused to accept the situation offered him under the new arrangement."[20] It was resolved to set aside the young Nawab and set up another man, the brother to the de-

[20] Muir, "The Making of British India," p. 219.

ceased, on the throne, on condition he agreed to the proposed terms. This was accordingly done.

Mysore. Hyder Ali of Mysore was a person of humble origin. By dint of his courage, ability, enterprise and resourcefulness, he rose to a position which enabled him to usurp the powers of state, setting aside the rightful Hindu prince, and reducing him to the position of pensioner. The British Government entered into treaty relations with him, recognising him as the ruler. His first quarrel with the British was due to their seizure of Baramahal, a port of the Kingdom of Mysore. Hyder retaliated, and "under the walls of Madras, dictated a new treaty with the company, which was to furnish him with seven battalions of *sepoys* in case any foreign enemy attacked his dominions." When, in 1778, the British, at war with the French, took possession of Pondicherry, they attacked Mahe, a small town in one of the provinces of Mysore. Hyder protested, and upon being disregarded, invaded the English possessions in Carnatic and exacted retribution. The great historian of Anglo-India, Mill, remarks: "Hyder was less detested as a destroyer than hailed as a deliverer . . . and the English commander himself testifies in an official letter that "There is no doubt that Hyder has greatly attached the inhabitants to him." Torrens remarks that later, when Pettah and Arcot were taken by Hyder, he treated the inhabitants "with humanity; no plundering or license was allowed; every one was continued in the enjoyment of his fortune, and all who held places under the Nawab retained them; to the English officers, Hyder gave money to provide for their necessities"—conduct which places his "barbarity" in favourable contrast with the "civilisation" of the English, when later they sacked his capital.

In the winter of 1782, before the war with the English had terminated, Hyder died, and his adversaries made a new treaty of peace with his son Tipu. The fidelity of Hyder's Brahmin minister has been handed down in history—he it was who concealed the death of his prince until Tipu reached the camp and claimed his inheritance.

Colonel Fullarton's "View of the Interests of India" contains an estimate of the character of Hyder and conditions during his reign. The writer of the Reform Pamphlet remarks:

> "Although most constantly engaged in war, the improvement of his country and the strictest executive administration formed his constant care. Manufacturer and merchant prospered . . . cultivation increased, new manufactures were established, wealth flowed into the kingdom . . . the slightest defalcation by the officers of revenue was summarily punished. He had his eye upon every corner of his own dominions and every court in India. . . . Though unable to write himself, he dictated in few words the substance of his correspondence to secretaries . . . he united minuteness of detail with the utmost latitude of thought and enterprise. . . . He bequeathed to his son, Tipu Sultan, an overflowing treasury, a powerful empire, an army of 300,000 men . . . and great territories."

The following is the substance of Moore's estimate of Tipu's administration.

> "When a person, travelling through a strange country, finds it well cultivated, populous with industrious habitants, cities newly founded, commerce extending,

towns increasing, and everything flourishing so as to indicate happiness, he naturally concludes the form of government congenial to the people. This is a picture of Tipu's government . . . we have reason to suppose his subjects to be happy as those of any other sovereign . . . no murmurings or complaints were heard against him, though the enemies of Tipu were in power, and would have been gratified by any aspersions of his character . . . but the inhabitants of the conquered countries . . . so soon as an opportunity offered, scouted their new master, and gladly returned to their loyalty again." [21]

Dirom, another writer pays an equally high tribute to the prosperity of Tipu's country.[22]

All this prosperity was not created entirely by Hyder or his son, whose sway did not last half a century. For the foundation of these flourishing conditions we must look to the ancient Hindu dynasty — they were the constructors of those magnificent canals which intersect Mysore and insure the people prodigal returns from the fertile soil.

In 1789 occurred the third war with Mysore, resulting in a peace in 1792 whereby Tipu was forced to pay a heavy indemnity and cede half his territories. It was reserved for the Marquis of Wellesley to wipe out the House of Hyder completely, by annexing a large part of his remaining lands, and restoring the superseded Hindu dynasty to a fraction of its former domain under the title of the Raja of the state of Mysore.

Northern India. From the south, we may now turn to the north to examine conditions preceding British

[21] Moore's "Narrative of the War with Tipu Sultan," p. 201, quoted in the Reform Pamphlet.

[22] Dirom's "Narrative," p. 249.

occupation. To avoid all suspicion of political or racial bias, we will let the English writers of the Reform Pamphlet speak.

Bengal.

In the year that Hyder established his sway over Mysore, Bengal,— the brightest jewel in the Imperial Crown of the Moguls, came into British possession. (Clive described the new acquisition as "a country of inexhaustible riches" and one that could not fail to make its new masters the richest corporation in the world. Bengal was known to the East as the Garden of Eden, the rich kingdom. Says Mr. Holwell: "Here the property, as well as the liberty, of the people, are inviolate. The traveller, with or without merchandise, becomes the immediate care of the Government, which allots him guards, without any expense, to conduct him from stage to stage. . . . If . . . a bag of money or valuables is lost in this district, the person who finds it hangs it on a tree and gives notice to the nearest guard. . . ."[23]

The rich province of Dacca was cultivated in every part . . . justice was administered impartially . . . Jeswunt Roy . . . had been educated in purity, integrity and indefatigable attention to business, and studied to render the government of his province conducive to the general ease and happiness of his people — he abolished all monopolies and the imposts upon grain.[24]

Such was the state of Bengal when Alivardy Khan . . . assumed its government. Under his rule . . . the country was improved; merit and good conduct were the only passports to his favour. He placed Hindus on an equality with Mussalmen, in choosing

[23] Howells' "Tracts upon India," Reform Pamphlet No. 9, p. 21.

[24] Stewart's "History of Bengal," p. 430, quoted in the pamphlet No. 9, p. 22.

Ministers, and nominating them to high military and civil command. The revenues, instead of being drawn to the distant treasury of Delhi were spent on the spot.[25]

But in less than ten years after Bengal had become subject to British rule, a great and sudden change came over the land. Every ship, Mr. Macaulay tells us, for some time, had brought alarming tidings from Bengal. The internal misgovernment of the province had reached such a pitch that it could go no further.

"What indeed, was to be expected from a body of public servants exposed to temptation such as Clive once said, flesh and blood could not bear it, armed with irresistible power, and responsible only to the corrupt, turbulent, distracted, ill-informed Company, situated at such a distance that the average interval between the sending of a despatch and the receipt of an answer was above a year and a half. Accordingly the five years which followed the departure of Clive from Bengal saw the misgovernment of the English carried to such a point as seemed incompatible with the existence of society. The Roman proconsul, who, in a year or two, squeezed out of a province the means of rearing marble palaces and baths on the shores of Campania, of drinking from amber and feasting on singing birds, of exhibiting armies of gladiators and flocks of camelopards; the Spanish viceroy, who, leaving behind him the curses of Mexico or Lima, entered Madrid with a long train of gilded coaches, and sumpter horses trapped and shod with silver, were now outdone. . . . The servants of the Company obtained for themselves a monopoly of almost the whole internal trade. They forced the natives to buy dear and sell cheap. They insulted with impunity the tribunals, the police and fiscal

[25] Stewart's "History of Bengal," quoted in the Reform Pamphlet No. 9, p. 22.

authorities . . . every servant of a British factor was armed with all the power of the Company. . . . Enormous fortunes were thus rapidly accumulated at Calcutta, while thirty millions of human beings were reduced to an extremity of wretchedness. . . . Under their old masters, . . . when evil became insupportable, the people rose and pulled down the government. But the English Government was not to be shaken off. That Government, oppressive as the most oppressive form of barbarian despotism, was strong with all the strength of civilisation." [26]

The Kingdom of Oude. The same testimony regarding the East India Company's destructive and rapacious misrule applies to Oude. While Mr. Warren Hastings was still vested with supreme rule over India, he describes a condition which he himself was instrumental in producing.

"I fear that our encroaching spirit, and the insolence with which it has been exerted, has caused our alliance to be as much dreaded by all the powers of Hindustan as our arms. Our encroaching spirit, and the uncontrolled and even protected licentiousness of individuals, has done injury to our national reputation. . . . Every person in India dreads a connection with us." [27]

Before dealings with the English commenced, Oude was in a high state of prosperity, yielding, without pressure on the people, an income of three millions, clear. By quartering upon the Nawab an army of soldiers, as well as a host of civilians, he was soon reduced to a state of bitterest distress and his country to poverty, his income being reduced in a few years

[26] Macaulay's "Essay on Lord Clive."
[27] Gleig's "Life of Hastings," Vol. II, quoted in the Reform Pamphlet No. 9, p. 25.

to half its former amount. "In nine years," Mill says, "unjustifiable extortions, to the amount of thirty-four lacs of rupees (£340,000) per annum, had been practised on that dependent province."[28] The extent of the salaries, pensions and encroachments of the company's service, civil and military, upon the Nawab's revenues and authority, says Warren Hastings

"have become an intolerable burden and exposed us to the enmity, and resentment of the whole country, by excluding the native servants and adherents of the Vizier from the rewards of their service and attachments. I am afraid few men would understand me were I to ask by what right or policy we levied a tax on the Nawab Vizier for the benefit of patronised individuals, and fewer still, if I questioned the right or policy of imposing upon him an army for his protection, which he could not pay, which he does not want; with what expression could I tell him to his face, 'You do not want it, but you shall pay for it!' . . . Every Englishman in Oude was possessed of an independent and sovereign authority. They learned . . . to claim the revenue of lacs[29] as their right, though they could gamble away more than two lacs (I allude to a known fact) at a sitting.[30]

The demands of the English increased from £250,000 to £700,000 per annum, under Lord Cornwallis, with a further increase under Lord Teignmouth. In 1801, Lord Wellesley, under threat of seizing the whole, extorted from the Nawab one-half his dominions, valued at £1,300,000 per annum. From 1815

[28] Mill, "History of India," Vol. V, p. 316.
[29] A *lac* is equal to a hundred thousand rupees.
[30] "Life of W. Hastings," Vol. II, p. 458. Reform Pamphlet No. 9, p. 26.

to 1825 more than four million pounds were extracted from the Nawab under the name of loans, for which he received the title of King, and a territory little better than a wilderness. Says the Reform Pamphlet, commenting upon the dealings in Oude:

"This is a brief history . . . not penned by those who have suffered, but by the doers themselves. It is based upon facts that are upon our records, and indisputable. If Oude then, is misgoverned,—if its people are impoverished and oppressed who is to blame—the native sovereigns, or those who have thus trampled upon the Native Sovereigns?"

At the time Lord Cornwallis, then Governor-General, was pronouncing Bengal to be in process of decay under British mismanagement, the Kingdom of Mysore, under the rule of Poorneah, was in a state of high prosperity, so much so, that the Duke of Wellington pronounced its government worthy of applause, and as a mark of his approbation, presented the Dewan Poorneah with his picture.

British publicists are fond of drawing the blackest possible picture of India under the administration of the Mahrattas. Sevaji, the great founder of the Mahratta Empire, has been termed a "robber" by them, but all classes of modern India hold him in memory as a hero worthy of universal respect. The following estimate of his character is based on Grant Duff's History of the Mahrattas, vol. II.[31]

"The 'robber,' Sevajee, who entered upon the scene in the latter part of the sixteenth century, and who shook the Mogul Empire to its foundation during the

[31] *Vide* the Reform Pamphlet, No. 9, pp. 14 and 15.

reign of Aurungzebe, was an able as well as skilful general. His civil government was regular, and he was vigorous in exacting from his provincial and village officers obedience to the rules he laid down for the protection of his people. His enemies bear witness to his anxiety to mitigate the evils of war by humane regulations, which were strictly enforced. Altogether, this robber hero has left a character which has never since been equalled or ever approached by any of his countrymen. None of his military successes raise so high an idea of his talents as his domestic administration, and the effect of this appears to have been permanent for eighty years after his death."

Anquetil du Perron, in his "Brief Account of a Voyage to India," published in the *Gentleman's Magazine* of 1762, gives an interesting glimpse of the state of the Mahratta Territory:

"From Surat, I passed the Ghats, . . . about ten in the morning, and when I entered the country of the Mahrattas, I thought myself in the midst of the simplicity and happiness of the golden age, where nature was yet unchanged, and war and misery were unknown. The people were cheerful, vigorous and in high health and unbounded hospitality was an universal virtue; every door was open, and friends, neighbours and strangers were alike welcome to whatever they found."

The successors of Sevaji were also rulers of sagacity and ability. Bajee Rao Bullal is said to have united the enterprise, vigour and hardihood of a Mahratta chief with the polished manners, wisdom and address which distinguished the Brahmins of Concan. He possessed eloquence, penetration and vigour, was simple in his habits, a successful military leader, who at all times partook of the privations of his soldiers. Ballajee Rao, who succeeded him, was characterised by the same political ability, devoting, amid the distractions of war, much time to the civil administration of his territory; in his reign the condition of the population was improved, the system of farming the revenues was abolished, and the tribunals of justice were rendered accessible to all. Following him came Mahdoo Rao, whose character as a sovereign was as conspicuous as were his military talents.

"He is deservedly celebrated for his firm support of the weak against the oppressive, of the poor against the rich, and . . . for his equity to all."

At that time, the Mahratta territory was more thriving than any other part of India. The celebrated Ram Shastree was the pure and upright minister who served Mahdoo Rao. The weight and soundness of his judgments have made them to this day precedents in Hindu law. By his unwearied zeal, he improved the condition of the people of all ranks. His integrity was never corrupted. It was the custom of this man of simple habits, never to keep in his house more food than sufficed for one day's consumption.[32]

The territory of the Peishwah was administered, for a quarter of a century, by Nana Furnawese, during the minority of Bajee Rao. He has been described as a minister of unequalled ability, who held together, by force and energy of mind, and the versatility of his genius, the incongruous interests of his empire. The wisdom, firmness and moderation of his government

[32] Grant Duff's "History of the Mahrattas," Vol. II, p. 208.

are testified to by Sir John Malcolm, who thus describes the condition of the country:

"It has not happened to me ever to see countries better cultivated, and more abounding in all the produce of the soil as well as in commercial wealth, than the southern Mahratta districts. . . . Poonah, the capital of the Peishwah, was a very wealthy and thriving commercial town and there was as much cultivation in the Deccan, as it was possible an arid and unfruitful country could admit." About another large part of the Mahratta territory under the sovereignty of Holkar we have the testimony of the same distinguished writers:

"With respect to Malwa, I saw it in a state of ruin, caused by the occupancy . . . of the predatory hordes of India. Yet, even at that period, I was surprised . . . to find that dealings in money to large amounts had continually taken place between cities, where bankers were in a flourishing state, and goods to a great extent continually passed through the province, . . . the insurance offices which exist through all parts of India . . . had never stopped their operations. . . . I do not believe that in Malwa the introduction of our direct rule could have contributed more, nor indeed so much, to the prosperity of the commercial and agricultural interests, as the re-establishment of the efficient rule of its former princes and chiefs. With respect to the southern Mahratta districts, of whose prosperity I have before spoken, . . . I do not think either their commercial or agricultural interests likely to be improved under our rule. . . . Their system of administration is, on the whole, mild and paternal. I refer their prosperity to be due . . . to the knowledge and almost devotion of the Hindus to agricultural pursuit; to their better understanding, or better practice than us . . . in raising towns and villages to prosperity, from the encouragement given to moneyed men, and the introduction of capital . . . but above all causes which promote prosperity, is the invariable support given to the village and other native institutions, and to the employment, far beyond what our system permits, of all classes of population."[33]

The same writer praises the administration of the Mahratta Queen, Ahalya Bai, the internal tranquillity of whose territory was as remarkable as her freedom from foreign attack. The object of her rule was to promote the prosperity of all her subjects; she was said to rejoice when she saw bankers, farmers, merchants and cultivators rise to affluence; she was regarded as the model of good government in Malwa. She built several forts, and constructed a road over the almost perpendicular Vindhya range. Among the princes of her own nation, all would have held it sacrilege to become her enemy, or to fail to defend her from hostile attack.[34]

The dominions of the Rajah of Berar, another member of the great Mahratta Confederacy, were equally flourishing. European travellers comment on the thriving districts, the industrious people, the fertile soil, the magnificent temples and the greatness of public works.[35]

From the Mahratta, let us pass to other States. The Reform Pamphlet quotes from a report from Commissions upon the Northwest Provinces, which it might be well to cite:

"In passing through the Rampore territory, we

[33] Reform Pamphlet No. 9, pp. 28, 29.
[34] Malcolm's "History of Central India," Vol. I, pp. 176, 195.
[35] See the authorities quoted in the Reform Pamphlet, pp. 32 and 33.

could not fail to notice the high state of cultivation to which it has attained when compared with the surrounding country; scarcely a spot of land is neglected and although the season was by no means favourable the whole district seemed covered with an abundant harvest. . . . The management of the Nawab Fyz-oolah Kahn is celebrated throughout the country. It was the administration of an enlightened and liberal landlord, who devoted his time and attention, and employed his own capital, in promoting the prosperity of the country. When works of magnitude were required . . . the means of undertaking them were supplied from his bounty. Watercourses were constructed, the rivulets made to overflow and fertilise the adjacent districts, and the paternal care of a popular chief was constantly exerted to afford protection to his subjects, to stimulate their exertions, to direct their labours to useful objects and to promote by every means the success of their undertaking."

"If the comparison for the same territory be made between the management of the Rohillas and that of our own government, *it is painful to think that the balance of advantage is clearly in favour of the former.* After seven years' possession of the country, it appears by the report that the revenue has increased only by two lacs of rupees, or 20,000 pounds. The papers laid before Parliament show that in the twenty years which have since elapsed, the collective revenues of Rohilcund and the districts forming the ceded province of Oude, actually declined 200,000 pounds per annum!

* * *

"While the surrounding country seemed to have been visited by a desolating calamity, the lands of the Rajahs Diaram and Bugwaut Singh under every disadvantage of season were covered with crops produced by better husbandry or greater labour." These neighbouring lands consisted *"of British territory, already five years in our occupation."*[36]

Bishop Heber, in his "Journal," Vol. II, pages 77–9 bears testimony to the enlightenment and prosperity of Oude at this period under Saadat Ali, whom he rates as a man of talents and acquirements, fond of business, with a penchant for science. He is described by Lord Hastings as a sovereign admirable for uprightness, humanity and mild elevation. The prosperous condition of the state of Bhurtpore under native rulers is likewise testified to.[36]

"This country . . . is one of the best cultivated and watered tracts which I have seen in India. The crops of corn on the ground were really beautiful; that of cotton . . . a very good one. What is a sure proof of wealth, I saw several sugar-mills, and large pieces of ground where the cane had just been cleared. . . . The population did not seem great, but the villages were in good condition and repair, and the whole afforded so pleasing a picture of industry, and was so much superior to anything I had been led to expect in Rajputana, *which I had seen in the Company's territories* . . . that I was led to suppose that either the Rajah of Bhurtpore was an extreme exemplary and parental governor, or that the system of management adopted in the British provinces was less favourable to the improvement and happiness of the country than some of the native states."

The British Government itself emphatically testifies to the high character of Pertaub Singh, the first Rajah of Sattara, and the prosperity of his kingdom. The government Records show a letter from the Court of Directors (1843, No. 569, page 1268).

[36] Bishop Heber's "Journal," Vol. II, quoted by the Reform Pamphlet.

"We have been highly gratified by the information from time to time transmitted to us from our Government, of your Highness's exemplary fulfilment of the duties of that elevated situation in which it has pleased Providence to place you.

"A course of conduct so suitable to your Highness's exalted station, and so well calculated to promote the prosperity of your dominions and the happiness of your people, as that which you have wisely and uniformly pursued, while it reflects the highest honour on your own character, has imparted to our minds unqualified pleasure and satisfaction. The liberality which you displayed in executing at your own cost, various public works of great utility . . . gives additional claim to our approbation, respect, and applause."

While the British Government was thus congratulating the Rajah on the prosperity of his dominions, the wretched state of some thirty millions of natives under British rule is described by Dr. Marshman, in *The Friend of India*, April 1, 1852:

"No one has ever contradicted the fact that the condition of the Bengal peasantry is almost as wretched and degraded as it is possible to conceive; living in the most miserable hovels, scarcely fit for a dog kennel, covered with tattered rags, and unable in many instances, to procure more than a single meal a day for himself and family, the Bengal ryot knows nothing of the most ordinary comforts of life. We speak without exaggeration when we say that if the real condition of those who raise the harvest, which yields between three and four millions a year, were fully known, it would make the ears of one who heard thereof tingle."

This, described by an unimpeachable eye-witness,

was the condition of Bengal, the "Garden of Eden" after almost a century of British rule! If this appalling state had been normal before the English came, what had the Government been doing for a century not to extricate the people from it?

But the words of Clive are still upon record—"Bengal, the country of inexhaustible riches, capable of making its masters the richest corporation in the world." What can the Government say for itself in the face of such a result? Lord Cornwallis said, in his time, that the people "were advancing hastily to a state of poverty and wretchedness." By multiplied exactions and heavy assessments, from 1765 to 1790 the British revenue system enriched itself and left the country exhausted and impoverished. Governor General Lord Hastings declared in 1827 (Parl. Papers, page 157):

"A new progeny has grown up under our hand; and the principal features of a generation thus formed beneath the shade of our regulation, are a spirit of litigation which our judicial establishments cannot meet, and a morality certainly deteriorated."

As with the judicial system, so with regard to person and property. Protection was so inadequate, that as stated in an article in *The Friend of India* (Aug. 28, 1851) "no man of property . . . can retire to rest with the certainty that he shall not be robbed of it before morning." Small wonder that Governor-General Lord Bentinck admitted that "Our administration had, in all its branches, revenue, judicial and police, been a failure." This was uttered in the first half of the nineteenth century.

Because of the gross ignorance on the part of the civilised world, regarding the facts discussed at such length, we have quoted somewhat lengthily from sources whose testimony, coming as it does, from the British camp, cannot be questioned. British publicists continue in their efforts to mislead the public mind by affirming that England rescued India from a state of widespread anarchy and confusion, and by conferring upon her, for the first time in her history, a settled government, saved her from herself. During her many centuries of political development, India was undoubtedly as good, and as bad, as the other evolving nations on the face of Mother Earth. She prospered under her beneficent rulers, and suffered under her bad ones. She had her periods of progress, as well as of stagnation. She had times of peace as well as of war. Her rulers were by no means immaculate. Her people were not always happy. They faced tyranny and oppression as often as good government and orderly justice. Were a chart of Indian politics for the past three thousand years to be compiled, it might be found that her eras of peace and prosperity perhaps exceeded those of any other country in the world. It is futile to pass judgment upon the India of the sixteenth century, from the pinnacle of twentieth century standards.

Even now there are native states in India which are admittedly better governed than British India. In several of them the rulers have introduced compulsory universal education, have established representative institutions and, last but not least, have started industries of their own to give employment to their subjects.

Dr. H. A. L. Fisher, the Minister of Education in the Lloyd George Cabinet says in his book "The Empire and the Future," "My impression is that the inhabitants of a well governed native state are on the whole happier and more contented than the inhabitants of British India. *They are more lightly taxed;* the pace of the administration is less urgent and exacting; their sentiment is gratified by the splendour of a native court and by the dominion of an Indian Government. They feel that they do things for themselves instead of having everything done for them by a cold and alien benevolence." [Italics mine. L. R.] We are sorry that consideration of space should have forced us to abridge many of the references given in this chapter. Independent enquirers are respectfully referred to the authorities quoted from.

PART TWO

CHAPTER II

INDIA AND THE BRITISH INDUSTRIAL REVOLUTION

Before Plassy. That India played a very definite part in the success of the British Industrial Revolution, is a fact almost universally acknowledged; vet how great a part India played in making for the industrial and economic prosperity of Great Britain is known to very few. It is our purpose to discuss that point in this chapter.

Let us consider first the respective economic positions of India and England at the time when the Industrial Revolution was brought about by the invention of the steam engine and of mechanical contrivances for the spinning and weaving of cloth.

We have already given the reader an idea, in the introductory chapter, of the economic prosperity of India in pre-British days. In the seventeenth and eighteenth centuries, India had enormous wealth; the treasuries of her rulers were full of money, bullion and precious stones of fabulous value; her industries and manufactures flourished, and she exported large quantities of goods in return for payment in gold and silver. Her trade with Asia, Europe and Africa was extensive, and she made enormous profits from the sale of her manufactured goods. Her cotton muslins, manufactured silks, woollen shawls, brass and bronzes had made her famous, all through Asia and Europe.

For centuries, the maritime nations of Europe had been trying to find a sea route to India in order to profit by trading with her and possibly with the motive of eventually conquering her. The discovery of America was only an accident. The goal which Columbus had in view was India. It is well known how, after Columbus, the Dutch and the Portuguese navigators kept up their search for a sea route to India until the efforts of Vasco da Gama bore fruit when he discovered the route around the Cape of Good Hope. For a long time before the East India Company was founded the Portuguese and the Dutch shippers had been making enormous profits from the Indian trade. The East India Company began its operations in 1603. In the first eighty years of its enterprise the company made a profit of 171 per cent. per annum on its investment. The details of its imports and exports show that while it took raw silk, fine calicoes, indigo, cloves and mace from India, it brought to India only bullion. It was in 1613 that the British East India traders first incorporated themselves into a sort of joint stock concern. Writing of that time, J. Bruce says [1] that the continent of India was " the seat of the most extensive and splendid monarchies on the surface of the globe."

In the four years following the incorporation, the character of the trade of the East India Company remained unchanged, though its profits were greatly reduced, reaching the modest figure of 87½ per cent.

Then came the embassy of Sir Thomas Roe in 1614

[1] " Annals of the East India Co.," by J. Bruce, Vol. I, p. 166; quoted by James Mill in his History, Vol. I, p. 30.

which resulted in the grant by the Mogul Emperor of Delhi, to the East India Company, of "the liberty of trading and establishing factories in any part of the Mogul dominions; Surat, Bengal and Sindh being particularly named."

At that time the Dutch and the Portuguese claimed the monopoly of the Eastern trade. The English Company had several naval encounters and military engagements with them in parts of Asia. In India, these Portuguese and Dutch traders maintained forts and garrisons by which they not only protected their factories but established a certain prestige in the eyes of the native rulers, which helped them in their business. The English wanted to follow their example and plant forts and garrisons as well, but Sir Thomas Roe persuaded them not to do so, on the ground that the expense of doing so would reduce their profits.

We are told that in 1617 "Cloths of India could best be obtained at Surat, though nothing could be disposed of, in return, except China goods, spices and money."[2] For more than a century and a half, the English trade in India consisted mainly of the export of cotton and silk goods, indigo and spices in return for bullion. During this period India imported *practically* nothing. Bruce says that "on the average of ten years, from 1747 to 1757, £562,423 bullion was exported to India, but after that year bullion was no longer exported there."[3]

How the East India Company made enormous

[2] Mill, Vol. I, p. 37.

[3] "Plans for British India," by J. Bruce, p. 316. See also "Outlines of English Industry," by Cunningham and McArthur, Cambridge University Press, 1895, p. 128.

profits (perfectly legitimate) from this trade is told by all the historians of the time. Macaulay says:[4]

"The company enjoyed during the greater part of the reign of Charles II, a prosperity to which the history of trade scarcely furnished any parallel and which excited the wonder, the cupidity and the envious animosity of the whole capital (London). . . . During the twenty-three years that followed the Restoration the value of the annual imports from that rich and popular district (the Delta of the Ganges) increased from £8000 to £300,000." And he adds that "the gains of the body (i.e., the company) were almost incredible . . . the profits were such that in 1676 every proprietor received as a bonus a quantity of stock equal to that which he held. On the capital thus doubled were paid, during five years, dividends amounting to an average of 20 per cent. annually."

In 1677 the price of the stock was 245 for every one hundred. In 1681 it rose to 300 and later to 360 and 500. The only limitations to the profits of the company were the exactions of the English crown, the demands of the English Exchequer, and the dishonesty of its servants.

At that time the balance of trade was entirely in favour of India. The British historian, Orme, in his "Historical Fragments" says that the manufacture of cotton goods was almost universal throughout India. The rupee, which now sells for 1s. 4d., was then worth 2s. 8d. Such was the economic condition of India.

Let us now consider the economic condition of Eng-

[4] Macaulay's "History of England," Vol. V, p. 2094.

land. "In the sixteenth century," says Robertson, "England was a backward country, and capitalists seeking investments looked towards it from all the monetary centres."

"Early in the seventeenth century," says Mill, "the English, whose country, oppressed by misgovernment or scourged by civil war, afforded little capital to extend trade, or protect it, were unequal competitors of the Dutch."

By the end of the seventeenth century, conditions had become alarmingly acute, not only in England, but throughout Europe, as has been shown by Brooks Adams. Adams says that towards the close of the seventeenth century Europe appeared to be on the brink of a contraction of money, due partly to the constant drain to Asia and the increasing demands of commerce. From the reign of Augustus commerce between Europe and Asia had usually favoured Asia. The lack of money led to a considerable depreciation of currency in England.

Speaking of the time of the Revolution Ruding says: "At that time the diminution of the value of money and counterfeiting had been so excessive that what was good silver was worth scarcely one-half of the current value, and a great part of the coins was only iron, brass, or copper plated, and some no more than washed over."

In the decade between 1710–1720 the actual export of bullion by the East India Company averaged £4,344,000.

The story of how England supplied her needs at this time is one of the most dramatic pages of history. As

Jevons has observed, "Asia is the great reservoir and sink of the precious metals." From time immemorial the oriental custom has been to hoard, and from the Mogul blazing with the diamonds of Golconda, to the peasant starving on his wretched pittance, every Hindu had, in former days, a treasure stored away against a day of trouble. "*These hoards, the savings of millions of human beings for centuries, the English seized and took to London,* as the Romans had taken the spoils of Greece and Pontus to Italy. *What the value of the treasure was, no man can estimate but it must have been many millions of pounds—a vast sum in proportion to the stock of the precious metals then owned by Europeans.*"[5]

We have already pointed out on the authority of Bruce that the last export of bullion from England to India took place in 1757, the year in which the battle of Plassy was fought. After that, bullion was no longer exported to India. "From this period on, the export of bullion to China very considerably decreased and it was only sent occasionally after the supply from India failed. This circumstance was explained in every letter sent by the directors to their servants at Madras and Bengal, which contained instructions to them to collect as much bullion as they could, to be ready for ships which would come out from Madras and China, and by the answers to the letters specifying the quantity sent by the different vessels."[6]

The circumstances in India at that time were very favourable to the collection of bullion by the servants

[5] Brooks Adams in "The Law of Civilisation and Decay," p. 305.

[6] J. Bruce, "Plans for British India," pp. 314–315.

of the East India Company. In the words of Macaulay, "Treasure flowed to England in oceans;" and what was lacking in England to make the fullest possible use of the mechanical inventions made by Watt and others, was supplied by India. The influx of Indian treasure added considerably to England's cash capital.

Brooks Adams remarks that after Plassy the Bengal plunder began to arrive in London and, "the effect appears to have been instantaneous, for all authorities agree that the Industrial Revolution — the current which divided the nineteenth century from all antecedent time — began with the year 1760."

It is an historic fact that prior to that time the machinery used for spinning cotton in Lancashire was as simple as it was in India. It was in 1760 that the flying-shuttle was invented. Hargreave invented the spinning jenny in 1764, Compton invented the mule in 1779, Cartwright in 1795 patented the power-loom, and Watt brought his steam engine to completion in 1768. Had these inventions been matured fifty years before the influx of Indian treasure and the expansion of credit which followed such masses of capital, they and their inventors would probably have perished for want of sufficient money to set them going, for it should be borne in mind that the factory system was not the father of the industrial revolution but the child thereof. In short, the accumulated masses of Indian treasure liberated the machines to furnish an outlet for the movement of the time. Adams points out how agriculture also was impelled by this new force.

A credit system based on Indian metal sprang up in

England, and the agriculturists who could borrow, imported cattle and improved tillage. This movement resulted in increasing the value of land. The wastes were enclosed, thus making the position of the yeomanry almost unbearable and provoking the far-reaching social revolution of the time.

England, favoured as she was with coal and iron mines and with credit, the easy vehicle of energy, soon dominated the European and American market and even undersold Hindu labour at Calcutta.

It is clear then that the "Industrial Revolution," the foundation on which England's economic prosperity was built up, was made possible only by the influx of Indian treasure, and that but for this capital, not loaned, but taken, and bearing no interest, the ascendency of the steam engine and mechanical appliances for mass production, might have remained unutilised. England's gain was India's loss,—a loss of treasure more than enough to starve her industries and retard the progress of agriculture. No country, however rich or resourceful, could bear such a drain unharmed.

The wound inflicted by wholesale exportation of India's wealth, was deepened by the way in which the treasure was collected. The wealth which England derived from India and invested in her industries at home, or otherwise used to her profit, may be classified thus:

1. Tributes and gratuities obtained from Indian rulers and potentates, in the name of, and for the East India Company.

2. Taxes raised from the people in the name of, and for the East India Company.
3. The profits of internal trade carried on by the servants of the East India Company in their own interests.
4. Bribes and gratuities obtained from the Native rulers, their relatives and connections who had any dealings with the East India Company. Some of these emoluments were obtained openly, others surreptitiously and by extortion.

Part of the money thus raised went to England in the shape of goods purchased from India for sale in England and elsewhere; the rest went in cash. For better understanding, the period may be considered under two divisions:

1. The economic effects of the battle of Plassy, 1757–60, under the governorship of Clive, and the revolutions and changes that took place in Bengal, 1760–65, during the absence of Clive in England.
2. Clive's second administration, 1765–67.

1. Effects of Plassy. The victory of Plassy was followed by a treaty with Mir Jaffar by which the latter agreed to pay to the East India Company about one and three-quarters millions pounds sterling, in cash, besides large tracts of land in permanent ownership.[7] In

[7] In addition to the sums defined in the treaty, Mir Jaffar after his enthronement made large gifts to the highest servants of the Company. The Select Committee of 1772 estimated the amount of these gifts at £1,250,000, of which Clive received £234,000 (Third Report, p. 311). But these were only "gifts proved and acknowledged." In 1759 Clive further received as a jaghir or estate, the right of receiving from the Company the tribute due from it for the territories referred to in the treaty as "the 24 parganas" or districts. Mir Jaffar also bequeathed him five lacs of rupees, £50,000 which he made over to the Company as a fund for pensioning disabled soldiers. See Muir, "The Making of British India," p. 59.

his "Essay on Clive," Macaulay has left a graphic description of the "shower of wealth" that began to fall after Plassy.

Within less than three years from this treaty, Mir Jaffar was declared a failure; during his rule, the greed and rapacity of the servants of the Company found full play, and Bengal was in a condition of anarchy. This state of things was the direct result of the conduct of the Company's servants. Muir says:

"The only persons who profited by these conditions were the individual servants of the Company, who found no check or control exercised over their high-handed pursuit of private profit." [8]

A change being necessary, Mir Jaffar was deposed, and his son-in-law, Mir Kassim, installed as Nabob. In return for this service, he ceded to the British three of the most prosperous districts of Bengal,—Burdwan, Midnapur and Chittagong,—in lieu of paying the army, which he was unable to do, his revenues being sadly depleted by the ravages and piratical demands of his masters, the servants of the Company. He also agreed to pay the balance of Mir Jaffar's unpaid account, and gave an extra present of five lacs of rupees, £50,000 to help pay the expenses of the Company's wars in the south. The amount given in presents to the English officers on this occasion totalled £200,269,—of which the governor took £58,333. Mir Kassim met his engagements with the Company, and in less than two years, had faithfully discharged his obligations.

Mir Kassim proved an unexpected set back to the de-

[8] "The Making of British India," p. 59.

signs of the British merchants. In place of being a mere tool in their hands, he turned out to be a far more efficient ruler than Mir Jaffar, and brought about a great improvement in conditions. But in the language of Professor Muir:

"He was never given a fair chance. From the outset he was an object of suspicion and hostility on the part of the majority of the Calcutta Council. They disliked the change from the nerveless rule of Mir Jaffar, because it interfered with their profits; and especially they resented the attempt to levy tolls on the trade carried on for their profit by the Indian gomastas."

Governor Verelst has left it on record that:

"A trade was carried on without payment of duties, in the prosecution of which infinite oppressions were committed. English agents or Gomastahs, not contented with injuring the people, trampled on the authority of government, binding and punishing the Nabob's officers whenever they presumed to interfere. This was the immediate cause of the war with Meer Cossim."[9]

A corroboration of this is furnished by the letter of Warren Hastings to the Governor on April 25, 1762:

"I beg leave to lay before you a grievance which loudly calls for redress, and will, unless duly attended to, render ineffectual any endeavours to create a firm and lasting harmony between the Nabob and the Company. I mean the oppression committed under the sanction of the English name. . . . I have been surprised to meet with several English flags flying in places which I have passed, and on the river I do not

[9] Quoted by Romesh Dutt, "India Under Early British Rule," p. 20.

believe I passed a boat without one. By whatever title they have been assumed (for I could trust to the information of my eyes without stopping to ask questions), I am sure their frequency can bode no good to the Nabob's revenues, the quiet of the country, or the honour of our nation, but eventually tends to lessen each of them. A party of Sepoys who were on the march before us afforded sufficient proofs of the rapacious and insolent spirit of those people where they are left to their own discretion. Many complaints against them were made me on the road, and most of the petty towns and Serais were deserted at our approach and the shops shut up from the apprehensions of the same treatment from us. You are sensible, sir, that it is from such little irregularities, too trivial perhaps for public complaint and continually repeated, that the country people are habituated to entertain the most unfavourable notions of our government."[10]

From the protests of the Nabob of Bengal we quote only one extract, viz., the one contained in his letter written in May, 1762:

"In every Perganah, every village, and every factory, they (the Company's Gomastahs) buy and sell salt, betel-nut, ghee, rice, straw, bamboos, fish, gunnies, ginger, sugar, tobacco, opium, and many other things, more than I can write, and which I think it needless to mention. They forcibly take away the goods and commodities of the Reiats, merchants, etc., for a fourth part of their value; and by ways of violence and oppressions they oblige the Reiats, etc., to give five rupees for goods which are worth but one rupee. . . . The officers of every district have desisted from the exercise of their functions; so that by means

[10] Quoted by Romesh Dutt, "India Under Early British Rule," p. 21.

of these oppressions, and my being deprived of my duties, I suffer a yearly loss of nearly twenty-five lakhs of Rupees. . . . By the grace of God, I neither have transgressed, nor do, nor will transgress the treaty and agreement which I have made; why then do the chiefs of the Englishmen render my government contemptible and employ themselves in bringing a loss upon me?"[11]

But a more graphic description is to be found in a letter from Sergeant Brago:

"A gentleman sends a Gomastah here to buy or sell; he immediately looks upon himself as sufficient to force every inhabitant either to buy his goods or sell him theirs; and on refusal (in case of non-capacity) a flogging or confinement immediately ensues. This is not sufficient even when willing, but a second force is made use of, which is to engross the different branches of trade to themselves, and not to suffer any person to buy or sell the articles they trade in; and if the country people do it, then a repetition of their authority is put in practise; and again, what things they purchase, they think the least they can do is to take them for a considerable deal less than another merchant, and oftentimes refuse paying that; and my interfering occasions an immediate complaint. These, and many other oppressions more than can be related, which are daily used by the Bengal Gomastahs, is the reason that this place (Backerjunj, a prosperous Bengal district) is growing destitute of inhabitants; every day numbers leave the town to seek a residence more safe, and the very markets, which before afforded plenty, do hardly now produce anything of use, their peons being allowed to force poor people; and if the Zemindar offers to prevent it, he is threatened to be

[11] Quoted by Romesh Dutt, "India Under Early British Rule," p. 23.

used in the same manner. Before, justice was given in the public Catcheree, but now every Gomastah is become a judge, and every one's house a Catcheree; they even pass sentences on the Zemindars themselves, and draw money from them by pretended injuries, such as a quarrel with some of the peons, or their having, as they assert, stole something, which is more likely to have been taken by their own people." [12]

One more quotation from William Bolts, an English merchant, and we have done with this part of this sad story:

"It may with truth be now said that the whole inland trade of the country, as at present conducted, and that of the Company's investment for Europe in a more peculiar degree, has been one continued scene of oppression; the baneful effects of which are severely felt by every weaver and manufacturer in the country, every article produced being made a monopoly; in which the English, with their Banyans and black Gomastahs, arbitrarily decide what quantities of goods each manufacturer shall deliver, and the prices he shall receive for them. . . . Upon the Gomastah's arrival at the Aurung, or manufacturing town, he fixes upon a habitation which he calls his Catcherry; to which, by his peons and hircarahs, he summons the brokers, called *dallals and pykars,* together with the weavers, whom, after receipt of the money despatched by his masters, he makes to sign a bond for the delivery of a certain quantity of goods, at a certain time and price, and pays them a certain part of the money in advance. The assent of the poor weaver is in general not deemed

[12] Quoted by Romesh Dutt, "India Under Early British Rule," pp. 23, 24.

necessary; for the Gomastahs, when employed on the Company's investment, frequently make them sign what they please; and upon the weavers refusing to take the money offered, it has been known they have had it tied in their girdles, and they have been sent away with a flogging. . . . A number of these weavers are generally also registered in the books of the Company's Gomastahs, and not permitted to work for any others, being transferred from one to another as so many slaves, subject to the tyranny and roguery of each succeeding Gomastah. . . . The roguery practised in this department is beyond imagination; but all terminates in the defrauding of the poor weaver; for the prices which the Company's Gomastahs, and in confederacy with them the Jachendars (examiners of fabrics) fix upon the goods, are in all places at least 15 per cent., and some even 40 per cent. less than the goods so manufactured would sell in the public bazaar or market upon free sale. . . . Weavers, also, upon their inability to perform such agreements as have been forced upon them by the Company's agents, universally known in Bengal by the name of Mutchulcahs, have had their goods seized and sold on the spot to make good the deficiency; and the winders of raw silk, called Negoads, have been treated also with such injustice, that instances have been known of their cutting off their thumbs to prevent their being forced to wind silk."

But agriculture also declined in Bengal under this system.

"For the ryots, who are generally both land-holders and manufacturers, by the oppressions of Gomastahs in harassing them for goods are frequently rendered incapable of improving their lands, and even of paying their rents; for which, on the other hand, they are again chastised by the officers of the revenue, and not infrequently have by those harpies been necessitated to sell their children in order to pay their rents, or otherwise obliged to fly the country." [13]

In fairness to Warren Hastings and the Governor Vansittart, it may be said that they recognised the force of the Nabob's complaints and tried to persuade their colleagues in Bengal to put matters right. But self-interest and greed prevented the latter from seeing the justice of the Nabob's complaints and the soundness of the proposals submitted by Warren Hastings and Vansittart in consultation with the Nabob to put an effective check on the company's servants. The Council rejected these proposals and when the Nabob heard of the rejection, he in a moment of " noble indignation and under an impulse of high-minded patriotism " resolved to sacrifice his revenues by abolishing all inland duties so that his subjects might have a chance of carrying on inland trade on equal terms with the servants of the East India Company. What the English merchants wanted, however, was monopoly and not equal opportunity. They accordingly protested against this action of the Nabob and made his protest the basis of a quarrel with him which eventually led to war. " The conduct of the Company's servants upon this occasion," says James Mill in his " History of British India," " furnishes one of the most remarkable instances upon

[13] Quoted by Romesh Dutt, "India Under Early British Rule," pp. 25, 26, 27.

record of the power of interest to extinguish all sense of justice and even of shame."

The move resulted in the defeat of Mir Kassim, who in a fit of fury caused the English prisoners at Patna to be massacred and then left his dominions for good. Mir Jaffar, the old puppet who had a few years before been declared a failure, was again set up as Nabob, but he died shortly after, and his illegitimate son Najm-uddaula was hastily created Nabob in 1765.

On these occasions the presents which the English officers received from Mir Jaffar and his illegitimate son amounted to £500,165 and £230,356 respectively. Besides these amounts received in presents (amounting within eight years to £2,169,665) other sums amounting to £3,770,833 were claimed and obtained as "restitution" within this period.[14] This amount was in addition to the income which the Company derived from the territories made over to them by the Nabobs, as well as the amounts agreed to be given under the different treaties as subsidies, gratuities and expenses of maintaining the army.

2. *The Second Administration of Lord Clive.* When the reports of the misdoings of their servants in India reached the directors of the East India Company in London they prevailed upon Lord Clive to return to India and set matters right. They seem to have been sincerely shocked at the turn things had taken and

[14] "House of Commons third report, 1773," p. 311, quoted by Romesh Dutt in his "India Under Early British Rule." See also the remarks of Lecky in his "History of England in the Eighteenth Century," Vol. III (1883), p. 76: "At every turn of the wheel, at every change in the system or personality of the Government vast sums of money were drawn from the national treasury," and so on.

condemned both the inland private trade carried on by their servants in defiance of old treaties, and the new treaty which had been "exacted by violence." Clive's views on the condition of Bengal at the time, may be gathered from the letters he wrote to the directors after his return to Bengal. In one of the letters he said:

"I shall only say that such a scene of anarchy, confusion, bribery, corruption, and extortion was never seen or heard of, in any country but Bengal; nor such and so many fortunes acquired in so unjust and rapacious a manner. The three provinces of Bengal, Behar, and Orissa, producing a clear revenue of £3,000,000 sterling, have been under the absolute management of the Company's servants, ever since Mir Jaffar's restoration to the *subaship;* and they have, both civil and military, exacted and levied contributions from every man of power and consequence, from the Nabob down to the lowest *zemindar.*

"The trade has been carried on by free merchants, acting as *gomastas* to the Company's servants, who under the sanction of their names, have committed actions which make the name of the English stink in the nostrils of a Hindu or a Mussulman; and the Company's servants themselves have interfered with the revenues of the Nabab, turned out and put in the officers of the government at pleasure, and made every one pay for their preferment." [15] These views were repeated, and proposals to remedy the evils were offered in another letter, which is an epoch making document and deserves extensive quotation, in any discussion

[15] Malcolm, "Life of Clive," II, p. 379.

of the events of these times. We give a few paragraphs below:

"Upon my arrival, I am sorry to say, I found your affairs in a condition so nearly desperate as would have alarmed any set of men whose sense of honour and duty to their employers had not been estranged by the too eager pursuit of their own advantage. The sudden, and, among many, the unwarrantable acquisition of riches, had introduced luxury in every shape and in the most pernicious excess. These two enormous evils went hand in hand together through the whole Presidency, infecting almost every member of each Department; every inferior seemed to have grasped at wealth that he might be able to assume that spirit of profusion which was now the only distinction between him and his superior. . . . It is no wonder that the lust of riches should readily embrace the proffered means of its gratification, or that the instruments of your power should avail themselves of their authority, and proceed even to extortion in those cases where simple corruption could not keep pace with their rapacity. Examples of this sort, set by superiors, could not fail of being followed in proportional degree by inferiors; the evil was contagious, and spread among the civil and military, down to the writer, the ensign, and the free merchant. . . .[16]

"The sources of tyranny and oppression, which have been opened by the European agents acting under the authority of the Company's servants, and the numberless black agents and sub-agents acting also under them, will, I fear, be a lasting reproach to the English name in this country. . . . I have at last, however, the happiness to see the completion of an event, which, in this respect as well as in many others, must be productive of advantages hitherto unknown, and at the

[16] Quoted by Dutt, "India Under Early British Rule," pp. 35, 36.

same time prevent abuses that have hitherto had no remedy: I mean the Dewanee, which is the superintendency of all the lands and the collection of all the revenues of the Provinces of Bengal, Behar, and Orissa. The assistance which the Great Moghul had received from our arms and treasury made him readily bestow this grant upon the Company; and it is done in the most effectual manner you can desire. The allowance for the support of the Nabob's dignity and power, and the tribute to His Majesty (the Great Moghul) must be regularly paid; the remainder belongs to the Company. . . .

"13. Your revenues, by means of this acquisition, will, as near as I can judge, not fall far short for the ensuing year of 250 lacs of Sicca Rupees, including your former possessions of Burdwan, etc. Hereafter they will at least amount to twenty or thirty lacs more. Your civil and military expenses in time of peace can never exceed sixty lacs of Rupees; the Nabob's allowances are already reduced to forty-two lacs, and the tribute to the King (The Great Moghul) at twenty-six; so that there will be remaining a clear gain to the Company of 122 lacs of Sicca Ruppees, or £1,650,900 sterling. . . ."[17]

He also submitted proposals to increase the salaries of the servants of the Company though he could not make up his mind to recommend a prohibition of private inland trade by them. In fact, such was his moral code, that on September 18, 1865, while he was probably drafting the letter of September 30, embodying his proposals about the Dewanee, he executed an indenture creating a partnership of himself and some of the other servants of the Company, to carry on joint inland trade in salt, betel-nut and tobacco for their personal profit, and so resolved was he

[17] Quoted by Dutt, "India Under Early British Rule," p. 37.

to carry on the trade even in defiance of the order of the directors that a clause was inserted in the indenture whereby he, as president of the Bengal Council, guaranteed the continuance of this trade even if the Court of Directors in England ordered its dissolution and discontinuance.

Later on when Lord Clive was charged with having allowed his private interests to get the better of his judgment in encouraging this evil, he tried to excuse himself on the ground that it was done to benefit friends whom he had induced to accompany him to Bengal on the understanding of being allowed to make money by such trade, yet he never denied that his own personal share in the profits of the transaction was the largest.[18] The directors, however, condemned the practice in the strongest terms and reiterated their disapproval of the practice which had in the past led to the acquisition of " vast fortunes " by " a scene of the most tyrannic and oppressive conduct that was ever known in any age or country." So in their letter of May 17, 1766, they refused to sanction Clive's scheme for continuing the private inland trade under the regulations framed by him. The trade, nevertheless, was continued for two years more under one pretence or another.

After Clive. Lord Clive left India for the last time in 1769. In the words of Professor Muir, " Clive had no sense of responsibility for the good government of Bengal. His sole desire was to preserve the Company's political ascendency by playing upon the weak-

[18] Mill, the historian of British India, holds that this plea does not in anyway lessen the shamelessness of the transaction, a view from which Wilson differs.

nesses of the Nabob and his subjects."[19] In all his writings there is no hint of a belief that the Company ought to insure good government to the people of Bengal. But in the language of Brooks Adams, "the takings of Clive either for himself or for the Government were nothing compared to the wholesale spoliation which followed his departure, when Bengal was surrendered a helpless prey to a myriad of greedy officials who 'were irresponsible and rapacious and who emptied the private hoards.'"

Speaking of the gains of Clive, Macaulay says: "As to Clive, there was no limit to his acquisition but his own moderation. The treasury of Bengal was thrown open to him. There were, well piled up, after the usage of Indian princes, immense masses of coin, among which might not seldom be detected the florins and byzants with which before any European ship had turned the Cape of Good Hope, the Venetians purchased the stuffs and spices of the East. Clive walked between heaps of gold and silver, crowned with rubies and diamonds and was at liberty to help himself." What followed his departure is thus summed up by the same authority:

"Enormous fortunes were thus rapidly accumulated at Calcutta, while thirty millions of human beings were reduced to the extremity of wretchedness. The misgovernment of the English was carried to such a point as seems hardly compatible with the very existence of society."

During the five years following Lord Clive's retirement from the service of the East India Company the servants of the latter left nothing undone to wring out

[19] "The Making of British India," Manchester (1915), p. 82.

as much money as they could, by every means, from the rulers and natives of Bengal. The "trade oppression" practised during this period may better be described in the words of William Bolts, a servant of the Company, from his "Considerations on Indian Affairs," published in 1772, a description which Professor Muir pronounces "substantially true."[20]

Says Mr. Bolts on page 73 of his book:

> "Inconceivable oppressions and hardships have been practised towards the poor manufacturers and workmen of the Country, who are, in fact, monopolised by the Company as so many slaves. . . . Various and innumerable are the methods of oppressing the poor weavers, which are duly practised by the Company's agents and gomastas in the country; such as by fines, imprisonments, floggings, forcing bonds from them, etc., by which the number of weavers in the country has been greatly decreased. The natural consequences whereof have been, the scarcity, dearness, and debasement of the manufactures as well as a great diminution of the revenues: and the provision of the Company's investment has thereby now become a monopoly, to the almost entire exclusion of all others, excepting the servants of the Company highest in station, who having the management of the investment, provide as much as their consciences will let them for the Company, themselves and their favourites; excepting also the foreign Companies who are permitted to make some small investments, to prevent clamours in Europe. . . ."

In this way, the servants of the Company ruined the trade of the country, and by coercion and oppression established their monopoly.

Mr. Bolts has dealt with the situation in Bengal at great length in his book where the interested reader may pursue his investigations further.

[20] Muir, "The Making of British India," p. 89.

This disposes of the first two items of what C. H. Peries in his "Industrial History of Modern England," p. 10, calls "the plunder of India."

The third item, the income derived from districts in possession of the Company, may be stated in the words of Mr. Verelst, one-time Governor of Bengal:

"In the provinces of Burdwan and Midnapur, of which both the property and jurisdiction were ceded to the Company by Mir Kasim in the year 1760, those evils which necessarily flowed from the bad policy of the Moorish Government had in no sort decreased. On the contrary, a plan was adopted in 1762 productive of certain ruin to the province. The lands were let by public auction for the short term of three years. Men without fortune or character became bidders at the sale; and while some of the former farmers, unwilling to relinquish their habitations, exceeded perhaps the real value in their offers, those who had nothing to lose advanced yet further, wishing at all events to obtain an immediate possession. Thus numberless harpies were let loose to plunder, whom the spoil of a miserable people enabled to complete their first year's payment."[21]

The net amount remitted to England by the representatives of the East India Company on account of revenues, after defraying all the civil and military charges from 1765 to 1771 amounted to a little over four million pounds sterling. The total amounts raised totalled a little over thirteen million pounds. Most of what constituted civil and military charges also went to England in one shape or another.

[21] "View of the Rise of the English Government in Bengal," by Harry Verelst, Esq., late Governor of Bengal; London, 1772; p. 70.

The whole matter was clearly put by Burke in the report of the select committee of the House of Commons appointed later to enquire into the affairs of the East India Company.

"This new system of trade, carried on through the medium of power and public revenue, very soon produced its natural effects. The loudest complaints arose among the natives, and among all the foreigners who traded in Bengal. It must have unquestionably thrown the whole mercantile system of the country into the greatest confusion. With regard to the natives, no expedient was proposed for their relief. The case was serious with respect to European powers. The Presidency plainly represented to the Directors that some agreement should be made with foreign nations for providing their investment to a certain amount, or that the deficiencies then subsisting must terminate in an open rupture with France."[22]

"Notwithstanding the famine in 1770, which wasted Bengal in a manner dreadful beyond all example, the investment, by a variety of successive expedients, many of them of the most dangerous nature and tendency, was forcibly kept up; and even in that forced and unnatural state it gathered strength almost every year. The debts contracted in the infancy of the system were gradually reduced, and the advances to contractors and manufacturers were regularly made; so that the goods from Bengal, purchased from the territorial revenues, from the sale of European goods, and from the produce of the monopolies, for the four years which ended with 1780, when the investment from the surplus revenues finally closed, were never less than a million sterling, and commonly nearer twelve hundred thousand pounds. This million is the lowest value of the goods sent to Europe for which no satisfaction is

[22] Ninth Report, p. 47; Burke, "Collected Works," Vol. III, quoted by Digby, p. 28.

made."[23] [The sale, to the amount of one hundred thousand pounds annually, of the export from Great Britain ought to be deducted from this million.]

"In all other countries, the revenue, following the natural course and order of things, arises out of their commerce. Here, by a mischievous inversion of that order, the whole foreign maritime trade, whether English, French, Dutch, or Danish, arises from the revenues; these are carried out of the country without producing anything to compensate so heavy a loss."[24]

[23] *Ibid.*, pp. 47-48.
[24] *Ibid.*, p. 50.

CHAPTER III

"TRIBUTE" OR "DRAIN"

General Observations. The question whether India pays tribute to England, or ever has paid it, has been and is the subject of bitter controversy among English publicists. One party asserts that India has been paying an enormous tribute to England and still pays it; that there has been going on a regular "drain" of India's wealth to England ever since British connection with India began; that under the direct administration of India by the Crown since 1858, that drain not only has not ceased but has actually increased; and that this drain has impoverished India beyond description. The other party holds that India has never paid any tribute to England; that there is no drain from India to England; that what has been paid by India has been received by England in lieu of services rendered or capital loaned for her improvement; and that under British rule India has attained a prosperity which she had never known before in her history. We intend to state the case of both parties, with as much fairness as we are capable of, considering that together with all Indian publicists we agree with the former and have no doubt of India's having been exploited and economically injured by British policy.

In the preceding chapter we have shown how England stood, economically, for more than two centuries, immediately preceding the battle of Plassy and thereabout; also how Indian treasure flowed to England and changed the whole economic outlook there. We do not know of a single publicist English or Indian who denies or questions the facts upon which the theory of drain is based. All parties are agreed that at least for thirty years, from 1757 to 1787, Bengal was "plundered" by the servants of the East India Company. What happened afterwards will be stated partly in the chapter relating to industries and completed in other chapters.

Drain: the Case Against England. In a letter of July 2, 1901, published in the *Morning Post*, London, Mr. H. M. Hyndman, the great Socialist leader, said:

"More than twenty years ago the late Sir Louis Mallet (I presume with the knowledge and consent of Lord Cranbrook, then Secretary of State for India, and of my friend the late Edward Stanhope, then Under-Secretary) put at my disposal the confidential documents in the India office, from Indian finance ministers and others, bearing on this question of the drain from India to England and its effects. The situation is, to my mind, so desperate that I consider I am entitled to call on Lord George Hamilton to submit the confidential memoranda on this subject, up to and after the year 1880, for the consideration of the House of Commons. I venture to assert that the public will be astonished to read the names of those who (privately) are at one with me on this matter. As to remedy, there is but one, and it is almost too late for that: the stanching of the drain and the steady substitution of native rule, under light English supervision, for our present ruinous system."

On page 208 of his book Mr. W. Digby gives the photographic reproduction of two pages from an Indian Blue Book containing admissions about the drain.

"Great Britain, in addition to the tribute she makes India pay her through the customs, derives benefit from the savings of the service at the three presidencies being spent in England instead of in India; and in addition to these savings, which probably amount to near a million, she derives benefit from the fortunes realised by the European mercantile community, which are all remitted to England." Parl. Paper, 1853 (445-II.), page 580.

The following extracts are made from the "Reports of the Committees of the House of Commons" (Vol. V, 1781–82, printed 1804). Comparing Indian rule with the rule of the East India Company, Mr. Philip Francis, once a member of the Bengal Council, wrote:

"It must give pain to an Englishman to have reason to think that, since the accession of the Company to the Dewanee, the condition of the people of this country has been worse than it was before; and yet I am afraid the fact is undoubted; and I believe has proceeded from the following causes: the mode of providing the Company's Investment; the exportation of specie, instead of importing large sums annually; the strictness that has been observed in the collections; the endeavours of all concerned to gain credit by an increase of revenue during the time of their being in station, without sufficiently attending to what future consequences might be expected from such a measure;

the errors that subsist in the manner of making collections, particularly by the employment of Aumils: These appear to me the principal causes why this fine country, which flourished under the most despotic and arbitrary Government, is verging towards its ruin while the English have really so great a share in the Administration."

Ten years later, says Mr. Digby "Prosperous British India," p. 215. Charles Grant, of the Indian House, the greatest panegyrist of British rule in India — and, at the same time, himself the worst disparager of the Indian people known in British-Indian literature — was constrained to admit: "We apply a large portion of their annual produce to the use of Great Britain."

The Honourable F. J. Shore, a retired Bengal administrator, says in his "Notes on Indian Affairs" (London, 1837, Vol. II, page 516):

"More than seventeen years have elapsed since I first landed in this country; but on my arrival, and during my residence of about a year in Calcutta, I well recollect the quiet, comfortable, and settled conviction, which in those days existed in the minds of the English population, of the blessings conferred on the natives of India by the establishment of the English rule. . . .

"I was thus gradually led to an inquiry into the principles and practice of British-Indian administration. Proceeding in this, I soon found myself at no loss to understand the feelings of the people both towards the Government and to ourselves. It would have been astonishing indeed had it been otherwise. *The fundamental principle of the English had been to make the whole Indian nation subservient, in every possible way, to the interests and benefits of themselves. They have been taxed to the utmost limit;*

every successive Province, as it has fallen into our possession, has been made a field for higher exaction; and it has always been our boast how greatly we have raised the revenue above that which the native rulers were able to extort. The Indians have been excluded from every honour, dignity, or office which the lowest Englishman could be prevailed upon to accept." [Italics ours.]

And elsewhere he writes:

"The halcyon days of India are over; she has been drained of a large proportion of the wealth she once possessed; and her energies have been cramped by a sordid system of misrule to which the interests of millions have been sacrificed for the benefit of the few."[1]

John Sullivan, also an eminent English administrator, who served in India from 1804 to 1841 and was examined by the Select Committee of the House of Commons when the question of the renewal of the charter of the East India Company came up in 1853, said:

"Do you suppose that they (the people of India) have traditions among them which tell them that the economic condition of the population was better in former times under their native rulers than it is now?

"I think, generally speaking, history tells us that it was; they have been in a state of the greatest prosperity from the earliest times as far as history tells us.

"How do you account for the superior economic state of the people, and for their ability to lay out the money which they did in canals and irrigation and tanks, if they were wasting more wealth, and sacrificing more lives in war, than we do now, especially seeing that the wars were carried on very much upon their

[1] *Ibid.*, p. 28.

own territories, instead of being beyond their limits?

"We have an expensive element which they were free from, which is the European element, civil and military, which swallows up so much of the revenue; from that cause our administration is so much more expensive; that, I think, is the great reason."

John Sullivan did not shrink from the logical conclusion of his opinions, when he was asked if he would restore British territory to native rule, keeping the military control of the Empire in British hands.

"4890. You would restore a great deal of territory to native rulers upon principles of justice?"

"Yes."

"Because we have become possessed of them by violence or by other means without any just right or title?"

"I would do so upon principles of justice and upon principles of financial economy."[2]

He also said:

"As to the complaints which the people of India have to make of the present fiscal system, I do not conceive that it is the amount altogether that they have to complain of. I think they have rather to complain of the application of that amount. Under their own dynasties, all the revenue that was collected in the country was spent in the country; but under our rule, a large proportion of the revenue is annually drained away, and without any return being made for it; *this drain has been going on now for sixty or seventy years, and it is rather increasing than the reverse*. . . . Our system acts very much like a

[2] Third Report of the Select Committee, 1853, pp. 19 and 20.

sponge, drawing up all the good things from the banks of the Ganges, and squeezing them down on the banks of the Thames. . . ." [Italics ours.]

Sir John Malcolm, Governor of Bombay in 1827 (one of the makers of British Empire in India) was examined before the select committee of the House of Commons in 1832.

"In your opinion, was the substitution of our government for the misrule of the native princes the cause of greater prosperity of the agricultural and commercial part of the population?

"I cannot answer this in every province of India, but I shall as far as my experience enables me. I do not think the change has benefited, or could benefit either the commercial, the monied, or the agricultural classes of many of the native States, though it may be of others. It has not happened to me ever to see countries better cultivated, and so abounding in all produce of the soil, as well as commercial wealth, than the southern Mahratta districts, when I accompanied the present Duke of Wellington to that country in the year 1803. . . .

"With respect to Malwa. . . . And I do not believe that the introduction of our direct rule could have contributed more, nor indeed so much, to the prosperity of the commercial and agricultural interests as the establishment of the efficient rule of its former princes and chiefs. . . .

"With respect to the southern Mahratta districts, of whose prosperity I have before spoken . . . I must unhesitatingly state that the provinces belonging to the family of Putwarden and some other chiefs on the banks of the Krishna present a greater agricultural and commercial prosperity than almost any I know in India. . . . Above all causes which promote prosperity is the invariable support given to the village and other native institutions, and to the employment, far beyond what our system admits, of all classes of the population." [3]

Sir George Wingate, who had held high posts in the government of Bombay, recorded the following observations for the consideration of his countrymen when the administration of the Empire passed to the Crown in 1858:

"If, then, we have governed India not merely for the natives of India but for ourselves, we are clearly blamable in the sight of God and man for having contributed nothing towards defraying the cost of that government. . . .

"With reference to its economic effects upon the condition of India, the tribute paid to Great Britain is by far the most objectionable feature in our existing policy. Taxes spent in the country from which they are raised are totally different in their effects from taxes raised in one country and spent in another. . . .

"The Indian tribute, whether weighed in the scales of justice or viewed in the light of our true interest, will be found to be at variance with humanity, with common sense, and with the received maxims of economical science." Again,

"Were India to be relieved of *this cruel burden of*

[3] "Minutes of Evidence taken before the Select Committee, &c., 1832," Vol. VI, pp. 30 and 31.

tribute and the whole of the taxes raised in India to be spent in India, the revenue of that country would soon acquire a degree of elasticity of which we have at present no expectation." "Our Financial Relations with India," by Major Wingate, London, 1859, pp. 56–64, quoted by Dutt "Early British Rule," pp. 618–20. [Italics ours.]

On page 126 of his book "India in the Victorian Age," Dutt quotes the opinion of Colonel Sykes, a distinguished director of the East India Company, who "spoke of the economic drain from India of £3,300,000 to £3,700,000 a year" and remarked that "It is only by the excess of exports over imports that India can bear this tribute."

Henry St. John Tucker, the chairman of the East India Company, (quoted by Dutt), said that this economic drain was an increasing quantity, "because our home charge is perpetually increasing," a prophecy which has been more than amply fulfilled.

Similarly another East Indian merchant quoted in the Parliamentary report of 1853, said: "I may say generally that up to 1847, the imports (of India) were about £6,000,000 and the exports about £9,500,000. *The difference is the tribute* which the company received from the country, which amounts to about £4,000,000."[4]

Mr. Montgomery Martin, a historian of the British colonies and dependencies, wrote in 1838:

"So constant and accumulating a drain, even on England, would soon impoverish her; how severe, then, must be the effect on India, where the wages of

[4] First Report, 1853.

a labourer is from two pence to three pence a day."[5]

Prof. H. H. Wilson, historian of India, says of the annual drain of wealth:

"Its transference to England is an abstraction of Indian capital for which no equivalent is given; it is an exhausting drain upon the country, the issue of which is replaced by no reflux; it is an extraction of the life-blood from the veins of national industry which no subsequent introduction of nourishment is furnished to restore."

Mr. A. J. Wilson, in an article in the *Fortnightly Review*, of March, 1884, wrote:

"In one form or another we draw fully £30,000,000 a year from that unhappy country (India), and there the average wages of the natives is about £5 per annum, less rather than more in many parts. Our Indian tribute, therefore, represents the entire earnings of upwards of six millions heads of families—say of 30,000,000 of the people. It means the abstraction of more than one tenth of the entire sustenance of India every year."

Lord Salisbury, the great English statesman, spoke in 1875 of India as a country from which "much of the revenue" was "exported without a direct equivalent."

Dr. J. T. Sunderland, a Unitarian minister of the United States, in his pamphlet "The Causes of Famine in India" (page 22), refers to the heavy drain of wealth that is going on as "the greatest of all the causes of the impoverishment of the Indian people."

[5] "History, etc., of Eastern India," Vol. II, p. 12. See also Dutt, "Early British Rule," p. 609.

This synopsis of opinions about the "tribute" which India pays and has been paying for more than a century and a half to England, or about the "drain" of India's wealth to England, is by no means exhaustive. In fact one could fill a volume with such extracts. Besides we have scrupulously kept back the opinions of those British statesmen (several of them very eminent Anglo-Indian administrators like Sir Henry Cotton — late Chief Commissioner of Assam, and once an M. P.; Sir William Wedderburn, retired member of the Bombay Council and once an M. P.; Mr. W. S. Caine, late M. P.; Mr. A. O. Hume, once a secretary to the Government of India; and many others), who have openly and actively identified themselves in one way or another, with the cause of Indian nationalism. Similarly we have made no mention of the opinions of Indians themselves. Some further opinions we hope to cite when we come to discuss the extent of the drain.

Drain: the Case for England. Now we give below a summary of the opinions on the other side. It should be noted, however, that this school which holds that India pays no tribute to England and that there is no drain of India's wealth to England is of comparatively recent growth. So long as the administration of India was vested in the East India Company, the presence of this tribute and the existence of this drain was admitted. It was hardly ever questioned. In fact that was the test by which James Mill judged the benefit to England of her occupation of India. It is more or less within the last thirty years that the fact of this drain has begun to be denied. We give below the explanation of the so-called drain, that is embodied in the new edition of the *Imperial Gazeteer of India* (an official publication), Vol. IV.

Discussing the "Home Charges" (which properly speaking should be called "Foreign Charges" met by Indian revenues), the compiler of the chapter says:

"These Home Charges have sometimes been erroneously described as a tribute which India pays to England in consequence of her subordination to that Country . . . figures will show that nearly 11 out of 17¾ million pounds consist of payments on account of Capital and materials supplied by England and belong to a Commercial rather than an administrative class of transaction. Of the balance 4½ millions represent furlough and pension payments and *are a necessary concomitant of the British Administration,* to which India owes her prosperity."[6] [Italics ours.]

We also make the following long quotation from a leaflet called "The Truth About 'The Drain,'" published and distributed free by the East India Association of London (April, 1909):

"What are the facts about the drain of India's wealth into Great Britain? It has been assumed that there is a drain, but the nature and extent of this drain has been highly exaggerated, and sometimes grossly misrepresented. The official 'drain' is included in what are known as the 'home charges,' and these 'Home charges' for the three years from 1904 to 1907 amount on the average to £19,000,000 a year, reduced to about £18,000,000 by deducting sundry receipts. These £18,000,000 can be roughly summarised and grouped under the following heads:

[6] "*Imperial Gazeteer of India,*" Oxford, 1907, Vol. IV, p. 194.

(1) Interest on money due or borrowed (chiefly for railways, etc.) about £10,000,000
(2) Purchase of stores............ £2,500,000
(3) Military charges (including pensions) £4,000,000
(4) Civil charges (including pensions) £2,500,000

"As will be seen (4) civil and (3) military charges, including pensions, amount to £6,500,000. This is no doubt a heavy charge, but it might well be regarded as a not unreasonable premium payable for insurance against foreign aggression and internal disturbance. The peace and security enjoyed in India may be taken as an adequate return for this outlay.

"It is not intended to justify every charge in the debt account, but (1) payment of interest on sums borrowed for the construction of railways, etc., or (2) disbursements on account of the purchase of stores, cannot fairly be described as a 'drain,' because in return for this money India has received adequate commercial equivalent in the shape of metals, machinery, railway plant, and miscellaneous stores. Such receipts have always been justly regarded as amongst the most valuable and permanent of commercial returns.

"It has, however, been urged that, in addition to these *known* payments, there is an unknown drain on India's resources in the shape of private remittances, and the extent of this drain has been estimated at between £10,000,000 and £12,000,000 a year. This is, of course, a mere guess, and the probabilities are against the accuracy of this guess. The sum mentioned is more than double the annual pay of all the European officials in India, civil and military, and it seems idle to contend that the comparatively few European merchants in India earn more than all the civil and military European officials put together. It is well known that European officials in India cannot remit a moiety of their pay to England. Many of them spend their pay (and even more) in India. It must surely be the same with some European merchants."

We give yet another quotation from a writer who may aptly be called the father of this school of Anglo-Indian economists. Sir John Strachey, who was Finance Minister of India in the administration of Lord Lytton, observes in his book, "India, Its Administration and Progress":

"During the last ten years the average value of the imports into India fell short of the value of the exports by about £16,000,000 a year. In this calculation are included imports and exports both of merchandise and treasure, on Government as well as on private account. For the excess India receives no direct commercial equivalent, but she receives the equivalent in another form.

"English capital to a very large amount has been, and is still being, invested in India by the State and by private individuals in railways, irrigation works, and industrial enterprises, and interest on these investments has to be remitted to England. In addition to this, large sums are required in England for what are really investments for India of another kind. It is an inevitable consequence of the subjection of India that a portion of the cost of her government should be paid in England. The maintenance of our dominion is essential in the interests of India herself, and, provided that she is not compelled to pay more than is really necessary to give her a thoroughly efficient Government, and in return for services actually rendered to her, she has no reason for complaint. The charges to be met in England are numerous: interest has to be paid on sterling debt incurred for India in England; there are, among others, charges for civil and military administration, interest and annuities on account of state railways, and interest on the ordinary public debt, furlough allowances, pensions, payments to the Government in England for British troops employed in India, stores of every kind, railway material for use in India, and the Secretary of State's administration at the India Office. The ordinary annual charge under the last-named head is about £200,000. The charges to be met in England necessarily vary from year to year; in 1909–10 they amounted to about £18,500,000.[7]

A pupil of Sir John Strachey, Sir Theodore Morison, a member of the India Council, discusses the question at some length in his book called "The Economic Transition in India" and concludes thus:

> "When viewed in this way I do not believe it is possible to resist the conclusion that India derives a pecuniary advantage from her connection with the British Empire [!!!] The answer, then, which I give to the question 'What economic equivalent does India get for foreign payments' is this:— India gets the equipment of modern industry, and she gets an administration favourable to economic evolution *cheaper* than she could provide herself."[8]

We have italicised the word "cheaper": the arguments and figures we will notice later on.

Drain: Weighing the Evidence. The reader is now

[7] 1911 Edition revised by Sir Thomas W. Holderness, K. C. S. I., Permanent Under Secretary of State for India.

[8] In this connection it will be of interest to compare the remarks of Sir John Strachey and Sir Theodore Morison with the following observations of Mr. Richard Jebb in his "Studies in Colonial Nationalism" (London, 1905), p. 322: "If it be objected that orderly Government is sufficient compensation to India for commercial exploitation, the ready reply is forthcoming that the administration is paid for separately in hard Indian cash; and so far from being a philanthropic service provides congenial and remunerative employment for a large number of Englishmen who could not have found the same opportunity elsewhere."

in possession of the views of both sides on the question of "tribute" or "drain." In forming his judgment he should consider that according to all sound systems of weighing evidence admissions by a party in his own favour are of little value. The question in essence is, whether Great Britain gets anything from India by virtue of her political domination of it and if so, what? One set of Britishers says she gets enormous sums for which India gets no "direct equivalent." This they call India's tribute or drain. Another set says she gets nothing as tribute, that what she gets is in lieu of "services" she renders. That she gets large sums is thus undisputed.

The only question that remains to be considered is the value of the services rendered. Every superior political authority, which exacts a tribute from an inferior, can justify the tribute on the same grounds on which the British do. So this quarrel seems to be nothing but a play on words. We do not intend, however, to leave the subject here and shall examine it more closely on the lines laid down by Messrs. Strachey and Morison.

In order to be absolutely clear on the point it is necessary to know (1) of what the drain consists, (2) the extent of that drain from 1757, when the political connection commenced, up to the present.

Speaking in general terms, whatever India has paid and still pays to England in money or in goods, without receiving an equivalent in money or in goods is the "drain." That is practically what Lord Salisbury said. This includes (1) the treasure which the East India Company and their servants accumulated from India in the early years of their reign from 1757 up to 1849, the year of the annexation of the Punjab, or for very nearly a century.

I do not know if what is known as the "loot" of India from 1757 to 1772 and then afterwards up to 1815 is denied by the school of politicians to which Sir John Strachey and Sir Theodore Morison belong. The period stands by itself. The extent of the treasure removed to England during this period is not to be estimated by the excess of exports over imports. This treasure consisted of gold, silver, precious stones and merchandise.

The period of 1772 to 1785 is represented by the administration of Warren Hastings. During this period very large amounts of money and very large quantities of merchandise were obtained from the princes and people of India, for which the only return made was in the shape of "*services rendered.*" These "services" resulted in wars in the then Northwest Province, Oudh and Deccan. These exactions were of two kinds, (1) those made in the name of the company, (2) those made by the servants of the company and of which from the very nature of things there is not and could not be a record anywhere. Then again during the administration of Wellesley large sums of money were obtained from the princes of India, during the war carried on by that pro-consul. This state of things continued more or less actively right up to the end of Dalhousie's administration. There is no record extant of the diamonds, rubies and other precious stones, worth millions, which were removed from India during this time. The Koh-i-noor, of almost fabulous value, which was last in the possession of Ranjit Singh, the ruler of independent Punjab, was only one of these. The system of international trade had not developed then and ways were open for the transference of wealth from one country to another otherwise than by means of trade. In fact it cannot be disputed that throughout India's connection with England quantities of Indian treasure were transferred to England, which are not shown in any account. In the days of the East India Company, this treasure consisted of "loot" during wars and of presents by princes and nobility either voluntary or under compulsion.[9] Since the assumption of the administration by the Crown this has consisted of presents given by, or obtained from, the native princes and nobility in the shape of jewels or valuable goods. That these presents are given and received is a matter of public knowledge in India and cannot be altogether unknown to the Anglo-Indian brotherhood of the East India Association. What the total value of these presents is, there is no means of ascertaining. But in no case can it be a trifling amount, and if we were to add compound interest, the amount would swell to a very large figure. One finds references to these presents scattered in histories, accounts of travellers, private letters published, and in other documents in the British Museum. That the recipients of these presents must

[9] Observes Mr. J. S. Cotton in "Colonies and Dependencies," Macmillan & Co., 1883: "The first generation of English rulers helped to drain the country of its inherited riches."

have rendered "services" to the givers thereof, there can be no doubt. But that India has been drained to that extent remains an indisputable fact. Then it must be borne in mind that throughout the British domination of India a large portion of that part of the revenue of India which was spent in India has gone into the pockets of Europeans employed in the civil and military departments of the company, and after them, of the Crown. For a long time the natives were employed only in the very lowest possible offices, as menials or clerks or sepoys. There were very few, if any, natives, in the subordinate ranks of civil and military offices during the first 80 years of the East India Company's rule. Even now a large portion of Indian revenues spent in India falls under that head. But in the days of the East India Company, especially from 1757 to 1833, when the services were at least in theory thrown open to educated natives the major portions of civil and military expenses went into the pockets of Europeans and with the exception of the sums spent in India were transferred to England.

It is clear that the amount of the treasure transferred from India to England during the century from 1757 to 1857 or to the present is not correctly represented by the excess of exports over imports; for to this excess should be added the amount of public debt that the East India Company contracted during this period.

The beauty of the English conquest of India lies in the fact that from the first to the last not one single penny was spent by the British on the conquest. India was conquered by the British, with Indian money and Indian blood. Further, almost all kinds of expenses incurred by the British in Asia, for the conquest of territories, for the expansion of trade, for research and inquiry, were borne by the Indian exchequer. The profits almost always went into the pockets of Britishers. The expenses and losses were debited to India.

R. C. Dutt points out how the total revenues of India have always been in excess of total expenditures incurred in India.

"The whole of the public debt of India, built up in a century of the company's rule, was created by debiting India with the expenses incurred in England."

The total Indian debt, bearing interest, was a little over seven millions in 1792. It had risen to ten millions in 1799. Then came Lord Wellesley's wars and the Indian debt rose to twenty-one millions in 1805. In 1807 it was twenty-seven millions. By 1829 it had risen to thirty millions. The total debt of India (registered debt + treasury notes and deposits + home bond debt) on April 30, 1836, was £33,355,536.[10] By 1844–45 the total debt of India had reached the figure of forty-three and one-half million pounds. This included the enormous expense of the Afghan war to which England contributed only a small part of the fifteen millions expended, although in the words of John Bright, the whole of this expenditure "ought to have been thrown on the taxation of the people of England, because it was a war commanded by the English cabinet, for objects supposed to be English."

[10] R. C. Dutt, "India in the Victorian Age," pp. 215–6 and footnote.

railways in India before 1850. When the Empire was transferred to the Crown it was provided that the dividend on the capital stock of the East India Company and other debts of the company in Great Britain and all the territorial and other debts of the company, were to be "charged and chargeable upon the revenues of India alone." Thus the annual interest which India had till then paid on the capital of the company was made permanent. Is there anything parallel to this in the history of the world?

By 1860, the public debt of India had risen to over one hundred million pounds. Since then it has gone upward by leaps and bounds. In 1913–14 the total liabilities of the Government of India stood at £307,391,121. The argument that the whole of this debt is a commercial transaction from which India got a return in the shape of productive works is on the face of it untenable. It is a pity that eminent Englishmen when dealing with the question of "drain" should ignore this phase of the question and always harp on the misleading statement that the interest paid in England represents interest on capital invested in India on productive works for which India got a fair return in the shape of materials supplied by England. The compiler of the *Imperial Gazeteer* from which we quoted above makes the bald statement that out of the total home charges amounting to seventeen and three-quarter millions (of what year it is not stated) nearly eleven millions "consist of payments on account of capital and materials supplied by England."

The Extent of the Drain: It is impossible to state

in pounds, shillings and pence, of how much India has been drained since 1757. We give the various estimates made by Englishmen themselves.

Montgomery Martin wrote in 1838:

"This annual drain of £3,000,000 on British India, amounted in thirty years at 12 per cent. (the usual Indian rate) compound interest to the enormous sum of £723,997,917 sterling; . . . So constant and accumulating a drain even on England would soon have impoverished her; how severe then must be its effects on India, where the wages of a labourer is from twopence to threepence a day?

"For half a century we have gone on draining from two to three and sometimes four million pounds sterling a year from India, which has been remitted to Great Britain to meet the deficiencies of commercial speculations, to pay the interest of debts, to support the home establishment, and to invest on England's soil the accumulated wealth of those whose lives have been spent in Hindustan. I do not think it possible for human ingenuity to avert entirely the evil effects of a continued drain of three or four million pounds a year from a distant country like India, and which is never returned to it in any shape."

Mr. Digby says:

"Estimates have been made which vary from £500,000,000 to nearly £1,000,000,000. Probably between Plassy and Waterloo the last-mentioned sum was transferred from Indian hoards to English banks.

"In estimating the loss to India in the nineteenth century the start must be made with Mr. Martin's figures:

"Loss to India, prior to 1834–35 compound interest, at twelve per cent.. £723,000,000

"The average annual loss, taking the trade tables alone, has been shown to be about £7,500,000. If that sum for the whole period be taken, and a charge of five per cent. compound interest be made (though the money and produce were worth vastly more than five per cent. to the Indian banker, merchant, cultivator, artisan, and to all others in India who would have been in a position to employ capital to good account, were worth at least three times five, but I have taken only five) the result is £4,187,922,732

Total £4,910,922,732

"Thus, the adverse balance of trade against India during the last century, even at the low rate of interest I have adopted, reached the enormous total of nearly £5,000,000,000. If one could follow the money in all the ramifications through which, in India, it might have passed, its fertilising effect in every one of the five hundred and forty thousand villages, its accumulating power ('money makes money') fructifying in a land where its expenditure would have led to an increase in substance, it would, even then, be impossible to put into words the grievous wrong which (unwittingly but, all the same, culpably) has been done to India.

"Now that I have reached this point in my exposition, I turn to page 372–373 of the latest issue of 'Financial and Commercial Statistics' for another purpose, and find that, in taking £7,500,000 as a fair estimate of India's annual payments to the India Office, I have greatly underestimated the facts. I ought to have reckoned those payments at £9,500,000 for each year. The 'Amounts received in England at the India Office on Account of India' during the period 1834–35 to 1898–99 were £610,389,135

"To this must be added debt in England existing at the end of 1898–99. £124,268,605

Total £734,657,740

("Prosperous British India," pp. 224, 225.)

"The figures indicating the drain of capital from India to England, given on page 225, must be amended.

"Loss to India, as already shown..£4,910,922,732

"*Add*, for remittances to England on official account, not shown in the trade returns, nearly £2,000,000 per annum, since (and including) 1834–5, at 5 per cent., per annum compound interest..£1,044,980,684

"Borrowings in England (net remaining after conversions, repayments, etc. ....£ 124,268,605

£6,080,172,021"

(Ibid, p. 230.)

Says Mr. H. M. Hyndman: [Bankruptcy of India, pp. 56, 57 and 58.]

"Now look at the trade figures for the twenty years: The total exports and imports of India, from 1857 to 1876 inclusive amount to £997,063,848 and £841,192,237 respectively. Discriminating between merchandise and bullion in the imports, we have merchandise to the value of £569,835,243 imported in that period, and £271,356,994 worth of bullion. Between 1857 and 1876 the total export and import trade together increased from £55,000,000 to £103,000,000, or very nearly doubled. Nothing could be more satisfactory is the general verdict. Trade doubled capital. Exports exceed imports — that is all right. Great inflow of bullion — the country *must* be getting richer.

"But to estimate correctly the above figures, which are calculated at the Indian ports, it is obvious that at least 15 per cent. must be added to the exports for profit, etc., and that therefore the value of the imports to balance these exports should not be less than £1,-145,000,000.[14] They were £841,000,000. Here is a discrepancy to start with of more than £300,000,000. Of the imports, however, £271,000,000 consisted of bullion. Now of this £271,000,000, certainly not less than £120,000,000 represents the proceeds of loans raised or guaranteed by Government, and brought into India as a borrowed fund, wherewith to pay the wages of labourers, engineers, etc., engaged on public works. It is a treasure which has been borrowed for a definite period, which is still owing, and which has to be repaid. This, therefore, is no trade import.

"We have thus the original disparity of more than £300,000,000 plus £120,000,000 as the drain from India in the twenty years. That amounts to £420,000,000, or £21,000,000 a year. It would be easy to show that the actual drain is much greater than this when the opium profits, and the import of treasure to carry on the increased private business (which is also a loan), are taken into account. The above figures are, however, sufficient to establish the principle for which I contend — that the export trade of India represents a most exhausting drain on the country.

"Even leaving out the profit and taking no account of the opium monopoly, India has sustained a drain of nearly £280,000,000 in the twenty years. The exports for 1876–7 were £65,000,000, and the imports, exclusive of bullion, were £37,427,000, with bullion, nearly £49,000,000."

14 "The reason for this is, that the estimate of value is made at the Indian ports, where freight, profit, and insurance are calculated in giving the value of the imports, but no such addition is made for the exports."

It is remarkable that the average of annual drain struck by Mr. Hyndman for the 20 years from 1857 to 1876 should coincide with the average estimate of "potential drain" found by Sir Theodore Morison on page 203 of his book, "The Economic Transition of India" (London, 1911).

He says:

"On the whole, I do not think that any one who studies the evidence and extends his calculations over a series of years will find any justification for estimating the potential 'drain' at more than £21,000,000 sterling."

Writing in 1882, Mr. A. J. Wilson, late editor of *Investor's Review,* an authority on finance, fixed the figure at thirty millions sterling a year.[15] Writing in 1906 Mr. Hyndman estimated the drain at forty millions sterling a year, but Mr. A. J. Wilson thought that thirty-five millions would be a safe figure, though in his own opinion it represented a low estimate.[16]

Figures. We have taken the figures up to 1898–99 from Mr. Digby's book. The figures from 1898–99 to 1913–14 are given below. The excess of exports over imports in the decade from 1899–1900 to 1908–09 is as below:[17]

1899–1900	13,841,000
1900–1901	10,983,000
1901–1902	17,989,000
1902–1903	18,570,000

[15] "An Empire in the Pawn," by A. J. Wilson, London (1911), p. 61.

[16] "An Empire in the Pawn," by A. J. Wilson, London (1911), pp. 64–65.

[17] These figures are taken from Sir Theodore Morison's book as being likely to be more accurate, though they do not fully tally with the figures given in the statistical abstracts.

1903–1904	24,893,000
1904–1905	20,227,000
1905–1906	22,360,000
a 1906–1907	13,713,000
a 1907–1908	2,665,000
a 1908–1909	5,271,000

a These were the years when the Swadeshi Boycott was in force in Bengal as also in other parts of India.

Total for the decade £150,512,000 or $752,560,000.

	Excess of exports	*Net Home charges*	*Total Disbursements in England from 1902–03 to 1913–14*
	£	£	£
1902–1903	....	17,667,016	25,730,325
1903–1904	....	17,399,728	31,491,699
1904–1905	....	18,827,654	31,168,251
1905–1906	....	17,666,233	51,429,591
1906–1907	....	18,333,943	43,047,986
1907–1908	....	17,768,630	36,669,171
1908–1909	....	18,323,419	37,925,455
1909–1910	22,794,990	18,411,709	40,082,753
1910–1911	29,097,946	18,605,706	51,411,496
1911–1912	27,224,951	18,865,246	43,092,806
1912–1913	18,925,775	19,302,292	52,717,391
1913–1914	14,228,512	19,455,055	45,274,370
	£112,272,174 Total for 5 years	£222,616,621 Total for 12 years	

The figures taken from the 48th and 49th Nos. of the Statistical Abstract relating to British India (1915 and 1916).

Mr. Digby's figures of drain are up to the end of the nineteenth century. We will leave it to the reader to add the figures for the 13 years of the twentieth century given above and find out for himself the grand total of the drain from India up to the end of 1913–14.

In the decade covered by Sir Theodore Morison's book, the total Home Charges (not total disbursements) amounted to £175,976,000, while the total excess of exports for the same period was only £150,512,000. This discrepancy is explained by Sir Theodore

Morison by adding loans raised in England and sent to India in the shape of "stores, rails, machinery, etc." as part of her imports. According to his calculations "the direct and guaranteed debt, charged on the revenues of India" increased by £41,931,036 during the decade from 1899–1900 to 1908–09. Adding this sum to the total excess of exports during the decade, he raises the sum that was available to meet the Home Charges to £19,244,000 per annum and argues that the margin of £3,502,000 per annum thus obtained, is sufficient "to defray the unknown remittances on private account." Following this line of argument he should have deducted from imports the proceeds of loans raised in England for the Government of India in bullion. Besides, it should be remembered that in fixing the amount of excess of exports over imports Sir T. Morison takes no notice of the fact that the imports include about 15 per cent. for freight, insurance, and brokerage and that the exports do not include any of these items.

Sir Theodore Morison obtained his figures about the capital liabilities of India from the India Office, but the figures available to the public are those given in the Statistical Abstracts from which we take the following information for the years 1909–1910 to 1912–13. In 1909–10 the permanent debt in England stood at £176,105,911; in 1912–13 it rose to £179,179,193. The total liabilities of the Government of India at the end of 1913–14 were £307,391,121; on these liabilities £5,912,796 was paid for interest in England and £4,210,848 in India.

It is to be noted that in 1905–06 the public debt of India was classified as follows:—

Railway	*Irrigation*	*Ordinary*
£149,035,455	£27,050,799	£54,425,226

In 1906–07 an alteration was made in the method of classifying the debt by which the portion "attributable" to Railways was raised to £168,344,748 and that "attributable" to ordinary debt reduced to £37,917,-252.

The question of the drain for India is thus complicated by several factors. The excess of exports over imports is not a safe guide (a) because the value of the imports include shipping charges, insurance and brokerage in addition to the profits made by the manufacturer and the importer (Messrs. Hyndman and Wilson have estimated these charges at 15 per cent. of the total value), while exports are represented by the cost price of goods (mostly raw produce at the Indian ports). The only thing they include over and above the price realised by the cultivator is the railway freight to the port of export and the profit and commission of the middleman.[18] (b) Because the debt raised in England is sometimes spent in England and must be added to the exports and the balance sent to India must be deducted from imports; (c) because private remittances sent by British servants of the Government and British merchants and manufacturers in India, *in many*

[18] See Hyndman's "The Bankruptcy of India," 1886, p. 57 footnote and also Mr. Wilson's "An Empire in the Pawn," p. 54; see also note to p. 462 of the "Oxford Survey of British Empire" (Asia), p. 462.

shapes, are not necessarily included in the account; (d) because many transactions are settled by exchange entries in books. Many English firms dealing with India have their branch offices in India and they pay for imports not always in exports. Sometimes they invest large sums of money in India.

Mr. J. S. Cotton a retired Government of India official, who was the editor of the *Imperial Gazeteer* says:

> "The trade for export, even in up country markets, is largely in the hands of a few European firms who make their purchases through brokers; and the business of shipping at the ports is almost entirely conducted by European firms to whom the Indian traders consign their purchases by rail. The import trade also is mainly in European hands." [19]

It might be added that a fair proportion of the exports are purchased by European firms directly from the producer.[20]

On the preceding pages we have given the various estimates made by Englishmen; those made by Messrs. Martin, Digby, Hyndman and Wilson on the one side and those made by Sir John Strachey and Sir Theodore Morison on the other. We have also shown how the latter explain away the "Drain." In the Statistical Abstract of 1912–13, the total interest paid in England in that year was £6,203,996 but in the table of Expenditure in England given on page 70 the interest on debt was as follows:

[19] "The Oxford Survey of British Empire" (Asia), p. 172.
[20] Ramsay Macdonald's "Awakening of India," p. 106, popular edition.

Ordinary	£2,296,498
Railways	8,979,898
Irrigation	124,730
Total	11,401,126

The total expenditure in England in 1912–13 was £20,279,572. If we deduct the interest paid on railway and irrigation debts, there will be left a balance of over eleven millions to be accounted for. Accepting the arguments of Sir Theodore Morison, we may also deduct the price of stores supplied.

Stationery and Printing	£ 85,314
Civil Departments	253,585
Marine Stores	84,727
Public Works	144,773
Military	788,309
Miscellaneous	9,563
Total	1,366,271

Roughly speaking that leaves a balance of a little less than ten million pounds as expenditure in England for which India got no return in any shape or form.

It will also be noticed that the Home Charges are always on an ascending scale and the excess of exports over imports has risen considerably of late; i.e., since 1908–09, the last year for which figures were given by Sir Theodore Morison. In comparing figures of past years with later years it should be remembered that the figures in sterling do not give an exact idea of the increase. The economic value of the rupee (the unit of Indian coinage) was 2s. in the seventies of the nineteenth century. It is 1s. 4d. now, and that makes a huge difference.

We think we have established beyond doubt that:

(1) There is a drain. India does pay a tribute, which the Imperialists call compensation for services rendered.

(2) The extent of the drain differs according to the way it is looked at by different persons.

Mr. Hyndman fixed the amount in 1906 at forty million pounds sterling per annum;

Mr. Wilson fixed it at thirty-five millions per annum;

Sir Theodore Morison fixed the amount of what he calls "potential drain" at twenty-one millions. Computed in rupees it will be much larger.

In any case this is sufficient to establish the fact that Great Britain does make a huge profit by her political ascendency in India.

CHAPTER IV

HOW INDIA HAS HELPED ENGLAND MAKE HER EMPIRE

"Perhaps the most striking testimony to the virtue of benevolent despotism is seen in the employment of native races to fight our battles for us. . . . Having extended the Empire by bringing the 'inferior races' under our sway, by a master stroke of genius we utilise them to still further extend and also to defend the Empire, and convert them into instruments for bestowing upon their brethren the boons which they themselves have obtained. It is very largely in this way that our Indian Empire has been built up."

—Mr. J. G. Goddard, M. P.—"Racial Supremacy."

India and "The Empire." The present generation of Englishmen, born into conditions of extreme prosperity, at a time when their country is at the zenith of her imperial glory, are apt to forget how much they owe to India. They ignore the fact that India is The Empire,—perhaps the only Empire they have. She is the pivot round which the whole Imperial edifice has been built and revolves. The self-governing dominions except in the present hour of war contributed little, if anything, to the prosperity and strength of the Empire. So far, they have laid more emphasis upon their rights than their duties, which they scarcely recognised at all. They rendered some help to Great Britain in the Boer War, and have splendidly borne their share in the present titanic struggle, but looking at their past history, they have got immensely more from the Empire than they ever gave it.

India, on the other hand, has always been the "milch-cow." She has supplied the British Isles with food, and with raw products to be turned into manufactured articles; she has supplied labour to develop the colonies; she has fought for the Empire in almost every hemisphere. She affords a vast field for all kinds of experiments; she is the training camp for engineers and generals from the British Isles. This point was frankly admitted by Lord Roberts in the evidence he gave before the Royal Commission on Indian Expenditures (97) when he said: "From the point of view of training, India is a very great strength to the United Kingdom."

But what is even more significant, India conquered most of her Empire for Great Britain. Her sons, her blood and her resources have been freely used by England to make new acquisitions, to put down revolts in existing dominions, and to maintain her prestige in Europe. At the time of the Boer War, India was the first to send an expedition to the Transvaal. The same thing happened in the present European war; the Indian expedition reached France very early in the conflict, and helped materially. Since then, Indian troops have been used at Gallipoli, in Mesopotamia and in Egypt. India herself has paid the bills. Yet when her sons talk of post-war reforms in the Administration, they are rebuked with a warning not to be sordid! It is their duty to shed blood for their great benefactor. For details of India's contribution to this war in men and money see the Post-Scriptum to the Preface.

In this chapter we purpose showing how India has helped England make her Empire. It would be well to remember, in this connection, that all the acquisitions of the East India Company in Asia were won through their Indian Government employing Indian troops, and paying the cost from Indian exchequers. It was the East India Company which acquired the Isle of France (Mauritius) the island of Ceylon, the settlement and port of Singapore, and other islands in the Indian Seas now in possession of England. It was the East India Company which originally obtained foothold in Persia and Arabia, conquered Burmah, and conducted military and naval operations for Great Britain whenever the latter was at war with France, Portugal or Holland, and desired to strike at their Asiatic and African holdings.

The following table, taken from the Report of the Royal Commission on Indian Expenditures, Vol. II, page 305, will show how India has been saddled with the expenses of the various wars she fought, or participated in, for the glory of the British Empire.

Foreign Wars Whose Cost Was Charged to India

Expedition	*Ordinary Charges paid by*		*Extra-ordinary Charges paid by*	
	India	*England*	*India*	*England*
1st Afghan War 1838-42	all	none	all	none
1st China War 1839-40	all	none	none	all
Persian War 1856	all	none	half	half

Expedition	*Ordinary Charges paid by*		*Extra-ordinary Charges paid by*	
	India	*England*	*India*	*England*
Abyssinian War 1867–68	all	none	none	all
Perak Expedition 1875	all	none	none	all
2nd Afghan War 1878–80	all	none	all except £5,000,000	£5,000,000
Egyptian War 1882	all	none	all except £500,000	£500,000
Soudan War 1885–86	all	none	none	all

To this table, we append the following extract from the same Report, showing India's expenditures for Great Britain's consular representation in Asia:

"The Persian mission was established in 1810 and maintained at the charge of Great Britain until 1823, when it was transferred to India. From 1823–31 it was wholly supported by Indian funds. In 1835 it was transferred to the British Foreign Office, the Indian Government contributing £12,000 a year towards its cost. Again, in 1859, the mission and consulate at Teheran, Tabriz and Resht were placed under the Government of India. The cost of the mission was then estimated at £15,000 a year, towards which Great Britain contributed £3,000, with £2,000 on account of the consulate. In 1860, the mission and consulate were re-transferred to the British Foreign Office and from 1860–1880, India contributed £12,000 towards the mission, leaving the consulate at the sole charge of Great Britain. In 1880–90, the Indian contribution was reduced to £10,000 and further reduced, in 1891, to £7,000."

That India has been unjustly and sometimes illegally treated in this respect, will be clear from a few extracts we submit from the evidence of British statesmen given before the Royal Commission. For fuller material, we refer the reader to the evidence itself and to the written statements of Colonel Hanna and Colonel Waterfield in Vol. II. India not only pays for a huge British garrison within her confines, but also for all the expenses incurred in connection with their enlistment, training and equipment; for all pensions earned by the men and officers as well as every cent spent on medical and various philanthropic institutions maintained for their benefit in England. The whole thing is so unjust, that rather than trust our own language to express our feelings, we will let Lord Northbrook, Sir Henry Brackenberry and Sir Edward Collen speak about it.

Lord Lansdowne on the Indian Army.

15,996—*Mr. Courtney*—"Have you considered, Lord Lansdowne, from the point of view of India herself, supposing she were isolated from Great Britain, whether it would be necessary to maintain a force such as is borrowed from the United Kingdom, and in the same degree of efficiency?" "Certainly not. The Indian army is organised with a view to its employment upon operations which have nothing to do either with the internal policy of the country, or the mere repression of tribal disorders on the frontier."

15,997. "Then the difference in the cost of training that force so borrowed, between what would be necessary for Indian purposes and the standard kept up for Imperial and Home purposes, should be borne by the home exchequer?" "Your question points to the principle which I was endeavouring in my answers to enforce."

15,998. "That we for home and Imperial purposes, keep the army at a higher standard of efficiency than India taken by herself, requires, and we should make that a consideration in settlement of charges between the two countries?" "Certainly."

Lord Roberts on India as Training Ground for British Army.

15,664. "The argument that India affords the best training ground for the British army during peace is a ground for reducing the home charges of British regiments in India. Any one who has served in India must admit it affords the best training ground for troops and this should not be lost sight of in apportioning home charges. I doubt if any country is so peculiarly well adapted for training troops as India. From the point of view of training, India is a very great strength to the United Kingdom."

Sir Henry Brackenberry on Indian Army Expenditure.

14,782. "The army in India is largely in excess of requirements for preserving internal peace. The foreign policy of India is directed entirely from England and is a part of British foreign policy in general. The object of British foreign policy is to secure British rule over the British Empire. If British rule were maintained in India only for India's sake, then it would be fair to make India pay everything that was due to Britain's rule over India. But I cannot but feel Britain's interest in keeping India under British rule is enormous. India affords employment to thousands of Britons; India employs millions of British capital; Indian commerce is of immense value to Great Britain. It seems to me Great Britain should pay her share of expenditures, and in estimating that share, she should behave generously, because England is a rich country and India a poor one;—also India has no representation; where a nation is arbitrarily governed, the governing power should behave generously."

14,896. "If this Royal Commission could see its way to recommend the abolition of all those accounts for military and naval services, for the Secretary of State's salary, and the expenses of the India Office, for diplomatic and consular charges in Persia and China and elsewhere, and to substitute for them a fixed contribution from India, many constant causes of irritation would be removed, and it would do much to convince all classes of India of the desire of this country which rules India, to treat her justly and generously."

Sir Edwin Collen on the Apportionment of Expenses.

6,197. "The division between the British and Indian Treasuries of the charges for European troops in India should be determined with special reference to the fact that the military forces of the United Kingdom are organised to meet the requirements of the whole Empire, that India has no voice in deciding on the nature of such organisation, and that she as a poor country is made to enter into partnership with England, one of the wealthiest in the world. India's contribution should be decided with reference to the relative wealth of India and England, to the fact that India, supplies a great training ground for the British part of the Indian army. That a contribution should be made by the Imperial Exchequer towards the cost of fortifications which have been erected on the frontier, or to defend the ports of India against attack by great European powers, and that England should bear a share of the cost of Aden, which is practically an Imperial fortress. That this is not to be regarded as a matter of generosity, but of justice and legality."

Lord Northbrook on Wars Outside India.

14,108. "Have you paid any attention to the arrangements made for the payment of troops lent by India for service outside the country?" "Yes, I have had occasion to give considerable attention to this matter."

14,109. "Do you think that fair treatment has been given to India in the apportionment of these charges?" "I think India has been hardly treated."

14,110. "Could you go through the various cases and give us your reasons?" "The cases will be found in Sir Henry Waterfield's Memorandum in the Appendix, page 364. . . ."

14,119. "Do you remember the ground upon which the Government decided that India had an interest in the Abyssinian Expedition?" "No, I should like to see it — I never heard of it. I believe a protest was made at the time."

14,120. "I am speaking from memory. Was it not put forward that the Government of India was concerned, because Abyssinia, being within the purview of India, you may say the prestige of the English name must not be endangered by allowing any official English subjects to be taken prisoner?" "The idea may have been put forward. I do not think any impartial person would have paid the slightest attention to it."

14,121 — *Mr. Courtney* — "I remember a French critic arguing at the time that the war was for the purpose of discovering a sanatorium for English troops?" "That would be a better reason than the one adduced as regards prestige. Then I come to the next case, — the Perak Expedition. I cannot conceive any one doubting that India has been hardly treated. An expedition beyond the frontier of India, and for which, to apply any portion of the Indian revenue, it is by statute necessary to address the Crown from both Houses of Parliament. I was Governor General at the time, and protested at this charge being put upon India. No notice was taken of the protest, made by the Government of India, and not even were the statutory addresses from both Houses moved, so the law was broken, and the charge made upon India has never been repaid."

14,124. "Have you mentioned the Egyptian operation of 1882?" "That is the next case. There was no doubt that as regards keeping the Suez Canal open, India had a substantial interest. The question was, what interest? It was intended that India should pay the whole cost of the expedition that was sent. The English Government was put to considerable cost, and we thought India would be put to small cost, so might fairly pay the cost of troops sent to Suez. The operations became very extended and the expedition from India became a large one. The whole cost was 1,700,-000 pounds. India paid 1,200,000 pounds and England 500,000. The Government of India thought it had been hardly treated, and looking at it now, I must say it would have been better if we had charged India half."

14,127—*Soudan War*—"Would you consider, under the original plan, India was sufficiently interested in the expedition to justify her being called on to contribute?" "No, certainly not. I do not think there was a substantial interest of India in any expedition to the Soudan. By statute, the Indian revenues are not to be used except after addresses from both Houses of Parliament; in my opinion, the continued employment of the Indian troops at Suakim as a garrison was not covered by the address. As to the force sent to Suakim last year, certainly India should not have been charged."

14,166. "To sum up what I have put before the Commission, I think if the ordinary charges of the Abyssinian War were 600,000 pounds, India has a fair and equitable ground to claim that sum. The whole of the Perak charges ought to be paid. The whole of the garrison charges at Suakim ought to be refunded to India. On equitable grounds, £350,000 ought to be given India for the Egyptian Expedition of 1882,—because India has been inequitably and in some cases, illegally treated during many years, I do not see any reason why that treatment should not be redressed by some action at the present time."

We will conclude this chapter with a few instances, illustrating further India's contribution to the making of the British Empire:

The First Treaty with Persia. The first British embassy to Persia was sent from India at the expense of the Indian exchequer. "The Embassy," to use the words of the negotiator, "was in a style of splendour corresponding to the character of the monarch and the manners of the nation, to whom it was sent; and to the wealth and power of that state from which it proceeded."

Commenting on the above quotation, Mill remarks:

"A language, this, which may be commonly interpreted, lavishly, or, which amounts to the same thing, criminally expensive."

The negotiator continues: "It was completely successful in all its objects. The King of Persia was not *only induced* by the British envoy to renew his attack upon *Khurassan,* which had the effect of withdrawing Zamanshah from his designs upon India; but entered into treaties of political and commercial alliance with the British Government."[1]

For the terms of the treaty, we quote again the language of Mill:

"It was stipulated that the King of Persia should lay waste, with a great army, the country of the Afghans, if ever they should proceed to the invasion of India, and conclude no peace without engagements binding them to abstain from all aggressions upon the English: that should any army belonging to the French, attempt

[1] Malcolm's Sketch, p. 31, quoted by James Mill, Bk. VI, Ch. 9, p. 187.

to form a settlement on any of the islands or shores of Persia, a force should be employed by the two contracting states to co-operate for their extirpation,— and if any individuals of the French nation should request permission to reside in Persia, it should not be granted. In the Furman, annexed to the treaty, and addressed to the governors and officers in the Persian Provinces, it was said: 'Should any person of the French nation attempt to pass our ports or boundaries, or desire to establish themselves either on the shore or frontiers, you are to take means to expel or extirpate them, and never to allow them to obtain a footing in any place, and you are at full liberty, and authorised, to disgrace or slay them.' Though the atrocious part of this order was no doubt the pure offspring of Persian ferocity, yet a Briton may justly feel shame that the ruling men of his nation, a century ago, could contemplate with pleasure so barbarous and inhuman a mandate, or endure to have thought themselves, except in the very last necessity, its procuring cause."

"The Embassy proceeded from Bombay on December 29, 1799. 'These treaties,' says Malcolm, 'while they excluded the French from Persia, gave the English every benefit they could desire from the connection.'"

It appears, from Wilson's "History of India" that the East India Company had been maintaining a Resident at Bagdad for many years before the English Government resolved to send an ambassador to the Persian Court. The allowances of "His Majesty's Envoy Extraordinary and Plenipotentiary, Sir Hartford Jones, and the cost of the mission" were defrayed by the Company, and the Envoy was to act under instructions from the Governor-General in India. The latter had meanwhile sent his own representative in the person of Sir John Malcolm, and protested against the English Government sending their own ambassador to the Court of Persia, but his protests were unheeded, and upon this precedent, ambassadors to Persia were from that time forward sent directly from the Court of St. James.

In 1819, expeditions were sent from Bombay for the subjugation of certain Arab tribes. A political station had been maintained for a time at Kishme Mocha, where an officer was employed by the Company to superintend the affairs of its subjects. This station was bombarded in 1879, and the Chief taken prisoner.

In 1828, the Indian Government paid to the Shah of Persia two hundred thousand *Tomans* as an equivalent for the final abrogation of the Treaty of Teheran.

Other Nations of Asia. In Chapter VI., Book 1 of his "History of India," Wilson speaks of Lord Minto being "busily and anxiously engaged in asserting the ascendency of the British Empire in India over the other nations of Asia." The cost of every expedition into the Persian Gulf, whether against the Persians, the Arabs or the Afghans, was of course, defrayed by the Indian Revenues. We are told besides, that "the attention of Lord Minto was earnestly fixed upon objects of European as well as Indian interest, arising out of the war which raged in the Western hemisphere." As a result of that interest, an expedition was sent from India, at the cost of India, to reduce the Portuguese possession of Macao in Chinese territory. The expedition failed, owing to the refusal of the Chinese to permit the British to occupy Macao, but this failure was "more than redeemed by the success which attended the employment of the resources of

British India in the furtherance of objects of greater importance to the nation."

Isle of France. It was reserved for Lord Minto's administration to effect the extirpation of the remains of French colonial possessions in the Eastern hemisphere, "that had so long been suffered to inflict humiliation and injury upon the subjects" of Great Britain. It was this motive and this excuse which actuated Lord Minto to attempt the conquest of the Isles of France and of Java. The expedition was successful, and though the Isle of Bourbon was subsequently restored to France when peace in Europe was declared, the Isle of France, or the Mauritius, is still subject to Great Britain as one of her Crown Colonies, quite apart from India.

The Muluccas. The Muluccas, Batavia, and other Dutch possessions, including Java, were also captured at this time by Indian expeditions sent out by Lord Minto. Under the Treaty of 1844 the Dutch possessions were restored to Holland.

Ceylon. In 1796, Ceylon was taken from the Dutch, as being identified with the Republic of France, by an expedition fitted out from Madras. For a short time it was subject to the government of Fort St. George, but in 1798 was annexed as a Crown Colony of the British Government.

Eastern Archipelago; Straits of Malacca and Singapore. According to the terms of the treaty of 1814, made with the Dutch, the latter's settlements in the East were restored to them, but "no provision was made for the continued observance of those compacts which had been formed by the English while occupying

Java, with the independent Native States." The Dutch consequently did as they pleased with the latter, and "extended their chains of supremacy over all the native princes, whom it was their interest to control — an invariable article of their engagements being the exclusion of all other European ships from their ports." This policy excited the resolve of the British Government to strengthen and preserve its own connection in the Archipelago so as to preserve the free passage of the Straits of Malacca, the other great thoroughfare to the China Sea. The Governor of Bencoolen was accordingly appointed "Agent to the Governor-General of India, in charge of British interests" to the eastward of the Straits, and in "anticipation of the sanction of the British Government," Singapore, the key to all maritime activities in the China Sea, was occupied.

Siam and Cochin-China. In November of the year 1821, the British-Indian Government sent a mission to Bangkok, capital of Siam, to open commercial intercourse with that country and Cochin-China. Failing to obtain its designs in Siam, the mission proceeded to Cochin-China and there obtained permission from the King of that country to trade in the principal ports on the same terms conceded to the Chinese.

Burmah. The first war with Burmah occurred in 1824, was conducted with Indian troops, and paid for from the Indian exchequer. It resulted in the annexation of Arakan, Tenaserim and other parts of Burmah to the British Dominions.

Malacca. In 1831, a revolt in Malacca was put down by an expedition of Indian troops sent there, resulting in the annexation of Nauring to Malacca.

The China Consular Representatives. The East India Company bore the whole expense of diplomatic intercourse with China as long as it enjoyed the monopoly of British trade with that country. The Company made the profit and the Indian people paid the expenses. The monopoly ceased in 1834, and thenceforth it was decided that Great Britain should pay two-thirds, India one-third of the cost of the superintendents of trade who were to represent diplomatic interests in China. In 1876, the arrangement was revised, and India paid a fixed contribution of £15,000 a year, reduced in 1891 to £12,500. This was put upon the ground of the opium trade with China, which has now been discontinued.

Aden. India bears the whole charge, civil and military, for Aden, which is not an Indian port but an Imperial dependency, from which the rest of the Empire, including Australia, derive more benefit than India.

The Zanzibar and Mauritius Cable. The Government of India pays one-half the subsidy for this cable, although Sir David Barbour, the Finance Minister at the time, objected to incurring this expenditure, because in his opinion, "the duty of protecting commerce on the high seas should devolve upon England."

The Red Sea Telegraph. India contributed one-half the £36,000 annuity which was payable until 1908 for this useless cable.

In conclusion, we cite the words of Mr. Thorburn, page 350 of his book, "The Punjab in Peace and War":

"The Government of India in their foreign proceedings are irresponsible and in pursuit of the chimera of high politics, sometimes a mere mount for vaulting ambitions, they plunge lightheartedly into adventures and wars which may benefit a few individuals, but injure the people of India collectively. When things go wrong in India, hardly a voice is raised against the wrong-doers; officers may not speak, the press has little information, and if it had more, is timid, *the line between treason and criticism being finely drawn;* and as for the masses — their horizon is the evening meal, and the next instalment of the revenue demand.

"We give the following instances:

1. Lord Lytton's Afghan Wars — 'India bleeds silently.'
2. In 1890, our wars of pinpricks cost six or seven million pounds sterling. Once more, 'India bleeds silently.'
3. An agent trails his coat in Chitral, a war follows, India pays and the agent is knighted and promoted.
4. The events of August 23, 1897, take place beyond the Khyber Pass, a serious war follows. Once more, India bleeds,— this time, happily, not quite in silence."

PART THREE

CHAPTER V

THE COTTON INDUSTRY OF INDIA

I

HISTORICAL SURVEY

"The birthplace of cotton manufacture is India, where it probably flourished long before the dawn of authentic history. Its introduction into Europe took place at a comparatively late period where, for a long time, it existed like a tropical plant in northern latitudes, degenerate and sickly, until, by the appliance of modern art and science, it suddenly shot forth in more than its native luxuriance." (Baines, History of Cotton Manufacture, 1835, page 2).

Early Mention. The arts of spinning and weaving, which rank next to agriculture, are supposed to have been invented very early in the world's history. In the time of Joseph, 1700 B. C., it is recorded that "Pharaoh arrayed him in vestures of fine linen"— and the writer quoted above adds; "it is extremely probable that cotton was manufactured in India as early as linen in Egypt."

Herodotus, writing about 445 B. C., stated that cotton was the customary wear of the Indians of that period. The subsequent writings of Europeans and Asiatics testify to the same fact. Strabo, whose authority is Nearchus, mentions "their flowered cottons, or chintzes, and the various and beautiful dyes with which their cloths were figured."

The first mention of cotton as an article of trade occurs in that valuable record of ancient commerce, "The Circum Navigation of the Erystheaen Sea," by Arrian, an Egyptian Greek living in the first or second century A. D. He describes particularly the imports and exports of several Indian towns, in their trade with the Arabs and Greeks. From this record, it appears that the Arab traders brought Indian cottons to Aduli, a port of the Red Sea; that the ports beyond the Red Sea had an established trade with Batala, on the Indus, Ariake and Bazygaza (the modern Baroach); receiving from them among other things, cottons of various weaves; that Barygaza largely exported calicoes, muslins and other cotton goods made in the province for which this was the port, as well as in the more remote provinces of the interior. Mosalia, or Masulipatam, was famous then as now for its manufacture of cotton piece goods, and the muslins of Bengal were superior to all others, receiving from the Greeks the name of Gangi,—i.e., made on the banks of the Ganges.

In the days of the Roman Empire, silk, both raw and manufactured, was an important article of commerce throughout India and Persia. Two Persian monks brought silk-worms and the art of silk manufacture from China to Constantinople, in the reign of Justinian, 352 A. D. Indian cotton goods were imported into the Eastern Empire in the same age, as they are found in the lists of dutiable goods in the Justinian Code.

From India, the art of cotton manufacturing went to

Arabia. The English word "cotton" is a modification of the Arabian "Quttan." Marco Polo states that cotton was abundantly grown and manufactured in all the provinces on the Indus,— and was the staple manufacture of the whole of India. In the thirteenth century, the art of cotton manufacture went to China and thence to Japan. In the tenth century it travelled to Spain, being introduced by the Moors, and thence to Italy about the fourteenth century. The Mohammedans introduced it into Africa even earlier. Thus it spread east and west, "from its native seat in India across the breadth of the old continent to Japan eastward and the mouths of the Tagus and Senegal westward." (Baines, page 47.)

Excellence of Indian Cotton Fabrics.

"The Indians have in all ages maintained an unapproached and almost incredible perfection in their fabrics of cotton — some of their muslins might be thought the work of fairies or insects, rather than of men," said Baines in 1835, when Indian fabrics were still being made. The Arabian travellers of the ninth century say; "In this country, India, they make garments of such extraordinary perfection, that nowhere else is their like to be seen,— sewed and woven to such a degree of fineness, they may be drawn through a ring of moderate size." Marco Polo (thirteenth century) says: "The Coast of Coromandel and especially Masulipatam, produce the finest and most beautiful cottons to be found in any part of the world."

Many authorities show the quality of cotton cloth manufactured in India up to the end of the eighteenth century. In spite of the raw material not being brought to its highest state of cultivation, despite crude machinery and little division of labour, the products were, according to Baines, "fabrics of exquisite delicacy unrivalled by any other nation, even those best skilled in the mechanic arts." He ascribes its excellence to the "remarkable fine sense of touch, and the patience and gentleness of the Hindus."

Even now, fine muslins are woven in India, but since the introduction of machine-made cloths, the industry has suffered both in quantity and in quality.

Extent of the Cotton Industry in Olden Times.

"On the coast of Coromandel and the province of Bengal, it is difficult to find a village in which every man, woman and child is not employed in making a piece of cloth. At present much of the greatest part of the provinces are employed in this single manufacture (409). The progress of the linen (cotton) manufacture includes no less than a description of the lives of half the inhabitants of Hindustan."[1]

Upon this and other testimony, Mr. Baines remarked in 1835 that cotton manufacture in India was not carried on in a few large towns or districts; it was universal. The growth of cotton was nearly as general as the growth of food. Bengal was noted for the finest muslins; Coromandel coast for chintzes and calicoes; Surat for strong and inferior goods of all kinds; table cloths of superior quality were made at Patna. The basius or basinets came from the northern Circars. Condaver furnished the beautiful handkerchiefs

[1] Orme: in "Historical Fragments of The Mogul Empire," p. 413; quoted by Baines, p. 65.

of Masulipatam, the fine colours of which are obtained from a plant growing on the banks of Kishna and the coast of Bengal. Chintzes and ginghams were made chiefly at Masulipatam, Madras, St. Thome and Paliam Cotta. Long cloths and fine petticoats came from Madras. Besides these, there were endless varieties of fabric known to the markets of Europe, Asia and Africa.

Indian commerce was extensive from the Christian era to the end of the eighteenth century. For many hundred years, Persia, Arabia, Syria, Egypt, Abyssinia and all the eastern parts of Africa were supplied with cottons and muslins from the markets of India. Owing to the beauty and cheapness of Indian fabrics, the manufacturers of Europe were apprehensive of being ruined by their Indian competitors. The Dutch traders and the East India Company imported large quantities of these cotton goods in the seventeenth century. As early as 1678, a loud outcry was raised in England against the admission of Indian fabrics, which "were ruining our ancient woollen manufactures." We quote from a pamphlet of the period:

> The woollen trade "is much hindered by our own people who do wear many foreign commodities instead of our own; . . . instead of green sey that was wont to be used for children's frocks, is now used *painted and Indian stained and striped calicoes;* . . . and sometime is used a *Bangale* brought from India, both for lynings to coats and for petticoats too. . . . It would be necessary to lay a very high impost on all such commodities as these are . . ."

A writer of 1696 laments the misfortune of Indian

muslins and silks becoming the general wear in England.

In 1708 Daniel Defoe wrote in his weekly review:

"The general fansie of the people runs upon East India goods to that degree that the *chintes* and *painted calicoes,* before only made use of for carpets, quilts, etc., and to clothe children and ordinary people, become now the dress of our ladies; and such is the power of a mode as we saw persons of quality dressed in Indian carpets, which but a few years before their chamber maids would have thought too ordinary for them; the chintz was advanced from being upon their floors to their backs, and even the Queen herself at this time was pleased to appear in China silks and calicoe . . . it crept into our houses; our closets, and bed chambers; curtains, cushions, chairs and beds themselves were nothing but calicoes or Indian stuffs, and in short, almost everything that used to be made of wool or silk, relating either to the dress of our women or the furniture of our houses, was supplied by the Indian trade."

Defoe's complaint was not of an evil existing in 1708 when he wrote, but of one a few years earlier, for the prohibition of Indian goods had taken place in 1700, by Acts 11 and 12 of William III, Cap. 10. The introduction of Indian silks and printed calicoes for domestic use as either apparel or furniture was forbidden under penalty of £200 on the wearer or seller, and as this did not prevent the use of Indian goods, other acts were passed at later date. This "evil" of the consumption of Indian manufactures did not disappear by 1728, and other countries of Europe were making similar efforts to penalise the import and use of Indian fabrics.

Baines says: "Not more than a century ago, the

cotton fabrics of India were so beautiful and cheap that nearly all the governments of Europe thought it necessary to prohibit or load them with heavy duties, to protect their own manufactures."

What, adds he, could not be achieved by legislation in Europe, was brought about by the exercise of political power in India. This is evidenced partly by the following petition submitted by the natives of Bengal to the British Government, in September, 1831:

"To the Right Honourable, the Lords of His Majesty's Privy Council for Trade, etc.

"The humble petition of the undersigned Manufacturers and dealers in Cotton and Silk Piece goods, the fabrics of Bengal;

"Sheweth; that of late years your petitioners have found their business nearly superseded by the introduction of the fabric of Great Britain into Bengal, the importation of which augments every year, to the great prejudice of native manufactures.

"That the fabrics of Great Britain are consumed in Bengal without any duties levied upon them to protect native fabrics.

"That the fabrics of Bengal are charged with the following duties when they are used in Great Britain:

"On manufactured cottons.... 10 per cent.
On manufactured silks....... 14 per cent.

"Your petitioners most humbly implore your Lordships' consideration of these circumstances, and they feel confident no disposition exists in England to shut the door against industry of any part of the inhabitants of this great empire.

"They therefore pray to be admitted to the privilege of British subjects, and entreat your lordships to allow the cotton and silk fabrics of Bengal to be used in Great

Britain free of duty or at the same rate which may be charged on British fabrics sold here.

"Your Lordships must be aware of the immense advantage the British manufacturers derive from their skill in constructing and using machinery, enabling them to undersell the unscientific manufacturers of Bengal in their own country; and although your Petitioners are not sanguine in expecting to derive any advantage from having their prayer granted, their minds would feel gratified by such a manifestation of good will towards them; and such an instance of justice to the natives of India would not fail to endear the British Government to them.

"They therefore confidently expect that your Lordships' righteous consideration will be extended to them as British subjects without exception of sect, country, or colour.

"And your Petitioners, as in duty bound, will ever pray."

The petition was signed by 117 natives of high respectability. (P. 82.)

In a footnote, Baines remarks that "this reasonable request has not been complied with, the duty on Indian cottons being still 10 per cent. The extra duty of 3½d. per yard on printed cottons was removed when the excise duty on English prints was repealed, in 1831. English cottons imported into India pay duty of only 2½ per cent." This document in his opinion furnished abundant proof how a manufacture which had existed without a rival for thousands of years withered away under the competition of a Power which had arisen but yesterday.

Decline of the Indian Industry. Let us enumerate the causes which made the English industry flourish while the Indian declined:

1. The invention of the power loom and other mechanical appliances ranks first. But these might have been of no avail had not the capital for their development been taken from India, as shown in a previous chapter.

2. The monopoly created by the East India Company in their own favour.

3. The imposition of a heavy tariff in England on Indian cottons. The following scale of duties on imported cotton goods is copied from Baines (P. 325).

Rate of Duty on Cotton Goods Imported

	East India White Calicoes per Piece					*East India Muslins and Nankeens Per cent ad val.*			*East India Dyed Goods Per cent ad val.*
	s.	d.	L.	s.	d.	L.	s.	d.	
1787	5	3 &	16	10	0	18	0	0	Prohibited
1797	5	9 &	18	3	0	19	16	0	
1798	5	9 &	21	3	0	22	16	0	
1799	6	8 &	26	9	1	30	3	9	
1802	6	8 &	27	1	1	30	15	9	
1803			59	1	3	30	18	9	
1804			65	12	6	34	7	6	
1805			66	18	9	35	1	3	
1806			71	6	3	37	7	1	
1809			71	13	4	37	6	8	
1813			85	2	1	44	6	8	
1814			67	10	1	37	10	0	

N. B. The importation of cotton goods other than from the East Indies, was inconsiderable until 1825.

Cotton Manufactures of all Sorts, Not Made Up.

1825 10 per cent. ad valorem, additional duty of 3½d. per sq. yd. if printed.

1832 Repeal of the additional duty of 3½d. per sq. yd. on printed goods.

Inspector General's Office, Customs House, London, January 21, 1834.

Signed; WM. IRVING.

In 1783 Parliament passed a law sanctioning bounties on the exportation of British printed cottons, viz.:

Under value of 5d. per yd.; (before printing) ½d. per yd.
Value 5d. under 6d. " " ; 1d. per yd.
Value 6d. under 8d. " " ; 1½d. " "

Besides the Drawback of the Excise Duty.

These bounties were continued for more than thirty years, when they were repealed. The duties on Indian goods were raised from time to time, till in 1813 and later, up to 1831, they stood at the figures quoted below. The following statement is taken from the evidence of Mr. Ricards given before the Select Committee of the House of Commons in 1813. (See Report Appendix, page 581.)

"The duties of many articles of East India produce are also enormously high, apparently rated on no fixed principle, and without regard to market price. . . . The rates of duty imposed on Indian imports into Britain when compared with the exemption from duty of British staples into India (cotton goods being subject to a duty of only 2½ per cent), constitute an important feature in the present question. Indians within the Company's jurisdiction, like English, Scotch, or Irish, are equally subjects of the British Government. To make invidious distinctions, favouring one class but oppressing another, all being subjects of the same empire, cannot be reconciled with the principles of justice; and whilst British imports into India are thus so highly favoured, I know that Indo-British subjects feel it a great grievance that their commodities when imported into England should be so enormously taxed."

The following charges on cotton manufactures in 1813 are significant:—

	£	s.	d.
Flowered or stitched muslins of white calicoes (for every £100 of value)	32	9	2
And further (for every £100 of value)	11	17	6
Calicoes and dimities (for every £100 of value)	81	2	11
And further (for every £100 of value)	3	19	2

	£	s.	d.
Cotton, raw (per 100 lbs.)	0	16	11
Cotton, Manufactured (for every £100 of value)	81	2	11
Articles of manufacture of cotton, wholly or in part made up, not otherwise charged with duty (for every £100 of value)	32	9	2

(Digby, p. 90.)

John Ranking, an English merchant, when examined by the Select Committee of the House of Commons in 1813, said that he looked upon these duties as "protecting" duties, to "encourage our own manufactures."

The real object of the Parliamentary Enquiry in 1813 was to promote the interests of the manufacturers of England. This is evident from the nature of the questions that were put to the witnesses that were examined then as also in 1831. For instance Warren Hastings was asked: "From your knowledge of the Indian character and habits, are you able to speak to the probability of a demand for European commodities by the population of India, for their own use?"

Similar questions were asked Sir John Malcolm and other witnesses, among them Sir Thomas Munro, who in reply to a question whether the civilisation of the Hindus could not be improved by the establishment of an open trade said:

"I do not understand what is meant by the civilisation of the Hindus; in the higher branches of science, in the knowledge of the theory and practice of good government, and in education which, by banishing prejudice and superstition, opens the mind to receive instruction of every kind from every quarter, they are much inferior to Europeans. But if a good system of agriculture, unrivalled manufacturing skill, a capacity to produce whatever can contribute to convenience or luxury; schools established in every village for teaching reading, writing and arithmetic; the general practice of hospitality and charity amongst each other; and above all, a treatment of the female sex full of confidence, respect and delicacy, are among the signs which denote a civilised people, then the Hindus are not inferior to the nations of Europe; and if civilisation is to become an article of trade between the two countries, I am convinced that this country (England) will gain by the import cargo." [2]

In less than seventy-five years (from 1757 to 1829) India was reduced from the position of a manufacturing country to that of a supplier of raw materials. By 1830 the English people had begun "to look to India for the means of rendering Great Britain independent of foreign countries for a considerable portion of raw material upon which her most valuable manufactures depend. . . ." [3] By this time the Manchester school of free traders had come into prominence who in the interests of English industrial workmen were anxious to have cheap food for them imported in exchange for the products of their manufactures, which had by then been well established. Cobden and Bright could not under the circumstances be expected to give a thought to the devastation of Indian industries, but what escaped their notice was observed by a German economist (quoted by Dutt) [4] as far back as 1866. He wrote:

"Had they sanctioned the free importation into England of Indian cotton and silk goods, the English cotton and silk manufacturers must, of necessity, soon come to a stand. India had not only the advantage of

[2] "Minutes of Evidence, &c., on the Affairs of the East India Company" (1813), pp. 124, 127, 131.

[3] Sir John Malcolm, Governor of Bombay in 1830.

[4] Dutt: "India Under Early British Rule," p. 300.

cheaper labour and raw material, but also the experience, the skill and the practice of centuries. The effect of these advantages could not fail to tell under a system of free competition.

"But England was unwilling to found settlements in Asia in order to become subservient to India in manufacturing industry. She strove for commercial supremacy, and felt that of two countries maintaining free trade between one another, that one would be supreme which sold manufactured goods, while that one would be subservient which could only sell agricultural produce. In the North American colonies, England had already acted on those principles in disallowing the manufacture in those colonies of even a single horse-shoe nail, and still more, that no horse-shoe nails made there should be imported into England. How could it be expected of her that she would give up her own market for manufactures, the basis of her future greatness, to a people so numerous, so thrifty, so experienced, and so perfect in the old systems of manufacture as the Hindus?

"Accordingly, England prohibited the import of the goods dealt in by her own factories, the Indian cotton and silk fabrics. The prohibition was complete and peremptory. Not so much as a thread of them would England permit to be used. She would have none of these beautiful and cheap fabrics, but preferred to consume her own inferior and more costly stuffs. She was, however, quite willing to supply the Continental nations with the far finer fabrics of India at lower prices, and willingly yielded to them all the benefit of that cheapness; she herself would have none of it."[5]

[5] The reader might also read the statement of Henry St. John Tucker, a British administrator on the panel in "Memorials of the Indian Government," being a selection from the papers of Henry St. John Tucker (London, 1883), p. 494, and also that of the historian H. H. Wilson in "Mill's History of British India," Wilson's Book I, Chapter VIII, note.

In 1840 the East India Company, who had now ceased to be directly interested in Indian trade, in their new character of administrator pure and simple, responsible for the good of the people of India, presented a petition to Parliament for the removal of invidious duties which discouraged and repressed Indian industries. A Select Committee of the House of Commons was appointed. One of the witnesses examined was a certain Mr. J. C. Melvill. We take the following questions and answers from his evidence:

"Have native manufactures been superseded by British?" Melvill was asked.

"Yes, in great measure," was his reply.

"Since what period?"

"I think principally since 1814."

"The displacement of Indian manufactures by British is such that India is now dependent mainly for its supply of those articles on British manufacturers?"

"I think so."

"Has the displacement of the labour of native manufacturers at all been compensated by any increase in the produce of articles of the first necessity, raw produce?"

"The export of raw produce from India has increased since she ceased largely to export manufactures; but I am not prepared to say in what proportion." [6]

Mr. Andrew Sym said that "the people of India deprived of their occupations," by the displacement of Indian labour by the introduction of English manufactures — clothing, tools, implements, glassware, and brass articles, turned "to agriculture chiefly."

[6] Questions 577, 578, 583, 584.

Testimony of G. G. de H. Larpent, and other Britishers. Mr. Larpent supplied the Committee with the following figures relating to the import of Indian cotton goods into England, and the export of English cotton goods into India.

Cotton Piece Goods Imported into Great Britain from the East Indies.

1814	1,266,608	pieces
1821	534,495	"
1828	422,504	"
1835	306,086	"

British Cotton Manufactures Exported to India.

1814	818,208	yards
1821	19,138,726	"
1828	42,822,077	"
1835	51,777,277	"

In spite of this decline in the Indian manufacture, and the increase of British manufacture, British cotton goods were still imported into India on payment of an *ad valorem* duty of 3½ per cent, while Indian cotton goods imported into England were subjected to an *ad valorem* duty of 10 per cent. Quoting from Mr. Shore, witness read: "This supersession of the native for British manufactures is often quoted as a splendid instance of the triumph of British skill. It is a much stronger instance of English tyranny, and how India has been impoverished by the most vexatious system of customs and duties imposed for the avowed object of favouring the mother country." Mr. Larpent did not agree with Mr. Shore in these observations to the full extent; but they showed the feeling of a distinguished servant of the Company, a feeling which was likely to prevail among the people of India.

Silk Goods. British silk goods were admitted into Calcutta on payment of a duty of 3½ per cent. Indian silk goods were subjected to an import duty of 20 per cent. in England. Corahs or Indian silk piece goods in the grey (unprinted), were imported into England mainly for being printed in England and then exported to other European countries. The following figures were given for Corahs imported into England:

	For Home Consumption Pieces	*For Re-export Pieces*
1838	16,000	310,000
1839	38,000	352,000

Bandannas or Indian printed pocket-handkerchiefs were imported into England in considerable quantities. Mr. Larpent pleaded strongly for the equalisation of duties between Great Britain and India with regard to silk goods. Mr. Brocklehurst, one of the members of the Select Committee, represented British silk manufactures, and necessarily desired the continuance of unequal duties to the advantage of England.

Mr. Brocklehurst.—You give your opinion without reference to the effect it would have on the British producer?

Mr. Larpent.—I have no doubt there would be, to a certain extent, a rivalry in competition with the silk manufactures of this country; but I submit on principle that India ought to be admitted as one of our own possessions. The argument has been used that while our manufactures are allowed to go into India at a very reduced duty, we ought to have admitted theirs on as low a duty.

Mr. Brocklehurst.—Is there any colony of this country whose manufactures are admitted on so low a scale as those of India?

Mr. Larpent.—There is no colony of this country whose manufacturers are of a magnitude calling for it. We have destroyed the manufactures of India. (And then the witness quoted the views of the Court of Directors, stated in Lord William Bentinck's minute of

May 30, 1829: "The sympathy of the Court is deeply excited by the report of the Board of Trade, exhibiting the gloomy picture of the effects of a commercial revolution productive of so much present suffering to numerous classes in India, and hardly to be paralleled in the history of commerce.")

But Mr. Brocklehurst was not convinced. He returned again and again to the subject.

Mr. Brocklehurst.—Are you aware that they have already so far displaced silk handkerchiefs made in this country, that attempts are now made to introduce a spurious article from waste silk as a substitute?

Mr. Larpent.—I have heard that an article is introduced made of waste silk; and that as I stated before, the ingenuity and science of the parties who are making those goods, will probably introduce into the home market a quantity of goods at a low price, which will be in very general use.

Mr. Brocklehurst.—Driving the British manufacturer to make inferior articles to maintain his ground in competition?

Mr. Larpent.—The articles alluded to are those made here; the British manufacturers have made those inferior articles.

Mr. Brocklehurst.—It would be more desirable perhaps that India should produce the raw material, and this country show its skill in perfecting that raw material?

Mr. Larpent.—The course of things in India is decidedly leading to that; and it is in the main articles such as we have already alluded to, that we do think every assistance should be given to the agricultural produce of India; but I submit that as this is the last of the expiring manufactures of India, the only one where there is a chance of introducing the native manufactures, at least let it have a fair chance, and not be oppressed with the duty of 20 per cent., in favour of the British manufactures.

Testimony of Montgomery Martin.

"I have examined at considerable length, and for a series of years, the trade of India. I have taken the utmost pains to arrive at correct conclusions by examining various documents which the Honourable Court of Directors of the East India House, with their usual liberality, permitted me access to. And I have been impressed with the conviction that India has suffered most unjustly in her trade, not merely with England but with all other countries, by reason of the outcry for free trade on the part of England without permitting to India a free trade herself." And he added that, "on all articles except those where we are supplanting the native manufacturers, and consequently impoverishing the country, there is a decreasing trade."

Cotton Goods. In 1815 the cotton goods exported from India were of the value of £1,300,000. In 1832 they were less than £100,000. In 1815 the cotton goods imported into India from England were of the value of £26,300. In 1832 they were upwards of £400,000. "We have during the period of a quarter of a century compelled the Indian territories to receive our manufactures; our woollens, duty free, our cottons at 2½ per cent., and other articles in proportion; while we have continued during that period to levy almost prohibitory duties, or duties varying from 10 to 20, 30, 50, 100, 500, and 1000 per cent. upon articles, the produce from our territories. Therefore the cry that has taken place for free trade with India, has been a free trade from this country, not a free trade between India and this country. . . . The decay and destruction of Surat, of Dacca, of Murshedabad, and other places where native manufactures have been carried on, is too painful a fact to dwell upon. I do not consider that it has been in the fair course of trade; I think it has been the power of the stronger exercised over the weaker."

Evidence such as this brought about a keen controversy between the witness and Mr. Brocklehurst, the representative of the British manufacturer.

Mr. Brocklehurst.—The fact being that weavers, either in the one country or the other, must be sacrificed, and that sacrifice having already taken place in India, you wish to revive the population of India at the expense of this country?

Mr. Martin.—I do not wish to revive it, but I wish to prevent continued injury to India. But it does not necessarily follow that the weavers of England would be destroyed by admitting the natives of India to compete with them in this country, because the natives of India have no power looms, and no means of employing skill and capital to the extent that the manufacturers of Glasgow and Manchester have.

Mr. Brocklehurst.—The questions that have been asked refer entirely to fine fabrics which cannot be woven by power. The question is, whether we are to give up fine weaving in this country, or retain it?

Mr. Martin.—If it is only to be retained at the expense of injustice to India, my answer is, that England ought to act with justice, no matter what the result may be. That she has no right to destroy the people of a country which she has conquered, for the benefit of herself, for the mere sake of upholding any isolated portion of the community at home.

Mr. Brocklehurst.—When the transfer of India to the Government of this country took place in 1833, the destruction of weaving in India had already taken place, and therefore it is not a question of destruction, for that is past; and we have it in evidence that India is an agricultural rather than a manufacturing country, and that the parties formerly employed in manufactures are now absorbed in agriculture. Does it occur to you that there is an opening in this country, if manufacturers are displaced, for the people to turn to agriculture?

Mr. Martin.—I do not agree that India is an agricultural country; India is as much a manufacturing country as an agricultural; and he who would seek to reduce her to the position of an agricultural country seeks to lower her in the scale of civilisation. I do not suppose that India is to become the agricultural farm of England; she is a manufacturing country, her manufactures of various descriptions have existed for ages, and have never been able to be competed with by any nation wherever fair play has been given to them. I speak not now of her Dacca muslins and her Cashmere shawls, but of various articles which she has manufactured in a manner superior to any part of the world. To reduce her now to an agricultural country would be an injustice to India.

Another committee with John Bright as chairman was appointed to inquire into the growth of cotton in India. The evidence given before this committee laid stress on the necessity of land assessments being reduced to put heart into the cultivator and also on the improvement of means of transportation. Some members also spoke of the economic drain. On the condition of the cultivators of Madras and Bombay the committee remarked that they were "almost wholly without capital or any of those means which capital alone can furnish by which industry may be improved and extended. They are in reality a class of cultivators in the most abject condition." Their other recommendations are not relevant to this part of our subject. Duties on the import of cotton (raw) into England from Bengal had been abolished in 1836, those on Bombay cotton in 1838 and those on Madras cotton in 1844.

II

THE HISTORY OF IMPORT DUTIES AND THE PRESENT STATE OF THE INDUSTRY

Legislative Acts.— Various acts were passed from time to time between 1833 and 1853 by the Indian Legislature to regulate trade and navigation and to fix the tariff. We have already stated in the previous section how the export of raw cotton was freed of any duty between 1836 and 1844. In 1853 the import duties ranged from 3½ per cent. to 5 per cent. *ad valorem* except in the case of foreign (i.e., non-British) cotton and silk goods, foreign cotton thread and yarn and foreign marine stores and foreign metals. These foreign goods had to pay double duty. These duties were imposed for revenue purposes and not for protection. In the case of cotton and silk manufactures there was no question of protection as there was no industry in India to be protected and later when the industry did come into existence, the duties were more than once remitted. The higher duties on foreign goods, though, were a sort of protection to British goods.

In 1858 when Queen Victoria assumed the direct sovereignty of the Indian Empire, the import duties, as before, stood at 3½ per cent. *ad valorem* upon cotton twist and yarns and at 5 per cent. on other articles of British produce and manufacture, including cotton piece goods. The duties on foreign articles were still double. In 1859, on account of the heavy financial pressure after the Mutiny, all differential tariffs were abolished; duties on all articles of luxury were raised to 20 per cent. *ad valorem;* duties on other articles, including cotton piece goods, were raised to 10 per cent.; and those on cotton twist and yarn to 5 per cent.

In 1860, only a year later, there was another change in favour of uniform tariff of 10 per cent. *ad valorem,* with special rates upon beer, wines, spirits and tobacco.[7] In 1861, the duty on cotton twist and yarn was reduced to 5 per cent. In 1862 it was further reduced to 3½ per cent. and the duty on cotton and other manufactures was reduced to 5 per cent. In 1863 the duty on imported iron was reduced to 1 per cent. In 1867 a great number of articles were added to the free list. In 1870 a new Tariff Act was passed which placed the import duties generally at 7½ per cent. on manufactured goods and raw materials, at 5 per cent. on piece goods, at 3½ per cent. on twist, at 1 per cent. on iron and at 10 per cent. on tobacco.

The law was again changed in 1871 but the alterations were not material.

A select committee of the House of Commons which sat from 1871 to 1874 took evidence on the operation of the duties, in which objection was made to the import duty on cotton piece goods and to the export duty on grains. At that time there were only two or three cotton spinning and weaving mills in Calcutta.

Sir Bartle Frere expressed himself in favour of keeping down the import duty on cotton piece goods *in order to foster the sale of British goods.* He confessed that " the interests of India and England on that point seemed to be at variance. No doubt some con-

[7] Export duties on Indian raw produce were abolished.

siderable increase of revenue might be realised by increasing the import duties; say upon piece goods and yarn, but the direct result of that would be to diminish consumption and to stimulate production on the spot," which, of course, he and his countrymen did not desire.

Mr. Walter Cassels, a Bombay merchant who had been a member of the Bombay Legislative Council, agreed that even the small import duty of 5 per cent. on cotton piece goods operated as a protective duty, though he added he did not desire its abolition on that ground. He stated that at that time there were twelve cotton mills in Bombay employing 319,394 spindles, 4199 looms and 8170 hands.

A glimpse into the helplessness of the Government of India in the matter of its fiscal policy can be had by a study of questions that were put to Lord Lawrence by Henry Fawcett and the answers given by the former. Lord Lawrence had tried to raise the export duties on jute and other Indian products in 1865, to get a little additional revenue and save the country from a deficit. But British interests had been too strong for him and the Secretary of State for India had disallowed his proposals. Eight years after, when he was questioned by Mr. Fawcett, he guardedly expressed his painful impressions of the influence of British trade over the financial policy of India. The British trade interests have virtually dominated the fiscal policy of the India Government ever since British occupation of India, and they do so to this day.

In 1874, the Lancashire manufacturers, by a memorial addressed to the Secretary of State for India, started their attack on the 5 per cent. and 3½ per cent. duties on cotton piece goods and cotton twist respectively, representing them as protective duties. The complaint was that on account of the duties a protected trade in cotton manufacture was springing up in British India to the disadvantage of both India and Great Britain. The reference to India is very amusing. The interests of India and of the poor people of India have always been present before the mind of the English merchant and his protector,—the Secretary of State for India. We shall find it referred to, in feeling terms almost every time a mandate has had to be issued to the Government of India for the furtherance of the interests of British trade, so often that we are afraid the reader might be disgusted by its constant reiteration and repetition in documents so palpably harmful to Indian interests.

The reply of the Secretary of State to this memorial being rather evasive on the main points raised by the memorialists, they found it necessary to state in so many words that what they objected to was the opening of new mills in India. They said:

"The statements as to the harmful operation of these duties on commerce, and on the best interests of her majesty's subjects, both in India (!!) and England are abundantly confirmed by the latest advices from Bombay, which show that, under protection extended by the levying of duties on imports, to the spinning and weaving of cotton yarns and goods in India, *a large number of new mills are now being projected.*[8]

[8] Quoted by Dutt from Government of India Resolution No.

On this, the Government of India appointed a committee to consider the question. All the members, we are told by Dutt, were English merchants and officials. Yet the committee was unanimous in rejecting the Manchester demand for the repeal of import duties on cotton yarns and goods.

Lord Northbrook, then Viceroy of India, a free-trader, refused to sacrifice a source of revenue which in his opinion did not operate as protection. A new Tariff Act was passed which retained the import duties on cotton yarn and goods; largely reduced valuation; and imposed a 5 per cent. duty on the import of long staple cotton "to prevent Indian Mills competing at an advantage in the production of the finer goods."[9] They also abolished all export duties except on indigo, rice and lac, reduced the general rate of import duties to 5 per cent. and raised the duties on spirits and wines. This resulted in a total loss of £308,000 to the Indian revenues. Meanwhile by the turn of the political wheel in England, the Conservative party had come into power and Lord Salisbury had been appointed Secretary of State for India, in the administration of Disraeli. In July, 1875, he wrote to the Viceroy:

"If it were true that this duty is the means of excluding English competition, and thereby raising the price of a necessary of life to the vast mass of Indian consumers, it is unnecessary for me to remark that it would be open to economical objections of the gravest kind. I do not attribute to it any such effect; but I cannot be insensible to the political evils which arise from the prevalent belief upon the matter.

2636 of August 12, 1875, forming an enclosure to Despatch No. 15 of 1875. The italics are ours.

[9] Dutt, "India in the Victorian Age," p. 404.

"These considerations will, I doubt not, commend to your Excellency's mind the policy of removing, at as early a period as the state of your finances permits, this subject of dangerous contention."

Lord Northbrook replied by cable that the Bill had been passed, giving the substance of its provisions. Lord Salisbury wired back his dissatisfaction and objections.

The dispute between Lord Salisbury and Lord Northbrook raised a question of principle, viz., the competency of the Governor General in Council to pass any important measure without obtaining the previous sanction of the Secretary of State for India. Finding himself unable to accept this principle, Lord Northbrook resigned his office. His resignation was accepted, and Lord Lytton appointed in his place. After this affair, Lord Salisbury laid down the principle in black and white, in a despatch to the Viceroy — a view from which two of his counsellors dissented. Ever since, the Government of India has been in theory as well as fact "a government by mandate."

With Lord Lytton succeeding Lord Northbrook to the Viceroyalty of India, the path of Lord Salisbury became smoother. He at once ordered the repeal of the import duty on cotton goods in spite of the dissent of three members of his council.

Lord Lytton, though quite willing to do the bidding of the Secretary of State, found that in the meantime the terrible famine of Madras had affected the financial situation of India so seriously that even he could not sacrifice this item of revenue immediately. So, with the concurrence of the Secretary of State, the import duties had to be continued for two years longer.

But the manufacturers of Lancashire were losing patience. The question was raised in the House of Commons and that august body resolved:

"*That, in the opinion of this House, the duties now levied upon cotton manufactures imported into India, being protective in their nature, are contrary to sound commercial policy, and ought to be repealed without delay, so soon as the financial condition of India will permit.*"

Lord Salisbury forwarded the Resolution to the Government of India and referred to the fact "that five more mills were about to begin work; and that it was estimated that by the end of March, 1877, there would be 1,231,284 spindles employed in India." (Letter to the Governor General in Council of August 30, 1877.)

So in the coming year, the Government of India began by exempting from duty certain kinds of imported goods with a calculated loss of £22,227 to the Indian revenue. Lancashire was not satisfied and pressure was brought to bear upon the Government of India to repeal the duties on cotton imports altogether. The Council of the Governor General, however, was not unanimous on the point and the minutes of the dissenting members speak for themselves.

Mr. Whitley Stokes' first objection was in the interests of Indian finance:

"We have spent our Famine Insurance Fund, or what was intended to be such. We are carrying on a costly war with Afghanistan. We may any day have to begin one with the King of Burma. We have now to borrow five crores (five millions sterling) in India, and we are begging for two millions sterling from England.

"*Secondly,* because the proposed surrender would eventually lead to the surrender of the import duty on all cotton goods. 'The powerful Lancashire manufacturers will be encouraged by their second victory to new attacks on our revenue. . . . If ever we have any true surplus, we should, in my opinion, lessen some of our direct taxes rather than abolish any of our moderate import duties.'

. . . .

"*Fifthly,* because, by the proposed repeal, 'the Manchester manufacturers *would practically compel the people of India to buy cotton cloths adulterated, if possible, more shamefully than such goods are at present.* The cost of the clothing of the people would thus be increased rather than lessened.'

"*Sixthly,* because Indian newspapers will proclaim in every bazaar that the repeal was made 'solely in the interest of Manchester, and for the benefit of the Conservative party, who are, it is alleged, anxious to obtain the Lancashire vote at the coming elections.' Of course the people of India will be wrong; *they always must be wrong when they impute selfish motives to the ruling race.*"[10]

Among other objections he also pointed out that the repeal was demanded by the manufacturers of Lancashire and not by the people of India.

Sir Alexander Arbuthnot pointed out that

"The people of India attribute the action which has been taken by her Majesty's Government in this matter to the influences which have been brought to bear upon it by persons interested in the English cotton trade; in

[10] The italics are ours.

other words by the manufacturers of Lancashire. It is notorious that this impression has prevailed throughout India from the time, just four years ago, when the Marquis of Salisbury informed a large body of Manchester manufacturers that the Government of India would be instructed to provide for the gradual abolition of the import duties on cotton goods.

"Nor is this feeling limited to the Native community. From communications which have been received from the Chambers of Commerce at Madras and Calcutta, it is evident that the feeling is shared by the leading representatives of the European mercantile community in those cities.

"It is equally shared by the great body of the official hierarchy throughout India. I am convinced I do not overstate the case when I affirm my belief that there are not at the present time a dozen officials in India who do not regard the policy which has been adopted in this matter as a policy which has been adopted, *not in the interests of India, not even in the interests of England, but in the interests or the supposed interests of a political party, the leaders of which deem it necessary at any cost to retain the political support of the cotton manufacturers of Lancashire.*" [The italics are ours.]

Similar protests were made by Mr. Rivers Thomson (afterwards Lieutenant Governor of Bengal) and Sir Andrew Clarke. Against all these protests, and in defiance of the opinion of the majority of his Council, Lord Lytton, with the concurrence of Sir John Strachey and Sir Edwin Johnson, exempted from import duty "all imported cotton goods containing no yarn finer than 30's." The Secretary of State of course approved of the act of Lord Lytton, though seven members of his own Council, including Sir Frederic Halliday, Sir Robert Montgomery, Sir William Muir, and Sir Erskine Perry, dissented.

This shows conclusively how even the Anglo-Indian Administrator is helpless to protect Indian interests, when the latter clash with the financial interests of Great Britain.

The question of cotton duties has been one of the most exciting questions that have exercised the public mind in India for the last fifty years. It is one of those few questions on which the Indians and the resident Anglo-Indians hold exactly the same views. It affects an industry, in the prosperity of which the Indian and the resident Anglo-Indian mill owners are equally interested. To proceed with the story, the tariffs were again tampered with during the viceroyalty of Lord Ripon, with the result that in March, 1882, the remaining import duties were also abolished, excepting those on salt and liquors.

For the next twelve years the matter remained at rest, until the financial embarrassments of the Government of India forced the latter to reopen the question in 1894, when the Indian Government had to face a deficit of more than two million pounds sterling.

A committee, called Lord Herschell's Committee, was appointed, which recommended the re-imposition of import duties except on cotton goods. When a tariff bill was brought before the Council, on the lines of the recommendations of the Committee, it met with strong opposition from the non-official members of the Council on the ground that it exempted a class of goods which should pre-eminently bear an import duty and a duty that would yield the best results, as "the volume of trade in cotton goods and yarns then represented nearly one-half of the total imports from abroad." It was argued that "the exemption of these important commodities when practically every single commodity was being subjected to an import duty could not be justified on its merits as a sound fiscal measure much less when it was an admitted fact that the Budget would still show a deficit."[11] The Government of India, however, could not accept these views, as they had a mandate from the Secretary of State for India which they dared not ignore. This Act was thus passed in the teeth of the strong and united opposition of the Indians and the Anglo-Indians, in March, 1894, but in December, 1894, the subject was re-opened under instructions from the Secretary of State who in the meantime found out another way of propitiating Lancashire without sacrificing revenue — viz., by imposing a counteracting excise duty upon yarns produced in Indian mills, which could possibly compete with Lancashire yarn. Accordingly two bills were introduced in the Legislative Councils, the first of which subjected cotton yarn and fabrics to the general import duty of 5 per cent *ad valorem* and the second imposed an excise duty on all cotton yarns of 20's and above produced by Indian mills. In introducing this latter bill, the then Finance Minister, Sir James Westland, stated in the Council that the policy underlying its provisions had been imposed on the Governments of India by the Secretary of State in pursuance of the resolutions of the House of Commons passed in 1877 and 1879. The law, however, satisfied nobody. The Indian mill owners were of course dissatisfied with the whole

[11] The Indian Year Book issued by the *Times of India* Press for 1915, p. 234.

policy but they also added another objection and pointed out how impossible it was to spin precisely to a particular count. Lancashire on the other hand contended that the bill left loopholes for evasion. Consequently the matter was reconsidered in 1895 and another Act (II of 1896) was passed by which yarn was altogether exempted from duty and a uniform duty of 3½ per cent. was imposed on all woven goods whether imported or manufactured in India. The measure was of course opposed by both Indian and Anglo-Indian non-official members. Mr. Stevens, afterwards Sir Charles Stevens, representing the Bengal Chamber of Commerce, said:

"I fear it must be owned that the measure has not received the support of the public as a whole. For this there are two main reasons. First, the suspicion existing in some quarters that it has been called for by the exigencies of party politics in England rather than by the wants of India; secondly, that the trade will be disturbed to the disadvantage of important industries and of poor consumers in this country."

What has happened since then may be stated in the words of the writer of the article on this subject in the Indian Year Book of 1915:

"*New Factors in the Situation.* Since the passing of this measure into law the policy of the Government of India in this respect has frequently been the subject of attack in the press and in the Legislative Councils while it has also formed the subject of continued representations by the industrial interests affected and political organisations. In more recent years the agitation in favour of the abolition of the Excise duties has been revived by the growth in England of a strong body of public opinion in opposition to the policy of Free Trade. Advantage has been taken of this new phase in English economic thought to press on behalf of India the acceptance of a policy of Protection, and the removal of the Excise duties is now claimed by the opponents to this measure as a necessary corollary of the application to the British Empire of the principles associated with the name of Mr. Chamberlain. A new factor in the situation which has strengthened the position of those who are in opposition to the Excise duties is to be found in the severe competition which Indian mills have to face in China as well as in India from the Japanese industry. The Japanese market was lost to India in the early years of this century. More recently, however, Japan has entered as a competitor with India into the China market, while within the last few years it has pushed its advantage as against the Indian millowner in the Indian market itself. Again it is claimed that the recent enhancement of the silver duty has materially affected the position of the Indian spinner who relied on the China market. On two occasions within the last five years the question of Excise duties has come prominently to the front as a result of debates in the Viceroy's Council. The official attitude is firmly based on the position that the Excise duties stand and fall with the import duties. Against such an attitude all arguments based either on the advantages of a Protectionist as opposed to a Free Trade policy or on the handicap to which the present system exposes the Indian millowner can, of course, make no headway. The Government of India are confronted with a heavy recurring loss in their revenues as a result of the abolition of the opium traffic. The import duties on cotton piece-goods represent nearly fifteen per cent. of the total revenue collected as Customs duty while the Excise duty itself realised no less than 47 lakhs in 1912–13. The strength of the arguments which support the Government position is so patent that the movement in favour of the total abolition of the Excise duty is gradually giving way to a feeling that a solution may be found in maintaining the Excise duty at its present rate while enhancing the import duties to the level of the general rate of Customs duty. This policy which is frankly of a protective character, can to some slight extent be supported by the change in the position of Lancashire in respect of the imports of cotton piece-goods. In 1894 when the duties were first imposed the share of Lancashire was no less than 98 per cent. of the total import trade in piece-goods. Foreign competition, notably from Japan has reduced its share to 91 per cent. and it may be expected that the success of this attack on the position of Lancashire will in the near future loom largely in the arguments of those who favour a modified form of protection within the Empire."

In spite of these drawbacks the cotton industry received a great and extraordinary stimulus by the Boycott and Swadeshi movements started by the Indian Nationalists in 1905 as a protest against the administration of Lord Curzon; but as the momentum created by the movement has declined by the force of time and change in circumstances the rate of progress in the development of the industry has also gone down.

In 1904 there were 191 mills in the whole of British India, working 5,118,121 spindles and 45,337 looms. By 1909 the number had risen to 259 mills, with 6,053,-231 spindles and 76,898 looms. In 1910 the number rose to 263 mills, covering 6,195,671 spindles and 82,-725 looms. In 1911 the number of mills remained stationary though there was a slight increase in spindles and looms. In 1913 the number of mills rose to 272 with a total of 6,596,862 spindles and 94,136 looms. In 1914 there has been no increase in the number of mills, though there has been a slight increase in the number of spindles and looms. The number of the latter stood on August 31, 1915 at 6,898,744 and 108,-009 respectively. The following figures about the trade in cotton goods might be useful for purpose of reference: In 1915–16 the Indian mills' outturn in yarn was a little over 722 million lbs. and in woven goods a little over 352 million lbs., of which 160 million lbs. of yarn and tweed and 113 million yards of piece goods were exported as against 198 and 89, in 1913–14 and 136 and 67 in 1914–15. In 1913–14 the total value of the exports of cotton manufactures from India, is given at a little over 8 million lbs. sterling. The imports of cotton manufactures in that year were valued at over 66 million pounds sterling. In March, 1916, at the time of the Budget discussion, Sir William Meyer informed the members of the Indian Legislative Council that in deference to the unanimous opinion of the non-official members, Lord Hardinge's Government had proposed to the Secretary of State the abolition of the excise duty and an increase in the duty on imported cotton goods, but that the Secretary of State had decided that the consideration of the matter might be postponed, during the war.[12] So while the Government of India increased the price of salt (manufactured in India and a Government monopoly) they had to submit to the decision of the Secretary of State in the matter of the duties on cotton goods. The matter has been thus summed up by the writer of the article on "Industrial and Eco-

[12] The duty has now been raised to 7½ per cent. The excise duty is being maintained (see P. S. Preface).

nomic Conditions" in the volume of the Oxford Survey of the British Empire dealing with Asia (pages 140, 141):

"It is but natural that Indian politicians should express dissatisfaction with the meagre results at present achieved in industrial enterprise. They complain that, in the interest of Lancashire, their cotton fabrics were first excluded from the English market and now suffer from unrestricted competition at home. They are not content with the exportation of raw materials as an indication of prosperity, but rather regret that these are not profitably used up in the country. They quote the dictum of Mill that 'nascent industries' may be legitimately protected. They point to self-governing colonies which are allowed to impose a tariff even against the mother country. They point also to the analogous case of Japan, whose industrial development, fostered by the State, already threatens rivalry in their own markets. These complaints, when uttered by Indian representatives in the reformed legislative Councils cannot be ignored, especially when it is known that Anglo-Indian opinion, both official and commercial, largely sympathises. As long as no fresh taxation is required, a final solution of the problem may possibly be postponed; but when the time comes it will test, as no other question has done, the altruism of English statesmanship."

Before bringing this chapter to a close, we must, in fairness to the other side, mention some "alleged recent discoveries" of a retired Indian Civil Servant, Mr. C. W. McMin, who in 1908 read a paper before the East India Association, extracts from which have since been incorporated into a pamphlet entitled: "Truths About India." The obvious purpose of this document, which may be had for the asking, is to show the world that the charge brought against England of the "destruction of indigenous Indian industries" is unfounded.

A few extracts, copied verbatim, are appended below, with comments by the author opposite.

EXTRACTS

A

"In a great work on 'Economic History' by R. C. Dutt, it is stated the British imposed 'unjust and enormous' duty on Indian cottons of 20 per cent; on reference to the quoted authority I find it was 4d. per cwt. As cotton was 5d. per lb., the rate was less than 1 per cent. This was not printer's deviltry, for taffetas, sugars, mats are similarly misstated. The truth was that foreign cotton was paying 5s 10d. per cwt. about 20 per cent, while Indian cotton had a preferential tariff, less than 1 per cent."

ANSWERS

A

Mr. Dutt's alleged mistake has nothing to do with *manufactured* cotton and silk goods. How England treated Indian raw cotton has not been treated in this book—it was to her interest to encourage the cultivation of *raw cotton* in India, and supply it as cheaply as possible to the Lancashire mills. So the point made in the extract is of no significance whatever.

EXTRACTS

B

"In 1789 England reduced the British tariff tax on tea to 12½ per cent, on piece goods to 18 per cent; and to make up the deficiency so created, in the Inland Revenue, imposed a window tax on the English people. This proved a hardship and evil to the poor and an annoyance to the rich. William Pitt did this; possibly he remembered that Indian trade had made his grandfather rich, and founded the fortune of Chatham. Up to 1860, in tariffs, Britain favoured India more

ANSWERS

B

The statement of duties on piece-goods in 1789 does not show Baines' scale of duties levied on "East Indian White muslins and Nankeen, to be in any way wrong. Baines' table covers 1787–1814, and shows that the duty varied from 18 per cent. to 44 per cent. *ad val.* and from £16 15s. 3d. in 1787 to £85 2s. 1d. per piece in 1813. East India dyed goods were absolutely prohibited. On the other hand, bounties were given for the exportation of English cottons. The table of duties or less. In 1838 there were 43 articles, every important article of necessity or luxury, for which there were preferential light duties for British possessions. For raw silk from Bengal there was a special light duty — it paid 4s. 6d. while the rest of the world paid 5s. 10d. per lb. British tariffs were not only just to India, but even benevolent from 1825 onward. Opium, indigo, tea, jute, cotton, were bringing wealth to the Empire surpassing the Moguls.

I admit that in Bengal especially for the first 20 years after the Company assumed the Dewani, there were most serious drawbacks to the peace and prosperity introduced by British rule. From 1785 amendment commenced due to a great improvement in Customs regulations, and lower tariffs on tea and piece-goods, dating 1780–4.

filed before the Select Committee of the House of Commons in 1813 shows the duty on "Calicoes" was £81 2s. 11d. for every "100 of value" (also cottons) while the duty on raw cotton was 16s. 11d. per 100 lbs. The duty on tea in 1761, customs and excise is given as £96 0s. 0d., etc. The statement that opium, indigo, tea, jute and ale brought wealth to the Empire is true if by "Empire" is meant England and English manufacturers, who monopolise those industries and the profits therefrom.

C

The East India Company, far from being hostile to Indian manufactures, spent about £160,000,000 in training artisans, establishing factories, buying and transporting to England the piece-goods, silk, salt-petre, indigo, sugar, which were the principal staples. They sold piece goods alone for 659 million pounds in forty years (1771–1810).

C

The last statement is too vague to be tested. The East India Company in its character as trader, was interested in certain industries of which it had the monopoly. We are not told how the £160,000,000 was spent; how much in "training artisans" or in what kind of work, how much in "establishing factories" or what sorts; nor what proportion went into the pockets of the Company's servants.

Nor was there anything remarkable in the "fact" that in forty years, 1770–1810, the East India Company should have sold goods to the value of 659 millions of pounds,—where and to whom is not stated. An industry like that of the piece goods industry of India could not have been destroyed in a day.

In conclusion it is well to recall the testimony of such competent witnesses as Henry St. John Tucker, Larpent, Montgomery Martin, and others.

That the number of those who depend on textile industries for their living is still declining is made clear by the results of the census of 1911. See Mr. Gait's report, chapter on occupations, wherein he says that "As compared with 1901, there has been a decrease of 6.1 per cent. in the number of persons supported by textile industries. This is due mainly to the almost complete extinction of cotton spinning by hand. Weaving by hand has also suffered severely."

Cotton duties—1917 developments. Since the above was written, the duty on cotton goods imported into India has been raised to 7½ per cent. *ad valorem* while the countervailing excise duty has been maintained at the old figure. The action of the Government of India, taken with the sanction and approval of the Secretary of State for India, as a part of the plan whereby the Government of India was to contribute £100,000,000 to the British war fund as a "free gift," from India has furnished occasion for a very interesting discussion on the point, between Lancashire and the Free Traders on one hand and the Tory Secretary of State for India and *The Times* on the other. In the course of the controversy certain admissions have been made in high quarters which corroborate and support the statements made in this chapter.

In the course of a letter addressed to the *Westminster Gazette,* Lord Curzon says:

"I have always regarded the attitude of Lancashire toward India in respect to the Import duties on cotton and still more of the countervailing excise *as an injustice and a wrong.* . . . When in India, as Viceroy, I more than once expressed myself in the same sense. On my return to England I made a speech in the House of Lords on May 21, 1908, in the course of which I said that *the fiscal policy of India during the last thirty or forty years has been shaped far more in Manchester than in Calcutta.* In the speech at Manchester in 1910, I alluded to the same facts, namely, to *the subordination of Indian fiscal policy to the Secretary of State and a House of Commons powerfully affected by Lancashire influence.*" [The italics are ours.]

Mr. Charles Roberts, M. P., said in the House of Commons: "Long ago we forgave ourselves for the selfish commercial policy of the eighteenth century which crushed out the beautiful fabrics of India by fiscal prohibition."

Mr. G. W. Forrest, writing to *The Times,* London, (March 14, 1917), said: "The tale of England's dealing with Indian industry was one of littleness and injustice. . . . By positive prohibition and by heavy duties, the Indian textile trade in England was destroyed and our own trade was fostered."

Mr. Harold Smith, M. P., also condemns "the uneconomic and indefensible protection which" the British cotton trade "has received at the expense and the exploitation of India. . . . It is impossible that India can forever remain satisfied with this throttling hold on her own natural development." (*Times*, London, March 14, 1917.)

The Times has defended India's right to levy duties on cotton goods in the course of several leading articles on the subject.

We beg to make a present of these opinions to the East Indian Association of London, with reference to their book called "Plain Truths About India." This addition to the cotton duties has, however, been characterised as a war measure and we are not quite sure whether it will be maintained after the war is over.

CHAPTER VI

SHIPBUILDING AND SHIPPING

Conditions in Former Times. Considering that India has a seaboard of more than 4000 miles and that except in the north, the north-western, and the north-eastern corners of the peninsula, the only outlets to the outside world are by sea, there is no wonder that for thousands of years before the advent of the British, India should have developed shipping and maritime trade to a marvellous extent. There is ample justification for the claim made for her by one of the Indian writers on the subject, that "the early growth of her shipping and shipbuilding, coupled with the genius and energy of her merchants, the skill and daring of her seamen, the enterprise of her colonists, . . . secured to India the command of the sea for ages and helped her to attain and long maintain her proud position as the mistress of the Eastern Seas."

The claim has been made good in an excellent brochure written by Prof. Radhakumud Mookerji of Calcutta, and published by Messrs. Longmans, Green and Co. of London. The work is called, "A History of Indian Shipping and Maritime Activity from the Earliest Times." The evidence collected in this volume is both indigenous and foreign and goes back to about 3000 years B.C. Dr. Sayce, the famous Assyriologist, has been quoted in support of the statement that *commerce by sea* between India and Babylon must have been carried on as early as about 3000 B.C. One remarkable feature of the foreign evidence collected by Professor Mookerji is that it establishes beyond doubt that for ages before the British period, India was a great manufacturing country known for the excellence of her fabrics and that as a rule she was principally an exporter of manufactured articles, importing only gold and silver and other precious metals. As early as the first century A.D. this flow of gold into India was the cause of alarm to Pliny, who deplored the "drain" from the Roman Empire to the Orient in exchange for articles of luxury.[1] There is abundant testimony of Greek and Mohammedan historians, of Chinese and other foreign travellers as to ships of war forming a regular and significant feature of the offensive and defensive equipment of Indian rulers. A Board of Admiralty was one of the six Boards which made up the War Office of Chandra Gupta, the Hindu Emperor of India, who reigned from 321 B.C. to 297 B.C. Coming to the time of Akbar, the great Mogul who was a contemporary of Elizabeth in the sixteenth century, we find elaborate details for the upkeep of the Admiralty given in the monumental work of Abul Fazal, known as the Ayeen-i-Akbari (the laws of Akbar). Akbar's Admiralty, we find in the Ayeen-i-Akbari, looked to the supply and building of ships. Bengal, Cashmeer and Thatta in Sindh were famous for their shipbuilding industry, though ships were built nearly everywhere on the banks of navigable rivers or on seaboard. The

[1] Mark the use of the word "drain" here.

organisation of a ship given in the Ayeen-i-Akbari, is sure to be of interest to modern readers and we therefore make no excuse for making the following lengthy extract from Professor's Mookerji's book.

"The *second* duty of Akbar's Admiralty was regarding the *supply of men*, of efficient mariners who knew the nature of tides, the depths of channels, the coasts to be avoided, and the character of the prevailing winds. Every ship required officers and men of the following titles and descriptions: (1) The *Nakhoda*, or commander of vessel, who directed the course of the ship; (2) the *Maullim* (the mate), who knew the soundings, the situation of the stars, and guided the ship safe to her destination; (3) the *Tundeil*, who was the chief of the *khelasses* or sailors; (4) the *Nakhodakhesheb*, whose duty it was to provide fuel for the people and assist in lading and unlading the ship; (5) the *Sirheng*, who had to superintend the docking and launching of the ship; (6) the *Bhandaree*, who had charge of the ship's store; (7) the *Keranee*, or ship's clerk, who kept the accounts and also served out water to the people; (8) the *Sukangeer*, or helmsman, of whom there were sometimes twenty in a ship; (9) the *Punjeree*, whose duty it was to look out from the top of the mast and give notice when he saw land or a ship, or discovered a storm rising, or any other object worth observing; (10) the *Goomtee*, or those particular *khelasses* who threw the water out of the ship; (11) the *gunners*, who differed in number according to the size of the ship; (12) the *Kherwah*, or common seamen who were employed in setting and furling the sails and in stopping leaks, and in case of the anchor sticking fast in the ground they had to go to the bottom of the water to set it free."

It might be noted in passing that Akbar was *practically* a free-trader; the duties on exports and imports never exceeded 2½ per cent.[2] India could afford to be a free-trader then. She may again become a free-trader under a national government, but the present policy of free-trade followed by a foreign Government is inimical to her industries.

The Venetian traveller Cesare di Fedrici, writing about the year 1565, states that such was the abundance of materials for shipbuilding in the eastern parts of Bengal that the Sultan of Constantinople found it cheaper to have his vessels built here than at Alexandria.[3] Even in the early days of the British the shipping industry was in a flourishing condition in India. The East India Company built many of its ships there. A building yard was maintained at Surat, up to 1735, in which year most of the work was transferred to Bombay. The foreman of the Surat shipyard was a Parsee Indian. In 1774 the grandsons of this foreman, Lowjee, built two ships of 900 tons each. Later on in the latter part of the eighteenth and the early part of the nineteenth century in this ship yard and under the supervision of Indian foremen were built nine ships, seven frigates and six smaller vessels for the British Royal navy. In 1802 the British Admiralty ordered men-of-war for the King's navy to be constructed at Bombay. The master builder was a Parsee. From 1736 to 1837, the position of master-builder was always held by an Indian.

In 1775, a visitor recorded the following observation about the shipyard:

"Here is a dockyard large and well-contrived with

[2] Ayeen-i-Akbari, by Gladwin, p. 193; quoted by Mookerji, p. 208.

[3] Taylor's Topography of Dacca. quoted by Mookerji.

all kinds of naval stores . . . and . . . forges for making anchors. It boasts such a dry-dock as is, *perhaps not to be seen in any part of Europe, either for size or convenient situation.*[4]

Lieut.-Col. A. Walker wrote in 1811: "The docks (i.e., those at Bombay) that have recently been constructed are capable of containing vessels of any force."

As for their quality the same authority said:

"It is calculated that every ship in the navy of Great Britain is renewed every twelve years. It is well known that teak-wood built ships last fifty years and upwards. Many ships, Bombay built, after running fourteen or fifteen years have been brought into the navy and were considered as strong as ever. . . . *No Europe built Indiaman is capable of going more than six voyages with safety.*"

As to their cost the same authority says: "Ships built at Bombay also are executed by a quarter cheaper than in the docks of England, so that the English-built ships requiring to be renewed every twelve years, the expense is quadruple."[5]

The East India Company maintained several ship-yards in Bengal, but gradually Calcutta came to be the centre of the industry.

In 1781 to 1800 inclusive, 35 ships with a total tonnage of 17,020, were built at Calcutta; in 1801, 19 ships of 10,079 tons; in 1813, 21 ships of 10,376 tons. Including the above from 1801 to 1821, both inclusive, there were built on the Hugli 237 ships of 105,653

[4] The History of the Indian Navy, by Lieutenant C. R. Low, L. N., and other authorities, quoted by Mookerji, p. 245.
[5] Mookerji, pp. 245, 246, 247.

tons, which, reckoned at an average cost of 200 Rs per ton (£20 then) cost £2,000,000.

Lord Wellesley, the Governor General of India, wrote in 1800:

"From the quantity of private tonnage now at command in the port of Calcutta, *from the state of perfection which the art of shipbuilding has already attained in Bengal* (promising a still more rapid progress and supported by abundant and increasing supply of timbers) *it is certain that this port will always be able to furnish tonnage to whatever extent* may be required for conveying to the Port of London the trade of the private British merchants of Bengal."

A Frenchman, F. Baltazar Solvyns has recorded the following observation (1811) about Indian ships:

"In ancient times the Indians excelled in the art of constructing vessels, and the present Hindus can in this respect still offer models to Europe—so much so that the English, attentive to everything which relates to naval architecture, *have borrowed from the Hindus many improvements which they have adopted with success to their own shipping.* The Indian vessels unite elegance and utility, and are models of fine workmanship."[6]

The Decline of the Industry. The decline of the Indian Marine, remarks Mr. Mookerji, began after 1840, no large ships having been built after that date. "It was finally abolished in April, 1863, shortly *after the assumption of the Government of India by the Crown.*"[7]

[6] Quoted by Mookerji, p. 250.
[7] Italics everywhere in this chapter are ours.

Reading the despatches of the directors of the East India Company of 1801 it appears that shipbuilding lingered in India for more than half a century against the wishes and inclinations of her masters. In a despatch quoted by Mr. Digby on page 101 of his book one can find "the reasons" against shipbuilding and shipmanning. One of the reasons was that Indian-built ships will have to be manned by Indian sailors which was "undesirable," "inadvisable" and "unpatriotic." While shipbuilding was stopped in India only sixty years later, the Europe-built ships running to the East continue to employ Indian sailors to a considerable number, though in the lowest capacities.

The changes represent (a) the destruction of the shipbuilding industry, (b) and the bar to the rank of officers.

"Scarcely anything has struck me more forcibly," says Mr. Digby, "than the manner in which the Mistress of the Seas in the Western World has stricken to death the Mistress of the Seas in the East." Statistics from the beginning of the century are not available—to me at least—but from the Statistical Abstracts I gather the following significant facts:

	Vessels	*Tonnage*
1857		
Indian (entered and cleared)	34,286	1,219,958
British and British-Indian	59,441	2,475,472
1898–99		
Indian (entered and cleared)	2,302	133,033
British and British-Indian	6,219	7,685,009
Foreign	1,165	1,297,604

In 1899–1900 the native craft declined to 1776 (109,813 tonnage). The present conditions (1912) may be judged from the following figures taken from Mookerji's "Conclusion."

Our oceanic trade represents 11,800,000 tons, our indigenous shipping represents only 95,000 tons or only about .8 per cent. Of the aggregate tonnage of 29.61 million tons in the inter-portal trade, only 3.24 million tons is our own and over 89 per cent foreign. Our national shipping at the present day consists of only 130 vessels of under 80 tons each, used in the oceanic trade and 7280 in the inter-portal trade of the country of under 20 tons each. . . . Our shipbuilding is now so contracted as to give employment to only 14,321 men, who build only about 125 galbats a year.

As for the status of the Indian sailor, he is after all only a *lostan,* at best only a *Tindal.* In 1912–13 the total number of ships (sail and steam) that entered the Indian ports was 4408, with a tonnage of 8,727,627. The number of those that cleared from Indian ports was 4341, with a tonnage of 8,756,764. Of these, British Indians were 313 and 296 respectively of 188,977 and 174,286 tonnage; and native craft 823 and 765 respectively (tonnage 65,076 and 62,822).

The following figures taken from the Statistical Abstract are of interest:

No. 179.—Number and Tonnage of Steam and Sailing Vessels which Entered with Cargoes or in Ballast from Foreign Countries, distinguishing Nationalities.

	British		*British Indian*		*Native*	
	No.	*Tons*	*No.*	*Tons*	*No.*	*Tons*
1904–05	2,843	5,820,723	522	55,398	1,022	62,840
1905–06	2,408	5,079,474	468	47,250	1,065	59,096
1906–07	2,476	5,461,686	351	80,171	1,394	93,323
1907–08	2,397	5,375,833	396	306,668	1,384	87,529
1908–09	2,144	4,936,332	325	203,338	1,117	79,400
1909–10	2,395	5,693,703	365	142,716	780	62,731
1910–11	2,417	5,916,437	312	162,695	1,049	70,564
1911–12	2,582	6,370,217	325	204,512	946	72,591
1912–13	2,544	6,521,527	313	188,977	832	65,076
1913–14	2,444	6,198,848	243	152,678	853	63,062

No. 180.—Number and Tonnage of Steam and Sailing Vessels which cleared with Cargoes or in Ballast to Foreign Countries, distinguishing Nationalities.

	British		*British Indian*		*Native*	
	No.	*Tons*	*No.*	*Tons*	*No.*	*Tons*
1904–05	2,790	5,723,410	509	48,197	938	58,340
1905–06	2,430	5,070,609	490	48,835	1,112	62,657
1906–07	2,442	5,422,275	388	99,190	1,174	76,809
1907–08	2,388	5,419,334	478	349,808	1,204	79,333
1908–09	2,094	4,886,545	386	247,387	946	67,579
1909–10	2,327	5,660,314	408	200,952	681	48,804
1910–11	2,334	5,799,263	325	187,788	1,075	68,362
1911–12	2,535	6,347,338	322	208,836	922	71,451
1912–13	2,577	6,613,992	296	174,286	765	62,822
1913–14	2,507	6,486,282	260	145,216	844	63,871

But even of greater interest are the figures of ships built at Indian ports.

Ships Built at Indian Ports

	1904–5		1905–6		1906–7		1907–8		1908–9	
	No.	*Tonnage*	*No.*	*Tonnage*	*No.*	*Tonnage*	*No.*	*Tonnage*	*No.*	*Tonnage*
Bengal										
Calcutta: Steam	..	.....	..	.....	2	335	1	73	1	160
Chittagong: Sailing	..	.....	1	26	..	.....	1	71	1	67
Bombay and Sind:										
Bombay: Steam	1	17	1	15	3	38	..	.....	1	12
Sailing	38	3,532	25	1,662	28	1,731	18	808	37	2,243
Karachi: Steam	..	.....	1	152	..	.....	1	14	..	.....
Sailing	11	399	10	778	7	239	18	1,004	17	838
Other Ports:										
Sailing	48	1,773	70	2,277	47	1,357	44	1,496	83	2,984
Madras:										
Various Ports:										
Sailing	45	1,411	44	1,915	30	1,641	28	796	36	1,510
Burma:										
Various Ports:										
Steam	..	.....	..	.....	..	.....	1	301	..	.....
Sailing	6	290	16	787	7	242	1	198	3	40
Total	149	7,422	168	7,612	124	5,583	113	4,761	179	7,854

Ships Built at Indian Ports — Continued

	1909–10		1910–11		1911–12		1912–13		1913–14	
	No.	Tonnage	No.	Tonnage	No.	Tonnage	No.	Tonnage	No.	Tonnage
Bengal:										
Calcutta: Steam	..	.....	1	163	..	.....	..	.....	5	349
Bombay and Sind:										
Bombay: Steam	..	.....	2	96	2	38	5	88	2	152
Sailing	19	1,412	15	1,162	18	851	28	2,256	17	1,199
Karachi: Steam	1	13	..	.....	..	.....	1	12	..	.....
Sailing	6	574	7	440	5	210	3	37	6	277
Other Ports:										
Sailing	56	2,110	40	1,505	50	1,015	73	1,782	81	2,038
Madras:										
Various Ports:										
Steam	..	.....	1	35	..	.....	..	.....	..	.....
Sailing	22	987	30	1,026	27	1,266	25	840	25	1,126
Burma:										
Various Ports:										
Steam	..	.....	1	248	8	1,060	..	.....	1	39
Sailing	4	145	1	16	2	42	1	17	4	131
Total	108	5,241	98	4,691	112	4,482	136	5,032	141	5,311

CHAPTER VII

MISCELLANEOUS INDUSTRIAL, AGRICULTURAL, AND MINING OPERATIONS

In the preceding pages we have related the story of the cotton industry and the shipbuilding industry: in what condition they were before the British took possession of India, and how they have fared since. In this section we give the reader a general idea about other industries and also about the general import and export trade.

Indigo. India from time immemorial had been famous for its beautiful dyes. The dyeing industry was closely connected with weaving, and the colours in which cotton and silk fabrics were woven increased immensely their price and their acceptability. Most of the dyes were produced from vegetables. "Indigo, lac, safflower and tumeric, moski, horitoki, maujestha and vandis flowers were the ingredients."

The trade in indigo was made a European monopoly in the very early days of British rule. It is one of the darkest chapters of the history of Bengal and Bihar that tells of the wrongs and oppressions committed on Indians by the European indigo planters. In his survey of Bengal made in the early years of the nineteenth century, Dr. Buchanan gives the details of the industry as he found it in each district and also of the way in which the European license holders treated the native growers.

Among other causes of complaint he mentions that the planter considers the growers "as his slaves, beats and confines them whenever he is dissatisfied," that the growers are "cheated both in the measure of their land and in the measure of the weed"; that the planters are "insolent and violent."

So frequent were the acts of violence committed by European indigo planters that the government was compelled to issue circulars to magistrates drawing their attention to "the offence" which had been established "beyond all doubt or dispute against individual planters."

The manufacture of indigo is not an important industry now. It has been killed principally by the imports of dyes from Germany.

Jute. The jute industry owes its growth to quite recent times. It is said that "about sixty years ago jute was almost unknown."[1]

The total area under cultivation (mainly in eastern and northern Bengal "exceeds three million acres, and the output may be estimated at more than eight million bags (of 600 lbs.) of which nearly half is exported raw, the rest being worked up in the mills near Calcutta."[2]

"The jute mills are nearly all concentrated in Bengal in the vicinity of Calcutta and are *mostly* in the hands of British firms."[3]

I have italicised the word "*mostly.*" It would have been perhaps nearer the truth to say "nearly all."

Woollen Mills. There were six woollen mills at

[1] "Oxford Survey" (Asia, 1911), p. 132.

[2] *Ibid.*

[3] "Parliamentary Blue Book Relating to the Moral and Material Progress of India for the year 1913-14," p. 63.

work at the end of 1913, containing 1086 looms and 38,963 spindles and producing goods valued at £374,-000 for the year.[4] They are most of them, if not all, in the hands of British firms.

Paper Mills. There were seven paper mills at work at the end of 1913, producing during the year sixty million pounds of paper valued at £535,800. (In the year 1913 we imported paper of the value of about nine millions sterling from foreign countries, of which about six millions' worth came from the United Kingdom alone.) The industry is principally in the hands of British firms, only two of the five larger mills being in native hands. In the Indian year book for 1917 the total number of paper mills in India at the end of 1915–16 is given at eleven, but it is said that only seven were in operation.

Breweries. This is a purely British industry in British hands. At the end of 1913 there were twenty-one breweries which produced during the year 3,654,-000 gallons of beer.

Rice Mills and Saw Mills. Rice mills and saw mills are most numerous in Burma, and " are mainly in European hands," being " the only large industries in Burma, organised and worked by Western methods." [5]

Iron. " Iron ore of rich quality is widely distributed over the country," says Mr. J. S. Cotton, editor of the *Imperial Gazeteer* and the writer of the chapter on Industrial and Economic Conditions in the " Oxford Survey of British Empire " (Asia, 1911).

[4] *Ibid.*

[5] " Blue Book on the Moral and Material Progress of India for 1913–14," p. 63.

"In former times iron smelting in little charcoal furnaces was a *common industry. The steel thus produced under the name of wootz, anticipated by many centuries the finest qualities of the modern European product.* Indeed the iron age in India . . . has been placed as early as 1500 B. C. *But no local industry has suffered more from importation than that of iron-smelting.* Apart from two Capitalist enterprises the total value of iron ore mined is estimated at only £15,000, while the annual imports of iron and steel exceed £4,000,000." [6]

Yet there is not a single good school for the teaching of mining in the country! The College of Engineering pretends to make a provision for teaching a mining course which was being pursued at the beginning of the session 1913–14 by a group of 16 students. We are further told that at lectures delivered at five centres in the Bengal coal fields under lecturers appointed by the mining Educational Board there were 360 registered students and, in June, 1913, 17 had qualified for certificates. The Mining and Geological Institute of India, which was inaugurated at the end of 1905, numbers 308 members.[7] The Tata Iron and Steel Works is an Indian concern, which is trying to revive the industry. They started work in 1912 and Mr. J. S. Cotton says that "it is interesting to learn that a much larger proportion of the labour is in the hands of trained Indians than was anticipated." Where did the Indians who are engaged in this industry secure their training? Most probably in America, perhaps some in Europe.

[6] "Oxford Survey" (Asia), p. 143. The italics are ours.

[7] "Blue Book Relating to Moral and Material Progress of India for 1913–14," p. 60.

The total output of Indian iron ore in 1914 was a little under 442,000 tons which in 1915 fell to about 390,000 tons. The amount of pig iron produced during the year by the Tata Company was 156,500 tons and by the Bengal Iron and Steel Company 87,285 tons. The former company produced 76,355 tons of steel including 16,871 tons of steel rails and the latter 25,634 tons of cast iron castings. ("The Indian Year Book, 1917," p. 332.)

Copper. "Copper ore is *likewise widely distributed over the country,* especially in the north, but it is nowhere now worked profitably, whereas the importation of copper amounts to nearly £2,000,000." [8]

Manganese. "More important than any of these is manganese ore," says Mr. Cotton, "the mining of which began in the last decade of the nineteenth century and has advanced so rapidly that India now ranks as the second country (after Russia) for the production of this substance. . . . The ores are exceedingly rich, and they are exported in bulk *to be smelted abroad.* The annual production has reached 900,000 tons valued at £577,000." [9] The number of manganese quarries worked in British territory alone is forty-one, employing more than 7000 persons. "The Indian Year Book for 1915" (published by the *Times of India* Office, Bombay) says that "India now takes the first place among manganese producing countries in the world." In 1915 the output was 450,416 tons, valued at £929,546.

[8] "Oxford Survey" (Asia), p. 144. Italics are ours.

[9] In 1913–14 the quantity produced was 815,047 tons, the value £1,211,036. See "Blue Book for 1913–14."

That is a matter of great satisfaction, except that the profits are almost exclusively monopolised by Europeans.

Coal. The total output of coal in 1913–14 was 16,208,000 tons, of which 723,641 tons were exported. In this year 559,190 tons were imported into India. In 1915–16, the Indian output was 17,103,932 tons, of which we exported 751,801 tons as against 175,000 tons imported. This is probably the only mineral product the profits of which go partly into the pockets of the Indians, because most of the coal raised in India comes from Bengal and the Bengal Zemindar has used his opportunities to advantage. In what proportion the industry is owned by Europeans and by natives, I have no means of saying.

Other Minerals. The following table gives the value of minerals produced in 1915:

	1915
Coal	£3,781,064
Gold	2,369,486
Petroleum	1,256,803
Manganese-ore	929,546
Salt	660,250
Mica	183,947
Saltpetre	373,891
Lead-ore and Lead	316,182
Tungsten-ore	296,772

Of these we have already dealt with coal and manganese; salt is a government monopoly; petroleum, gold, mica, lead-ore, lead and tungsten-ore are principally in European hands; saltpetre and building materials and road metals are shared by both but probably by far the larger share is in native hands.

Tea and Coffee. Both these industries are in the hands of Europeans and have been the source of untold misery to the people of India for the reason that in the interest of European capital the Government of India has been lending itself to make special legislative provisions for the supply of indentured labourers for the tea plantations in Assam.

"Of crops grown with European capital and under European supervision by far the most important is tea," says Mr. Cotton in the "Oxford Survey of British Empire" (Asia), page 133. In 1915 the area under cultivation for tea was 636,218 acres. In 1915, the total production was 371,836,668 pounds, of which 291,795,041 pounds were exported. The capital of joint stock companies engaged in this business was about £20.7 millions in 1915, of which £17,670,760 is owned by companies registered in Great Britain and Ireland. The balance, less than three millions, belongs to companies registered in India, which does not mean that they are constituted of Indians.[10] The great bulk of the Indian companies also are European in membership; so practically the whole profits of this industry go to European pockets. The coolies employed under special laws enacted for the benefit of the European capitalist have the hardest possible time and get practically slave wages. The total exports of tea in 1915 amounted to 340,433,163 lbs.

Coffee planting is confined to Southern India where it is said to be "pursued by Indians as well as by Eu-

[10] "The Indian Year Book for 1917," published by the *Times of India* Press.

ropeans." The industry is "stationary, if not declining." The total exports in 1915 amounted to 290,000 cwts.

CHAPTER VIII

AGRICULTURE

India's Greatest Industry. In the preceding chapters we have discussed the "minor" industries of India. We have shown how the cotton and silk industries were crushed in the early days of British rule; to what extent they have been revived and what hampers their further growth; how the shipping industry has vanished; and how the country stands in the matter of its mineral produce. We have also shown who controls and benefits from the other principal modern industries of India, such as jute, tea and coffee.

In this chapter we propose to discuss what, by common consent, is the greatest industry of India. "In India," says Mr. J. S. Cotton in the Oxford Survey, "agriculture forms the one predominant industry to an extent which is difficult for those to realise who are familiar only with the conditions prevailing in England. According to the occupation returns of the census of 1901, almost two-thirds of the total population of 294 millions are supported directly by agriculture proper and the subordinate industry of cattle raising; but if those supported indirectly be included it has been estimated that the proportion would rise to nine-tenths, leaving only one-tenth for all the towns inhabited by as many as 5,000 persons each."

The annual harvests are therefore a subject of supreme concern not only to the cultivators themselves, but also to the Government, and it might be added, to the people at large. Nay, one might go a step further and say that they are of supreme importance to the workers of Great Britain, as well.

The failure of a single harvest in India means *famine,* which may possibly result in a temporary fall in revenue collections but which does certainly involve a heavy expenditure for famine relief and also a certain decline in imports. The revenue from land is the principal source of government income, the realisation from land tax alone forming about one-third of revenue proper of the Government of India. In the budget figures of 1914–15, the realisation from the land tax was shown to be a little less than 21½ million pounds sterling out of a total of slightly over 85 millions sterling, the estimated income from all sources including railway receipts, proceeds of opium and canal receipts for 1913–14. Customs in India bring only a paltry sum. In 1913–14 there was an income of 7½ millions sterling from customs, while the realisation from the income tax was £1,950,250. In 1914–15 the figures were £5,960,469 and £2,036,733 respectively.

The land tax is not levied on the actual produce of the year. It is generally assessed for a number of years varying from ten to thirty years, except in certain areas where it has been permanently fixed. The failure of harvest therefore does not necessarily mean a reduction in Government income. Suspensions of one year are as a rule made good in another, and remissions are few. On the other hand, the sufferings of the people assume so terrible a shape that the Government is compelled to spend large sums of money on "famine relief." Of famines, of deaths from famine, of collections of revenue during famine years, and of the government expenditure for famine relief, we will speak in detail later on. A famine year is generally a bad one for imports, and a falling off in imports affects British industries. A failure of harvest in India thus spells not only disaster to India but loss to Great Britain as well. The very fact that 90 per cent. of the population should depend almost solely on such a precarious industry as agriculture is sufficiently condemnatory of the system of administration that has failed to look ahead and make provision for other sources of national income which would secure variety of occupation to the workers of the country and insure them against unemployment and starvation in the event of agriculture failing them.

The total cropped area (net after deducting area cropped more than once) in 1914–15 was 227,611,132 acres out of a total net area by professional survey of 619,392,157 acres.

By crops the area stood as below:—

	1913–14 for British India Acres	*1914–15 for whole India Acres*
Rice	60,320,000	77,668,882
Wheat	20,476,000	25,451,330
Other food grains (chiefly millet and pulse)	76,217,000	93,479,555
Barley	5,844,000	7,904,783
Total food grains and pulses	162,966,000	204,504,550
Oil seeds	12,675,000	15,333,591
Sugar crops	2,432,000	2,458,865
Cotton	15,665,000	15,221,787
Jute	2,817,000	3,308,718

The yield returns are given for the whole of India including the native states.

	1913–14 Area in Acres	1913–14 Estimated Yield	1914–15 Area	1914–15 Estimated Yield
Rice	70,583,000	563,332,000 cwts.	76,181,000	27,964,000 cwts.
Wheat	27,697,000	8,427,000 tons	32,230,000	10,269,000 tons
Sugar	2,519,800	2,262,000 tons	2,315,000	2,367,000 tons
Tea	610,000	307,250,000 lbs	622,600	312,976,000 lbs
Jute .... (1914)	3,359,000	10,444,000 bales	2,377,000	7,429,000 bales
Cotton	24,595,000	5,201,000 bales	24,632,000	5,232,000 bales
Oilseeds	15,720,000	2,565,000 tons	Not Given	

The figures for 1913–14 are taken from the "Parliamentary Blue Book on India for 1913–14," and those for 1914–15 from the "Indian Year Book for 1917." The yield returns are taken from Blue Books.

India produces almost half the rice of the world. All exports of rice are subject to a duty of about six shillings ten pence per ton. In 1913–14 India exported rice to the value of £17,738,000 (as valued at Indian ports) as against £21,704,000 worth of rice exported in the year before. The figures for 1914–15 are not given in the Blue Book, but it is said that there was a falling off in exports.

The export figures of wheat and wheat flour are subject to great fluctuations. It is said that "in a famine year, the export falls to a *trifling quantity*," which fact is not borne out by the table of exports given in the margin of the Blue Book which shows the maximum quantity of wheat exported in 1904–05 at 2,150,000 tons. Except in one year during the ten years, the quantity exported did not fall below 801,400 tons. The only exception is for the year 1908–09 when the quantity exported fell to 109,750 tons of wheat and 30,100 tons of wheat flour. In 1914–15 the exports of wheat were 706,400 tons and of flour 54,000 tons.

The following are the export figures of tea, jute, cotton, and oilseeds for 1913–14 and 1914–15:

	1913–14	*1914–15*
Tea	289.5 millions of lbs.	300.8 millions of lbs.
Jute	768,000 tons of the value[1] of £39,400,000	3,046,000 bales
Cotton ..	10,626,000 cwts.	10,349,000 cwts. valued at £22,326,000
Oilseeds .	31,652,000 cwts.	19,078,000 cwts.

To what extent India meets the requirements of the United Kingdom in the matter of raw produce may be judged from the following figures for the years 1903–04 to 1912–13 taken from the Statistical Abstract for British India:

IMPORTS OF AGRICULTURAL PRODUCE FROM INDIA INTO GREAT BRITAIN

Raw Jute

1903–04	£3,480,398
1904–05	3,298,003
1905–06	4,876,823
1906–07	7,707,883
1907–08	4,683,345
1908–09	5,601,794
1909–10	4,289,508
1910–11	3,885,292
1911–12	6,530,513
1912–13	7,352,171
1913–14	7,826,358

The United Kingdom is the largest importer of raw jute from India.

Raw Wool

1903–04	£ 891,011
1904–05	1,139,181
1905–06	1,337,108
1906–07	1,547,306

[1] The values of exports are those of the ports from which these articles were shipped.

1907–08	£1,365,631
1908–09	1,364,536
1909–10	1,850,846
1910–11	1,867,323
1911–12	1,659,622
1912–13	1,704,785
1913–14	1,621,111

The United Kingdom is not only the largest importer of raw wool, but practically the whole of the raw wool exported by India goes to the United Kingdom. Out of a total of £1,756,448 worth of raw wool exported in 1912–13, the United Kingdom took of the value of £1,704,785.

Rice

1903–04	£1,047,551
1904–05	1,096,965
1905–06	993,008
1906–07	836,225
1907–08	1,096,369
1908–09	790,195
1909–10	842,946
1910–11	1,022,480
1911–12	932,871
1912–13	1,305,463
1913–14	1,129,677

Wheat

1903–04	£6,032,913
1904–05	7,994,302
1905–06	4,276,648
1906–07	4,396,807
1907–08	5,052,461
1908–09	836,956
1909–10	7,130,489
1910–11	7,113,542
1911–12	6,741,190
1912–13	8,380,442
1913–14	5,694,757

The United Kingdom is not only the largest buyer of wheat from India but in some years takes practically the whole of the total quantity exported. That was so until 1908–09. In 1909 and 1910, she took more than £7,000,000 worth out of a total of almost £8,500,000 worth exported. In 1911–12 she took £6,741,190 worth of wheat of a total of £8,898,972 exported and in 1912–13 £8,380,422 worth out of a total of £11,795,816.

Barley

	£
1903–04	10,777
1904–05	3,548
1905–06	2,765
1906–07	74,157
1907–08	239,459
1908–09	39,796
1909–10	67,954
1910–11	54,172
1911–12	873,948
1912–13	1,737,542
1913–14	817,562

The United Kingdom is the greatest consumer of Indian barley. In seeds, again, we find that the United Kingdom heads the list of importers from India.

Tea

	U. K.	*Total*
1903–04	4,726,074 pounds	5,705,288 pounds
1904–05	4,473,166 "	5,643,657 "
1905–06	4,593,453 "	5,898,402 "
1906–07	5,049,684 "	6,571,843 "
1907–08	5,056,618 "	6,866,899 "
1908–09	5,223,037 "	6,929,141 "
1909–10	5,885,463 "	7,804,936 "
1910–11	5,915,923 "	8,277,579 "
1911–12	6,353,755 "	8,630,952 "
1912–13	6,325,049 "	8,862,651 "
1913–14	7,232,049 "	9,983,372 "

More than two-thirds of the tea exported from India goes to the United Kingdom.

Similarly the United Kingdom gets the largest quantity of raw skins, dressed or tanned hides and dressed or tanned skins.

Land Tax. For the latest figures of land revenue and the official explanation of the policy underlying them, we make the following lengthy quotation from the Parliamentary Blue Book for 1913:

"From time immemorial a share of the produce of the land has been the chief source of public revenue in India. Land revenue is still the mainstay of the Government, constituting about 36 per cent. of the total net revenue that accrues to the Indian Exchequer.[2]

"Owing to its far-reaching social and political effects the proper administration of the land revenue has always been one of the chief problems of the Indian Government, and during the early years of British rule the best methods of assessment were keenly debated. In 1793 Lord Cornwallis introduced into Bengal a permanent settlement, by which the demand of the State was fixed and made for ever unalterable. Other systems were gradually evolved, and at length over the greater part of India a system of periodical settlements was established, under which the State demand is revised at recurring periods of twenty to thirty years, the latter period prevailing in all the larger provinces except the Punjab and the Central Provinces, where settlements are usually made for twenty years, and in Burma, where the term of twenty years is now being adopted. Under the system of periodical revisions of the land assessment the State secures a share in the increased rental value arising from the general prog-

[2] The statement is repeated every year.

ress of the community. Of late years measures have been taken to exempt improvements from assessment, and generally to make the enforcement of the rights of the State as little burdensome as is possible to the revenue-payer. Periodical revision also affords the opportunity of reducing the assessment in villages or tracts which have declined in prosperity and of correcting inequalities arising from any cause.

"When the revenue is assessed by the State permanently or temporarily, on an individual or community owning an estate, and occupying a position identical with, or analogous to, that of a landlord, the assessment is known as *zamindari;* where the revenue is imposed on individuals who are, or who represent, the actual occupants of holdings, the assessment is known as *ryotwari.* Under either system there may be rent-paying sub-tenants. In Southern India, where most of the land is held by petty occupiers direct from the State, the occupiers have the right to retain their holdings so long as they pay the revenue due from them. The permanently settled districts, in which all holdings are *zamindari,* cover most of Bengal and Bihar, and parts of Madras and the United Provinces. As regards temporarily settled districts, *zamindari* estates, held by proprietary groups or large individual proprietors, are chiefly found in the Punjab, the United Provinces, the Central Provinces, and Orissa, while in Bombay and Sindh, Burma, Assam, Berar, and two-thirds of Madras the system of *ryotwari,* or peasant proprietors, prevails.

"*Revenue Assessments and Incidence.* Land revenue is realised in the form of an annual payment of cash, the assessment rates being subject to no alteration during the term of a settlement, though the amount leviable in any year may vary according to the area actually cultivated or to the condition of the harvest.[3] Except in Bombay (where assessment is not fixed in terms of produce) the land revenue is assessed so as to represent a share, not of the gross, but of the *net* produce (or net assets). In the zamindari, or landlord settlements, that widely prevail in Northern India, the cultivating tenant pays rent to a landlord. *Of this rent the Government usually takes rather less than 50 per cent. as land revenue.*

"It is certain that the Government NOW[4] *takes a very much smaller share of the gross product than was customary in pre-British days.* The incidence of ordinary land revenue for all British India in 1913–14 works out at 1s. 8d. per head of the population.[5]

"The Government makes liberal reductions of assessments in cases of local deterioration, where such reductions cannot be claimed under the terms of settlement."

The fiscal policy of the British Government is an anomaly from more than one point of view. It insists on imposing a heavy tax on land and agriculture in pursuance of the "universal practice of the country" but ignores:

(a) That under the best Hindu and Mohammedan rulers the Land Tax was *practically* the sole tax levied

[3] This is true only of the small area of land settled on the basis of every year's produce called fluctuating assessment.
[4] Mark the force of the word *now* put in capitals by me.
[5] It varies from 4s. per head in Berar, over 3s. 5d. in Bombay to 11d. in Bengal.

upon the people. A great many of the other taxes imposed by the British Government were unknown to the country. There was no income tax, no tax on justice, no stamp tax and no duty on succession.

(b) That all the proceeds of the tax were spent *in the country* and returned to the people in different forms like showers of rain from clouds formed of water sucked by the rays of the sun in the hottest months of the year.

(c) That except under the Moguls, the Government share was taken in produce. There was no fixed cash assessment. Besides, there were many ways of avoiding the giving of the full share, which cannot be used under the British system organised as it is to the minutest detail.

(d) Excessive demands were opposed or stopped by threats of revolt which kept the demands within proper bounds. A revolt of the peasantry under the British rule is *impossible*. The rate at which the Land Tax is fixed in India is unheard of in any other part of the globe and is the principal if not the only cause of the appalling poverty of the agricultural masses.

(e) Formerly large numbers were employed in other industries which have been driven out of existence under British rule. The numbers supported by industries other than agriculture have been steadily falling off (see the 1911 census report of India, by Gait, I. C. S., chapter on occupations). It is no credit to an enlightened Government like the British that they should justify their policy on the ground of the "universal practice of the country." Under the light of modern civilisation many an immemorial practice has been discontinued and even the British Government in India has given aid to stop and prohibit practices which were considered immoral and iniquitous.

The tests which should be applied are: Is the land tax just? Is it moderate? Is it fair? Does it leave sufficient margin to the agriculturist to live a *decent* life? Does it not result in an unequal distribution of the burdens of Government in favour of the moneyed classes? Judged by these standards there can be no doubt that the rate at which land tax is assessed is unjust, unfair and excessive. It tells extremely heavily on the very class which ought to be protected by an enlightened system of administration. The poor require protection against the wealthy; the weak against the strong, yet the present system of taxation maintained under the plea of [6] "an immemorial practice" tells most heavily on the poorest and the weakest. It is they who have to live on insufficient food from day's end to day's end; it is they who are not only underfed but also underclothed, and whose children have to go without education and are crushingly handicapped in the struggle for life and in the race for progress. Yet it is they who fight for the Empire and lose life and limb in the service of the Government. Many a noble-minded Englishman has felt the injustice of the system.

But one strong feature of the British system in India is that the Home Government, while it professes to support the man on the spot in all measures of repression, in all things which affect the dignity and privilege

[6] See Thorburn's "The Punjab in Peace and War" (1904), p. 175.

of the ruling classes, in all recommendations which refuse to make concessions to public opinion, in all things which tend to perpetuate power in the hands of the bureaucracy to the detriment of the people, has in numerous instances overruled the men on the spot when the latter made recommendations favourable to the people. Men realising large revenues, inventing new sources of income, have been honoured and promoted; men making light assessments have been dismissed, deported or censured. The Government has often used the authority of eminent Anglo-Indian Administrators in support of its policy, ignoring those portions of their opinions or recommendations which were favourable to the people. They have always accepted what was likely to bring them larger revenues, rejecting safeguards provided against hardship.

The economic history of India amply shows how the recommendations of the men on the spot in favour of a just and more considerate treatment of the cultivator in the matter of land tax, as also their recommendations in favour of import duties in the interests of Indian industries, have from time to time been vetoed by the authorities in England. In the preceding chapter we have referred to the praiseworthy attempts of Anglo-Indian Administrators in the matter of import duties. In this chapter we show how the efforts of eminent Anglo-Indian statesmen in the matter of securing a fixity of land revenue demand and of moderation in the rates have from time to time failed. The history of the land tax is as full of painful incidents as the history of Indian industries.

Bengal. The first chapter of the history of land

administration by the East India Company opens with the management of districts made over to them in Bengal and in the Karnatic by the native ruling princes in payment of debts incurred on account of subsidies promised, but not paid. It also includes the story of the management of lands or tracts the revenues of which were assigned to European servants of the East India Company in liquidation of the private debts advanced by the latter to the ruling Princes of Bengal and Karnatic and swelled to fabulous sums by all the methods of chicanery and fraud known to money-lenders. These lands were not crown lands that could be given away by the ruling princes without any regard to the rights of those who owned them or held them. They were lands which in many cases had been owned and held for generations in the families of the then existing owners, occupiers or holders thereof. The only right which the ruling Princes had was the Government's share of the produce, call it revenue or rent as you please. Yet the East India Company and its European servants treated these assignments of revenue as if the lands themselves had been given to them in complete ownership, regardless of the rights of those to whom they had belonged or by whom they had been cultivated or held in some sort of tenure for generations. Estates held for generations were put to auction and given over to the highest bidder. "In the provinces of Burdwan and Midnapur," wrote Governor Verelst in a letter to the Directors of the East India Company on December 16, 1769, "those evils which necessarily flowed from the bad policy of the Moorish Government had in no sort decreased. On the contrary, a plan was adopted in 1762 productive of certain ruin to the province."

"The lands were let by public auction for the short term of three years. Men without fortune or character became bidders at the sale; and while some of the former farmers, unwilling to relinquish their habitations, exceeded perhaps the real value in their offers, those who had nothing to lose advanced yet further, wishing at all events to obtain an immediate possession. Thus numberless harpies were let loose to plunder, whom the spoil of a miserable people enabled to complete their first year's payment."

The intense cruelty and heartlessness with which revenues were collected in Bengal is proved by documentary evidence on the subject. In a letter of the Directors of May 9, 1770, occur the following sentences:

"The famine which has ensued, the mortality, the beggary, exceed all description. Above one-third of the inhabitants have perished in the once plentiful province of Purneah, and in other parts the misery is equal." On the 11th September they wrote: "It is scarcely possible that any description could be an exaggeration of the misery the inhabitants . . . have encountered with. It is not then to be wondered that this calamity has had its influence on the collections; but we are happy to remark they have fallen less short than we supposed they would."

On the 12th February they wrote: "Notwithstanding the great severity of the late famine and the great reduction of people thereby, some increase has been made in the settlements both of the Bengal and the Behar provinces for the present year."

On the 10th January, 1772, they wrote: "The

collections in each department of revenue are as successfully carried on for the present year as we could have wished."

It is painful to read of this rigorous collection of the land tax during years of human sufferings and deaths, perhaps unexampled in the history of mankind.

It was officially estimated that in the famine of 1770 about one-third of the population of Bengal or about ten millions of people had died. Wrote Warren Hastings on November 3, 1772:

"Notwithstanding the loss of at least one-third of the inhabitants of the province, and the consequent decrease of the cultivation, the net collections of the year 1771 exceeded even those of 1768. . . . It was naturally to be expected that the diminution of the revenue should have kept an equal pace with the other consequences of so great a calamity. That it did not was owing to its being violently kept up to its former standard.[7]

Later on, when the East India Company had the Dewani or the revenue administration of the three provinces of Bengal, Behar and Orissa, conferred on it by the Great Mogul, a dual system was set up by which the collection of revenue was done by the servants of the Nabob under the superintendence of supervisors appointed by the Company's Government. This system was bad enough for the landlord and the cultivator, but the worst was yet to come. In 1776 Warren Hastings and Barwell proposed that estates should be sold by public auction or farmed out on leases, and

[7] Extracts from India Office Records, quoted in Hunter's "Annals of Rural Bengal," 1868, p. 381.

settlements should be made with purchasers or lessees for life. This was of course in utter disregard of the rights of those who had held the lands for generations before. Philip Francis, another member of the Bengal Council, saw the evil and proposed a permanent settlement. The most valuable part of his minute, however, is that in which he describes the system then in vogue. But the Directors would not agree to letting the land on lease for years or in perpetuity. In 1778, 1779 and 1780 the system of five year leases was given up and estates were let annually.

In 1781 a new settlement was affected, this time preference being given to Zemindars (landlords), though for one year only, by which the land revenues increased by about £260,000.[8]

Similarly harsh measures were adopted in the Upper Provinces, which the rapacity of Warren Hastings managed to bring under the control of the East India Company. How Warren Hastings coerced the Raja of Benares and then the Nabob Vizier of Oudh are matters of political history.[9]

Bengal, however, soon obtained relief by the permanent settlement of Lord Cornwallis, effected with the Zemindars on a basis of *nine-tenths* of the actual rental then received by them. But the Upper Prov-

[8] What happened to the great families of Bengal under this system has been stated by Mr. R. C. Dutt in his book "India Under Early British Rule" as also by Torrens in "The Empire in Asia."

[9] A brief synopsis of these most oppressive transactions is given by Mr. R. C. Dutt in his "India Under Early British Rule," pp. 70-76, or the reader may read the account in James Mill's "History of British India." The revenue which was to accrue from these acquisitions was estimated at £237,000.

inces did not receive the full benefit of this concession because at that time they were still nominally under native government. It will be interesting to compare the results of this settlement in the field of revenue with those of native rulers previous to the advent of the British. We take the figures from the famous "Minute" of Mr. Shore, afterwards Lord Teignmouth, of June 18, 1789:

By Todar Mall's settlement, 1582	£1,070,000	or	$5,350,000
By Sultan Suja's settlement, 1658	1,312,000	or	6,560,000
By Jaffar Khan's settlement, 1722	1,429,000	or	7,145,000
By Suja Khan's settlement, 1728	1,425,000	or	7,125,000

The actual collections, however, of the five years immediately preceding British rule were:

1762–63	£646,000	or	$3,230,000
1763–64	762,000	or	3,610,000
1764–65	818,000	or	4,090,000
1765–66	1,470,000	or	7,350,000

The last year was the first year of the Dewani granted to the British by the Mogul. The collections were made by Mohammed Raza Khan under the dual authority of the Nabob and the Company.

The collections made by the British in 1790–91 were £2,680,000 or $13,400,000, which was nearly double the assessment of Jaffar Khan and of Suja Khan in the early part of the century; it was three times the collection of Maharaja Nandkumar in the year 1764–65, and it was nearly double the collection made by Mohammed Raza Khan under British supervision in the first year of the Company's Dewani. Yet it was a relief to the people of Bengal because it was final and permanent.[10]

[10] It was Bengal which had suffered terribly from the rapac-

Madras. From Bengal let us turn to Madras. The story begins with the assignments of land revenues made by the Nabob of Karnatic in payment of his debts to the Company and its servants. The results of the system were testified to by one, Mr. George Smith, in his evidence before the Parliamentary Committee in 1782.

"George Smith, Esquire, attending according to order, was asked how long he resided in India, where, and in what capacity? He said he arrived in India in the year 1764; he resided in Madras from 1767 to October, 1779. Being asked what was the state of trade at Madras at the time when he first knew it, he said it was in a flourishing condition, and Madras one of the first marts in India. Being asked in what condition did he leave it with respect to trade, he replied at the time of his leaving it, there was little or no trade, and but one ship belonging to the place. Being asked in what state the interior country of the Karnatic was with regard to commerce and cultivation when he first knew it, he said at that period he understood the Karnatic to be in a well-cultivated and populous condition, and as such consuming a great many articles of merchandise and trade. Being asked in what condition it was when he left Madras with respect to cultivation, population, and internal commerce, he said in respect to cultivation, greatly on the decline, and also in respect of population; and as to commerce, exceedingly circumscribed."

Speaking of the Principality of Tanjore, in the Province of Karnatic, one Mr. Petrie said in his evidence before the Committee of Secrecy in 1782:

ity of the early British Administrators and if she has prospered under the permanent settlement, she has well earned that prosperity by her early losses.

"Before I speak of the present state of Tanjore country it will be necessary to inform the Committee that not many years ago that province was considered as one of the most flourishing, best cultivated, populous districts in Hindustan. I first saw this country in 1768, when it presented a very different picture from its present situation. Tanjore was formerly a place of great foreign and inland trade; it imported cotton from Bombay and Surat, raw and worked silks from Bengal; sugar, spices, etc., from Sumatra, Malacca, and the eastern islands; gold, horses, elephants, and timber from Pegu, and various articles of trade from China. It was by means of Tanjore that a great part of Haidar Ali's dominions and the north-western parts of the Mahratta empire were supplied with many European commodities, and with a species of silk manufacture from Bengal, which is almost universally worn as a part of dress by the natives of Hindustan. The exports of Tanjore were muslins, chintz, handkerchiefs, ginghams, various sorts of long-cloths, and a coarse printed cloth, which last constitutes a material article in the investments of the Dutch and the Danes, being in great demand for the African, West Indian, and South American markets. Few countries have more natural advantages than Tanjore; it possesses a rich and fertile soil, singularly well supplied with water from the two great rivers Cavery and Coleroon, which, by means of reservoirs, sluices, and canals, are made to disperse their waters through almost every field in the country; to this latter cause we may chiefly attribute the uncommon fertility of Tanjore. The face of the country is beautifully diversified, and in its appearance approaches nearer to England than any other part of India that I have seen. Such was Tanjore not many years ago, but its decline has been so rapid, that in many districts it would be difficult to trace the remains of its former opulence. . . .

"At this period (1771), as I have been informed, the manufacturers flourished, the country was populous and well cultivated, the inhabitants were wealthy and industrious. Since the year 1771, the era of the first siege, until the restoration of the Raja, the country having been during that period twice the seat of war, and having undergone revolutions in the government, trade, manufactures, and agriculture were neglected, and many thousands of inhabitants went in quest of a more secure abode."

How fabulous fortunes were made by the servants of the East India Company; how their interests came into conflict with the interests of the Company; how the latter censured the former; how the matter was eventually brought before Parliament for final settlement of the debts claimed from the Nawab by individuals once in the employ of the Company; how seats in Parliament were purchased by one of them, Mr. Paul Benfield, and how eventually all debts were realised up to the last penny, are matters which do not properly fall within the scope of the chapter. Mr. Dutt has described them with some detail and they may be studied there. The following quotation from James Mill's "History of British India" and from Burke's speech delivered in the discussion on the Nawab of Arcot's debts, may however be given here as a sample of how things were managed in those days:

"It was to hold the corrupt benefit of a large parliamentary interest, created by the creditors and creatures, fraudulent and not fraudulent, of the Nawab of Arcot, that . . . the Ministry of 1784 decided that they should all, whether fraudulent or not fraudulent, receive their demands."[11]

"Paul Benfield is the grand parliamentary reformer.

[11] Mill's "History of British India," book vi. chap. I.

What region in the empire, what city, what borough, what country, what tribunal in this kingdom, is not full of his labours? In order to station a steady phalanx for all future reforms, the public-spirited usurer, amidst his charitable toils for the relief of India, did not forget the poor rotten constitution of his native country. For her he did not disdain to stoop to the trade of a wholesale upholsterer for this House, to furnish it, not with the faded tapestry figures of antiquated merit, such as decorate, and may reproach, some other Houses, but with real, solid, living patterns of true modern virtue. Paul Benfield made, reckoning himself, no fewer than eight members of the last Parliament. What copious streams of pure blood must he not have transfused into the veins of the Present. . . .

"For your Minister, this worn-out veteran (Benfield's agent) submitted to enter into the dusty field of the London contest; and you will remember that in the same virtuous cause he submitted to keep a sort of public office or countinghouse, where the whole business of the last general election was managed. It was openly managed by the direct agent and attorney of Benfield. It was managed upon Indian principles and for an Indian interest. This was the golden cup of abominations . . . which so many of the people, so many of the nobles of this land, had drained to the very dregs. Do you think that no reckoning was to follow this lewd debauch? That no payment was to be demanded for this riot of public drunkenness and national prostitution? Here you have it, here before you. The principal of the grand election manager must be indemnified. Accordingly the claims of Benfield and his crew must be put above all inquiry." [12]

An account of what happened to Madras under the British Land Administration system may profitably be

[12] Burke's speech on the Nawab of Arcot's debts.

preceded by a brief description of the condition of things before the British took charge of the country. It appears from the reports made by the Committee of Secrecy that had been appointed by the Court of Directors (originally in 1775, abolished in 1778, revived in 1783) to inquire into the state of the Northern Circars in the Madras Presidency that land in that part of the country was held partly by Zemindars and partly by cultivators direct under the ruling authority. In the fifth report of this inquiry is given an account of the village community which is too valuable to be omitted.

"A village, geographically considered, is a tract of country comprising some hundreds or thousands of acres of arable and waste land; politically viewed, it resembles a corporation or township. Its proper establishment of officers and servants consists of the following descriptions: The *potail*, or head inhabitant, who has the general superintendence of the affairs of the village, settles the disputes of the inhabitants, attends to the police, and performs the duty, already described, of collecting the revenues within his village, a duty which his personal influence and minute acquaintance with the situation and concerns of the people renders him best qualified to discharge; the *curnum*, who keeps the accounts of cultivation and registers everything concerned with it; the *talliar* and *totie*, the duty of the former appearing to consist in a wider and more enlarged sphere of action, in gaining information of crimes and offences, and in escorting and protecting persons travelling from one village to another, the province of the latter appearing to be more immediately confined to the village, consisting, among other duties, in guarding the crops and assisting in measuring them; the *boundary-man*, who preserves the limits of the village or gives evidence respecting them in case of dispute; the *superintendent of tanks and water-courses* distributes the water therefrom for the purpose of agriculture; the *Bramin,* who performs the village worship; the *schoolmaster,* who is seen teaching the children in the villages to read and write in the sand; the *calendar Bramin,* or astrologer, who proclaims the lucky or unpropitious periods for sowing and threshing; the *smith* and *carpenter,* who manufacture the implements of agriculture and build the dwelling of the Ryot; the *potman,* or potter; the *washerman;* the *barber;* the *cowkeeper,* who looks after the cattle; the *doctor;* the *dancing-girl,* who attends at rejoicings; the *musician,* and the *poet.* These officers and servants generally constitute the establishment of a village; but in some parts of the country it is of less extent, some of the duties and functions above described being united in the same person; in others it exceeds the number of individuals which have been described.

"Under this simple form of municipal government the inhabitants of the country have lived from time immemorial. The boundaries of villages have been but seldom altered, and though the villages themselves have been sometimes injured, and even desolated, by war, famine, and disease, the same name, the same limits, the same interests, and even the same families have continued for ages. The inhabitants give themselves no trouble about the breaking up and divisions of kingdoms; while the village remains entire, they care not to what power it is transferred or to what sovereign it devolves; its internal economy remains unchanged;)the Potail is still the head inhabitant, and still acts as the petty judge and magistrate and collector or renter of the village."

These village communities were not confined to the South. They existed more or less all through India,

North, South, East and West. They have now vanished, though in some places the name is still kept up. The substance, however, is gone, perhaps never again to appear. The causes that have operated to bring about the result have been stated by Mr. R. C. Dutt as follows:

"Two causes, however, operated from the commencement of the British rule to weaken the old village communities. An extreme anxiety to enhance the land revenue to its very utmost limits induced the administrators to make direct arrangements with every individual cultivator. An equally unreasonable anxiety to centralise all judicial and executive powers in their own hands led the modern rulers to virtually set aside those village functionaries who had so long exercised these powers within the limits of their own villages. Deprived of their functions, the village communities rapidly fell into decay, and the Indian administration of the present day, better organised in many respects than the administration of the past, suffers from this disadvantage, that it is more autocratic, and rests in a far less degree on the co-operation of the people themselves."

The history of the Zemindari settlements in the Northern Circars (Madras) may be stated in a few words. These lands were settled with Zemindars until 1778; then Sir Thomas Rumbold made a five-years' settlement. In 1783 the practice of annual settlements was resumed and continued until 1786, when a three-years' settlement was concluded on an increased revenue demand. In 1789 a settlement for three and eventually for five years was concluded, and the Zemindars were assessed *at two-thirds of their gross collections.* For the lands not occupied by the Zemindar was adopted the system which has since become known as the Ryotwari system. So far back as 1787 two different methods were adopted for collecting the revenue due on these lands. "In some places they collected it directly from the cultivators in kind by taking a share of the produce as the Government revenue; and in other places they farmed out the lands for stipulated sums." The principle of the system was "dealing direct with the cultivator." As other parts of the country came into the possession of the Company, the principle of settling directly with individual cultivators was made universal and the rights of all middlemen were swept away. The one name which is indelibly written on the Land Administration of the Madras Presidency is that of Thomas Munro, who afterwards rose to the Governorship of the Presidency under the title of Sir Thomas Munro. His assessments were *fairly moderate*. In no instance, said he, in one of his letters of October 7, 1800, was the Government share "more than one-third. In many it was not more than one-fifth or one-sixth, and in some not more than one-tenth of the *gross produce*."[13] Even under those moderate assessments he showed an increase of 50 per cent., i.e., from £402,637 to £606,909, within seven years. From the context of a letter published by Mr. Dutt in his book "Early History of British Rule" (page 126) it appears that but for fear of being overruled by the Directors Munro's assessments should have been even more moderate. He had before him the example of a friend "who was about to be removed from the

[13] The share of Government under the Hindus varied from 1/10 to 1/6 but never exceeded that amount.

service because he had made assessments which the Board of Revenue had considered too low" (page 127).

While Munro was making the Ryotwari settlements in districts not held by Zemindars, steps were taken in the latter by which it was attempted to oust the proprietors from their holdings. The Zemindars, called the Polygars, revolted and had to be punished. In addition to the death sentences passed on some of the rebels, their lands were confiscated and subjected to Ryotwari settlement. With fourteen of these Southern Polygars permanent settlement was made in 1803. The revenues fixed varied *from 41 per cent. to 51 per cent. of the gross rental.* Similar settlements were made with the Polygars in Sivaganga and Ramnad. Permanent settlements were also made with the Western Polygars in 1802. But the Polygars of Chitoor were mostly expelled from their estates as a punishment for having resisted British claims by show of force.

The policy of Lord Wellesley was to "obtain for Government the utmost that the land will yield in the shape of rent."[14] The Ryotwari system was found to be most favourable to this object and was almost universally adopted. The greatest champion of the system was Thomas Munro who had settled several districts on those principles and had recommended the universal adoption of them for the rest of the country. Before his departure for Europe in 1807 he made a report recommending a Ryotwari settlement for the

[14] Henry St. George Tucker, "Memorials of Indian Government, London, 1853," p. 113.

ceded Districts adding (a) that the assessment should be permanent and that (b) "the exorbitant revenue he had raised,"[15] viz., 45 per cent. of the gross produce, be reduced by a quarter.

Munro's recommendation of a permanent Ryotwari settlement was confirmed by Lord William Bentinck, the then Governor of Madras, and six years later when Munro was examined by the Committee of the House of Commons, in connection with the renewal of the East India Company's Charter in 1813, he repeated his views most forcibly. In the meantime the Board of Revenue at Madras had started another idea, viz., that of a permanent village settlement, which differed from both the Bengal Zemindari settlements and Munro's Ryotwari settlements in so far as the settlement was to be made neither with individual landlords nor with individual cultivators but with each village community as a unit. The Board of Revenue also supported Munro's recommendation for a reduction of 25 per cent. in the government demand. The recommendations of the Board of Revenue were accepted by the Government of Madras, which authorised the "conclusion of triennial village settlements as a preparatory measure to the introduction of a permanent village settlement."[16] And on the expiration of these triennial settlements they proposed to the Court of Directors the conclusion of a decennial settlement to become permanent if approved by the Directors.[17]

[15] R. C. Dutt, "India Under Early British Rule," p. 135.

[16] Letters of the Government of Madras of 25th May, 1808, quoted by R. C. Dutt in his "India Under Early British Rule," p. 142.

[17] Letter of the 29th February, 1812, quoted by R. C. Dutt in his "India Under Early British Rule," p. 142.

The Directors, however, refused to sanction the element of permanancy. The Government of Madras made two different appeals to the Court of Directors in favour of a permanent settlement, but in vain. We give the following quotations from these dispatches:

"That agriculture was regarded as the basis of national wealth and prosperity; that it was considered essential to the improvement and extension of agriculture to restrict the demands of Government upon landed property; that it was not supposed Government could lose by this restriction, since without it agriculture would never be improved and extended, nor the resources of the country increased. . . . In offering the foregoing remarks, we have considered the Permanent Settlement strictly as a question of fiscal policy. But it does not need to be shown that it is of vital importance also, as being calculated to give to the mass of the people, who are engaged in agriculture, a deep and permanent interest in the stability of our Government."[18]

In the following year, the Government of Madras made a still more eloquent appeal to the Court of Directors in favour of permanent village settlements and against permanent Ryotwari settlements.

"If the primary object of a Permanent Settlement be to give the people the management of their own affairs, from the belief that their affairs will be indefinitely managed by themselves than by public officers, how little would that object be attained under such a system (the Ryotwari system)? How entirely would all management still remain in those hands from which it was meant to transfer it. It is singular that, under such a system, professedly designed to protect

[18] Letter dated 5th March, 1813.

the rights and interests of landed proprietors, they are to forfeit all property in any land which through general or peculiar calamity or indolence or mismanagement, they may any year fail to cultivate, and their property in it is, on every such occurrence, to escheat to the Government; assuredly a more violent encroachment on landed property, where it really exists, than ever was attempted under any other system. . . .

"He (the cultivator) is not secure against a fraudulent measurement on the estimation of the land he quits or the land he occupies; nay, if to escape from the mode of oppression he resolves not to alter his limits, the current business of agriculture, the means of irrigation, the distribution of Tuccavy, or of an abatement of rent on account of calamity, all must be regulated by men who have no interest in his property, no sympathy with his feelings. Surely it were better that confidence should be reposed where self-interest affords a security against its being abused, and that the people should be left to improve the country in their own way, without the encumbrance of useless and ill-judged aid from public officers, and without the dread of their oppression and rapacity. At any rate, we own that the Ryotwari system, proposed by Colonel Munro, seems to us in no respect to deserve the name of a Permanent Settlement of the land revenue, but, on the contrary, to leave land revenue and landed property as unsettled as ever, and the people liable to all that prying, meddling interference of public officers under which no private concern can prosper. . . .

"The grand difference between the view at present taken in England regarding Indian land revenue and that taken here, seems to be, that in England the fear is that the public demands upon the resources of India may not keep pace with its prosperity; while here the universal sentiment, we believe without any exception whatever, is, that the prosperity of the country is so much depressed by the public demands, that, without the most liberal and judicious management, there is more danger of its resources declining than room to hope for their speedy increase. This is a sentiment which we cannot too strongly convey to your Honourable Court. It is addressed to your wisdom, to your sense of justice, to your humanity; it concerns the successful administration of your Government no less than the welfare and happiness of a numerous population and the prosperity of an extensive country, favoured by nature, protected from internal commotion and foreign assault, and requiring only moderation in the demands of Government upon its resources to render it rich and flourishing. Compared with the attainment of these great ends, of how little value appears every sacrifice which can be made for them?"[19]

In 1818, the Board of Revenue repeated its views on the desirability of a permanent village settlement in a minute which R. C. Dutt calls "one of the most exhaustive and memorable minutes ever written in India" and from which we make the following extracts:

"The ancient Zemindars and Polygars were, in fact, the nobility of the country, and though the origin of some of their tenures would not bear too minute a scrutiny, they were connected with the people by ties which it was more politic, more liberal, and more just to strengthen than to dissolve. Had our power in the Circars been as strong on the acquisition of these provinces as it subsequently became at the period of the transfer of the Ceded Districts, the ancient Zemindars, like the Polygars of the latter country, might perhaps have been removed from their lands and reduced to the situation of mere pensioners on our bounty; but when the attachment of the people to their native chieftains and the local situation of many Zem-

[19] Letter dated 12th August, 1814.

indaris are considered, it may be greatly doubted whether such a policy would not have been as unwise as it would have been ungenerous.

. . . .

"In the Northern Division of Arcot, all these superiorities (special rights of Mirasdars or hereditary peasant proprietors) were also resumed and incorporated with the public revenue. In short, the survey assessment was raised so high as to absorb in the Government revenue any little rent remaining to the landholders. No intermediate person was acknowledged between the State and the actual cultivator. . . .

"The Ryotwari settlement, in fact, was made annually, frequently by the Tehsildars and Sheristadars (subordinate low-paid officers), and was not in general concluded until after the crop had been raised; the system then was to make as high a settlement as it was practicable to realise. If the crop was good, the demand was raised as high within the survey rates as the means of the Ryots would admit; if the crop was bad, the last farthing was notwithstanding demanded, and no remission was allowed unless the Ryot was totally unable to pay the rent. On this point the most severe scrutiny was instituted, for not only was the whole of the Collector's detailed establishment of servants employed in an investigation of his means, but each of his neighbours were converted into inquisitors by being themselves made liable for his failure unless they could show that he was possessed of property. . . .

"He (the cultivator) was constrained to occupy all such fields as were allotted to him by the revenue officers, and whether he cultivated them or not, he was, as Mr. Thackery emphatically terms it, saddled with the rent of each. To use the words of Mr. Chaplin, the Collector in Bellary, one of the most able of Colonel Munro's former assistants, and still one of the most strenuous advocates of the Ryotwari system, it was the custom under it, 'to exert in a great degree the authority, which is incompatible with the existing regulations, of compelling the inhabitants to cultivate a quantity of ground proportionate to their circumstances.' This he explains to have been done by 'the power to confine and punish them,' exercised by the Collector and his native revenue servants; and he expressly adds, that if the Ryot was driven by these oppressions from the fields which he tilled, it was the established practice 'to follow the fugitive wherever he went, and by assessing him at discretion, to deprive him of all advantage he might expect to derive from a change of residence.'

"Ignorant of the true resources of the newly-acquired countries, as of the precise nature of their landed tenures, we find a small band of foreign conquerors no sooner obtaining possession of a vast extent of territory, peopled by various nations, differing from each other in language, customs, and habits, than they attempt what would be called a Herculean task, or rather a visionary project even in the most civilised countries of Europe, of which every statistical information is possessed, and of which the Government are one with the people, viz., to fix a land-rent, not on each province, district or country, not on each estate or farm, but on every separate field within their dominions. In pursuit of this supposed improvement, we find them unintentionally dissolving the ancient ties, the ancient usages which united the republic of each Hindu village, and by a kind of agrarian law, newly assessing and parceling out the lands which from time immemorial had belonged to the Village Community collectively, not only among the individual members of the privileged order (Mirasdars and Kadeems), but even among the inferior tenantry (Pykaris), we observe them ignorantly denying, and by their denial abolishing private property in the land, resuming what belonged to a public body (the Gramamanium), and conferring in lieu of it a stipend in money on one individual; professing to limit their demand to each field, but in fact, by establishing such limit, an unattainable maximum, assessing the Ryot at discretion, and, like the Mussulman Government which preceded them, binding the Ryot by force to the plough, compelling him to till the land acknowledged to be over-assessed, dragging him back to it if he absconded, deferring their demand upon him until his crop came to maturity, then taking from him all that could be obtained, and leaving him nothing but his bullocks and seed grain, nay, perhaps obliged to supply him even with these, in order to renew his melancholy task of cultivating, not for himself, but for them."

The village system advocated by the Board of Revenue was rejected, but what pains the student of Indian History is that the permanency of the assessments, recognised and admitted by the Madras Government down to 1862 in accordance with the promises and declarations of Sir Thomas Munro, has since been ignored and the Government demand is being altered at each recurring settlement, which leaves the agricultural population of Madras in a state of perpetual uncertainty and chronic poverty.

Sir Thomas Munro returned to Madras as Governor in May, 1820, and the Ryotwari system was generally introduced in the same month. All opportunities were seized of acquiring Zemindaris and breaking up village tenures through the high rate of assessments by which the state demand was fixed at 45 per cent. or 50 or 55 per cent. of the field produce. . . . In the Administration report of Madras for 1855–56, it was stated that "the Ryot cannot be ejected by Government so long as he pays the fixed assessment. The Ryot under the system is virtually a proprietor on a simple and perfect title, and has all the benefits of a perpetual lease." In 1857 the Board of Revenue said that "a Madras Ryot is able to retain land *perpetually* without an increase of assessment. In 1862 the Government of Madras wrote to the Government of India that "there can be no question that one fundamental principle of the Ryotwari system is that the government demand on the land is fixed for ever." (Letter of February 18, 1862.) Yet none of these declarations and assurances availed the Madras Ryot. Since 1855 he has had "no fixity of rental and no security against enhancement." In 1858, on the transference of the administration of India from the East India Company to the Crown, Lord Halifax laid down the policy of the Government in the matter of land tax. He fixed it at half of the rent, but in practice, says R. C. Dutt, the land tax in Madras sweeps away the whole of the economic rent, particularly in small holdings.

Northern India. Turning to Northern India we find the same story of over-assessments and broken pledges. Benares was permanently annexed in 1795 by Lord Cornwallis.

Six years after, the Nawab of Oudh was compelled by a series of unjust coercive measures, fully noted by James Mill in his "History of British India," to cede to the East India Company "more than one-half and not much less than two-thirds" of his territory. These districts were settled under orders of Henry Wellesley, the brother of the Governor General. That they were over-assessed has been practically admitted by Henry Wellesley himself, who in his work called "Papers Relating to East India Affairs," has said that although he "was still apprehensive" that the settlement had been made upon an erroneous calculation of the existing assets of the country and that the amount would be with difficulty realised, he "determined not to annul the enforcements which had been recently concluded by the collectors from an apprehension that any immediate interference on my part might tend to weaken their authority,—which at that critical period it appeared to him so necessary to support." The sentiments expressed in this extract furnish the keynote of British policy in India. If the "man on the spot" errs on the side of the Government he is to be supported; if he errs on the side of the people, he is to be investigated and overruled. The following figures taken from the statement appended to the report of Henry Wellesley show the increase in the revenue made by the British:

Amount of the Nabob's land Revenue Assessment	£13,523,474
British assessment of the first year	15,619,627
British assessment of the second year	16,162,786
British assessment of the third year	16,823,063

In 1803 a Regulation was enacted (XXV of 1803) recognising the triennial settlement of the land revenue already made, and notifying that, at the expiration of that term, another settlement would be made for three years, to be followed by a settlement for four years, at the expiration of which a permanent settlement would be concluded.

"In these terms," says the Select Committee of the House of Commons in their report of 1812 (Fifth Report, page 51), "the Supreme Government pledged itself to the land holders for the introduction of a Permanent Settlement" at the expiration of an aggregate of ten years from the first settlement of Henry Wellesley.

In 1803 and 1805 first conquests were made in Northern India and practically the whole country between the Jumna and the Ganges now known as the United Province of Agra and Oudh with the exception of parts of Oudh that remained with the Nabob till Dalhousie made short business of him, came under British sway. The Regulations recently introduced in the Ceded Districts of Oudh were introduced into the "Conquered Provinces" also and "the same pledge which had been given to the land holders of the former country" about the permanency of the settlement after ten years "was given in the latter. . . . Two years later the pledge was repeated, but with the proviso that the conclusion of the permanent settlement would depend on the confirmation of the Court of Directors."[20]

Then came the famous discussions on the question of a permanent settlement in Northern India; the Special Commissioners R. W. Cox and Henry St. George Tucker submitted their report, "admitting the benefits of a Permanent Settlement, but declaring themselves adverse to the immediate conclusion of such a settlement in the Ceded and the Conquered Provinces."[21]

The arguments of the Special Commissioners were replied to by H. Clebrooke, who said:

"3. Government is pledged, by the proclamations of the 4th July, 1802 and 11th July, 1805, to conclude a Permanent Settlement with the landholders, at the expiration of the periods there specified, for such lands as may be in a sufficiently improved state of cultivation to warrant the measure, on fair and equitable terms. It was judged expedient, on full consideration of the subject, and with ample knowledge of the circumstances now alleged, to anticipate these periods; and accordingly, in June, 1807, the Governor-General in Council notified to the Zemindars and other proprietors, by Regulation X., 1807, that the Jumma assessed for the last year of the ensuing settlement shall remain fixed for ever, if they be willing to engage, and the arrangement shall receive the sanction of the Court of Directors.

"4. The pledge which has thus been solemnly contracted cannot be forfeited without such a glaring violation of promise as would lose us deservedly the confidence of the people. . . .

"9. The argument on which, if I mistake not, the

[20] Regulation X of 1807.

[21] R. C. Dutt, "India Under Early British Rule," p. 178.

late Commissioners chiefly rely, is that the right of participating in future improvement ought not to be relinquished, because Government is in a manner the landholder and proprietor of a vast estate. . . .

"26. Upon the important occasions of the Permanent Settlement of Bengal and Behar, and of the territories on the coast of Coromandel, and after mature deliberation, a claim of participation in the future improvement of the waste lands was relinquished to a greater extent than the proportion at which they are computed by the late Board of Commissioners in the Ceded and Conquered Provinces.

"27. The happy result of the measure is now witnessed in Bengal. The reviving prosperity of the country, its increased wealth and rapid improvement, are unquestionably due to the Permanent Settlement, the principle of which was so wise that even the serious errors that were committed in filling up the outline of the plan could not ultimately disappoint its views. . . .

"32. I appeal to this experience in preference to any speculative argument. . . . It was expected that the improvement of estates by the culture of waste lands would enrich the landholder by the increase of his usual income, and enable him to meet the variations of seasons and temporary calamities of drought and inundation without needing remissions of revenue.

"33. These expectations have been realised. . . .

"38. It appears to be a very prevalent opinion that the British system of administration is not generally palatable to our Indian subjects. Admitting this opinion to be not unfounded, it follows that while they taste none but the unpalatable parts of the system, and while the only boon which would be acceptable to them is withheld, the landed proprietors and with them the body of the people, must be more and more estranged from the Government, in proportion to the expectations which they formed, and the disappointment which they will have experienced. . . .

"63. I shall conclude by declaring my concurrence in the Commissioners' recommendation, that steadiness, moderation and justice should be the features borne by the administration of Government. But it is not by abandoning a measure deliberately resolved on, and beneficial to our subjects, that we shall prove our steadiness. It is not by grasping at the highest revenue and wringing from our peasants the utmost rent, that we shall evince our moderation; nor is it by depriving the sons of our petty landholders of their birthright that we shall demonstrate our sense of justice." (Colebrook's minute of 1808.)

Lord Minto, then Governor-General, supported H. Colebrook and said that on a mature consideration of all the documents connected with the establishment of a Permanent Settlement in the provinces of Bengal, Behar, Orissa, and Benares, and in the territories dependent on the Presidency of Fort St. George, and of all the reports and minutes respecting the proposed Permanent Settlement in the Ceded and Conquered Provinces, he was entirely satisfied of the sound policy, or rather of the urgent necessity, of the measure. (Letter dated September 15, 1808.)

The Directors, however, had made up their minds. They replied:

"No settlement shall be declared permanent in Cuttack or in any other of our Provinces till the whole proceedings preparatory to it have been submitted to us, and till your resolutions upon these proceedings have received our sanction and concurrence."

Nine months after, they again wrote that "the object of the present despatch is to caution you in the most pointed manner against pledging us to the extension of the Bengal fixed assessment to our newly acquired territories." (Despatch of 1st February, 1811, and 27th November, 1811.)

The Government of India naturally resented this and pointed out that the pledges given in the Regulations of 1803 and 1805 and the Proclamation which formed a part of Section 29 of Regulation XXV of 1803 were unconditional; that these pledges had been given by the responsible servants and agents of the company and were therefore binding on them. "Had the Honourable Court's dissent," wrote the Indian Government, "to the arrangements established by the Regulations of 1803 and 1805 been signified at an early period after the enaction of those regulations, the inherent powers of control possessed by the court might have been urged in support of such dissent, although those regulations contained no reserve of the court's approval; but now that the whole term of the contract has expired in the ceded provinces, and two-thirds of it in the conquered countries, the annulment of it, at this distant period, could not, we apprehend, as already intimated, be reconciled to the dictates either of policy or justice." [22]

Lord Minto, in a minute recorded by himself, endeavoured to construe the directors' recent orders in a restricted sense, as he could not reconcile a literal construction of those orders "with the maintenance of the faith of government so publicly and so solemnly pledged to the landlords." [23]

One more protest was submitted by Lord Minto against the directors' orders before he left India in

[22] Letter dated 9th October, 1812.
[23] Minute dated 11th July, 1812.

1813. He pointed out that a permanent settlement involved no sacrifice of revenues; that a variable land-tax had been condemned even by Adam Smith in his "Wealth of Nations," as a discouragement to improvements in land; that a permanent settlement could be effected for the estates actually held by the landlords in Northern India without including the waste lands; and finally if the object of good government was "to ameliorate generally the conditions of the natives, it is our firm conviction that no arrangement or measure will tend so speedily and effectually to the accomplishment of those important objects as the establishment of a permanent settlement."[24]

But the directors of the company were obdurate. Their professed desire for the good of the people of India would not move them to surrender their own profits. They had indeed fixed upon a plan of getting out of the pledges given in 1803 and 1805. They suggested an evasion which would not be held valid by any court of justice, and which was unworthy of honest merchants, not to speak of the rulers of an empire.

"Continued possession and a punctual discharge of the dues of government during the triennial leases formed only one part of the condition on which government pledged itself to a permanent settlement with the landholders. There was another and still more important clause in the condition, viz., that the land should, in the interval, be brought to a sufficiently advanced stage of cultivation to warrant us in fixing perpetual limits to our demand upon it. The precise

[24] Letter dated 17th July, 1813.

point of improvement at which such a measure might become expedient, or even justifiable, was not determined by the Regulation of 1803 and 1805, and would not, indeed, be determined by any prospective Regulation. The question was left completely open for the future exercise of the judgment of Government; nor is there anything in these Regulations by which its decision can, or ought to be, in the smallest degree fettered."[25] No Permanent Settlements were made in any estates in 1813, nor have any been made since, which shows that the argument was only a subterfuge to evade a solemn pledge.

Repeated efforts were made by responsible English officers to secure a Permanent Settlement for the Ceded and the Conquered Provinces in accordance with the pledge mentioned above, but the Directors remained obdurate.

All these efforts failed and the policy of the Government as to land tax was embodied in Regulation VII of 1822. The settlements were to be revised periodically. In estates held by superior landlords the assessments were to be so regulated as to leave the landlord a net profit of 20 per cent of the Government demand. When the lands were held by cultivators in common tenancy the State demand might be raised to 95 per cent of the rents. In actual practice it came to "over 83 per cent" in one case and to practically the whole of the economic rent in another.[26]

[25] Letter dated 16th March, 1813.

[26] In this connection it will be interesting to read the following extracts from a minute of Sir Charles Metcalfe about the nature of Indian Village Communities.

"The Village Communities are little Republics, having

The system introduced by Regulation VII of 1822 was found to be impracticable and oppressive. It "broke down ultimately by reason of its own harshness." A new policy was laid down by Regulation IX of 1833, by which the Government demand was re-

nearly everything that they want within themselves, and almost independent of any foreign relations. They seem to last where nothing else lasts. Dynasty after dynasty tumbles down; revolution succeeds to revolution; Hindu, Pathan, Moghal, Mahratta, Sikh, English, are masters in turn; but the Village Communities remain the same. In times of trouble they arm and fortify themselves; a hostile army passes through the country; the Village Community collect their cattle within their walls, and let the enemy pass unprovoked. If plunder and devastation be directed against themselves and the force employed be irresistible, they flee to friendly villages at a distance, but when the storm has passed over they return and resume their occupations. If a country remain for a series of years the scene of continued pillage and massacre, so that the villages cannot be inhabited, the scattered villagers nevertheless return whenever the power of peaceable possession revives. A generation may pass away, but the succeeding generation will return. The sons will take the places of their fathers, the same site for the village, the same position for the houses, the same lands, will be reoccupied by the descendants of those who were driven out when the village was depopulated; and it is not a trifling matter that will drive them out, for they will often maintain their post through times of disturbance and convulsion, and acquire strength sufficient to resist pillage and oppression with success.

"The union of the Village Communities, each one forming a separate State in itself, has, I conceive, contributed more than any other cause to the preservation of the people of India through all revolutions and changes which they have suffered, and it is in a high degree conducive to their happiness and to the enjoyment of a great portion of freedom and independence. I wish, therefore, that the Village Constitutions may never be disturbed, and I dread everything that has a tendency to break them up. I am fearful that a Revenue Settlement with each individual cultivator, as is the practice in the Ryotwari Settlement, instead of one with the Village Community through their representatives, the headmen, might have such a tendency. For this reason, and for this only, I do not desire to see the Ryotwari Settlement generally introduced into the Western Provinces."

duced to *two-thirds of the gross rental* and the settlements were made for thirty years. In accordance with the Regulation, settlements were made by a "very just and humane officer" of the name of Robert Bird, but so high was the Government demand that numerous villages were deserted by the peasants and vast tracts of the country became waste until the Government felt bound to reduce the Government share to 50 per cent. of the net rental in 1855. This continues the basis on which settlements are now made in Northern India.

Bombay. To complete the story of the development of the land tax in India, we have to state what was done in the Bombay Presidency. Bombay was more fortunate than the other provinces, in so far as the administration of its affairs and the settlement of the country, after its annexation in 1817, were entrusted to a man noted for his broad sympathies and statesmanlike desire to promote the prosperity of the people put in his charge. This man was Mountstuart Elphinstone (afterward Sir Mountstuart Elphinstone, author of a monumental history of early and Moslem India).

Elphinstone's "Report on the Territories Conquered from the Peshwas," submitted to the Governor-General in October, 1819, is a masterly account of the country as it was then, and of the measures adopted for its settlement by the British. From it we make the following extracts:

Village Communities. "In whatever point of view we examine the Native Government in the Deccan, the first and most important feature is, the division into villages or townships. These Communities contain in miniature all the materials of a State within themselves, and are almost sufficient to protect their members, if all other governments are withdrawn. Though probably not compatible with a very good form of Government, they are an excellent remedy for the imperfections of a bad one; they prevent the bad effects of its negligence and weakness, and even present some barrier against its tyranny and rapacity.

"Each village has a portion of ground attached to it, which is committed to the management of the inhabitants. The boundaries are carefully marked and jealously guarded. They are divided into fields, the limits of which are exactly known; each field has a name and is kept distinct, even when the cultivation of it has long been abandoned. The villagers are almost entirely cultivators of the ground, with the addition of the few traders and artisans that are required to supply their wants. The head of each village is the Patil, who has under him an assistant, called a Chaugulla, and a clerk called a Kulkarni. There are, besides, twelve village officers well known by the name of Bara Baloti. These are the astrologer, the priest, the carpenter, barber, etc., but the only ones who are concerned in the administration of the government are the Sonar or Potdar, who is silversmith and assayer of money, and the Mhar, who, in addition to various other important duties, acts as watchman to the village. Each of these classes consists of one or more individuals, according as their original families have branched out. The Mhars are seldom fewer than four or five, and there are besides, where those tribes are numerous, very frequently several Phils or Ramoshis, employed also as watchmen, but performing none of the other duties of the Mhar.

"The Patils are the most important functionaries in the villages, and perhaps the most important class in the country. They hold office by a grant from the Government (generally from that of the Moguls), are entitled by virtue of it to land and fees, and have various little privileges and distinctions, of which they are as tenacious as of their land. Their office and emoluments are hereditary, and saleable with the consent of the Government, but are seldom sold, except in cases of extreme necessity, though a partner is sometimes admitted, with a careful reservation of the superiority of the old possessor. The Patil is head of the police and of the administration of justice in his village, but he need only be mentioned here as an officer of revenue. In that capacity he performs on a small scale what a Mamlatdar or a Collector does on a large; he allots the land to such cultivators as have no landed property of their own, and fixes the rent which each has to pay; he collects the revenue for Government from all the Rayats; conducts all its arrangements with them, and exerts himself to promote the cultivation and the prosperity of the village. Though originally the agent of the Government, he is now regarded as equally the representative of the Rayats, and is not less useful in executing the orders of the Government than in asserting the rights, or at least in making known the wrongs of the people.

"A large portion of the Rayats are the proprietors of their estates, subject to the payment of a fixed land tax to Government; their property is hereditary and saleable, and they are never dispossessed while they pay their tax, and even then they have for a long period (at least thirty years) the right of reclaiming their estate on paying the dues of Government. Their land tax is fixed, but the late Mahratta Government loaded it with other impositions, which reduced that advantage to a mere name; yet so far, however, was this from destroying the value of their estates, that although the Government took advantage of their attachment to make them pay considerably more than an Upri, and though all the Mirasdars were in ordinary cases obliged to make up for failures in the payment of each of their body, yet their lands were saleable, and generally at ten years' purchase. . . .

"An opinion prevails throughout the Mahratta country, that under the old Hindu Government all the land was held by Mirasis, and that the Upris were introduced as the old proprietors sank under the tyranny of the Mohammedans. This opinion is supported by the fact that the greater part of the fields now cultivated by Upris are recorded in the village books as belonging to absent proprietors; and affords, when combined with circumstances observed in other parts of the peninsula, and with the light Land Tax authorised by Manu, a strong presumption that the revenue system under the Hindus (if they had a uniform system) was founded on private property in the soil."

Changes Under the British Rule. "The outline of the revenue system adopted since our acquisition of the country is contained in my letter dated July 10th, conveying instructions to the Collectors, and in that dated July 14th, enclosing instructions for Mamlatdars. The leading principles are to abolish farming, but otherwise to maintain the native system; to levy the revenue according to the actual cultivation, to make the assessment light, to impose no new taxes, and to do none away unless obviously unjust; and, above all, to make no innovations. Many innovations were, however, the result of the introduction of foreign rulers and foreign maxims of government; but in the revenue department most of them were beneficial." . . . Then follow certain detailed recommendations which Elphinstone made for the future administration of the country. In conclusion he said:

"But with all these defects, the Mahratta country flourished, and the people seem to have been exempt from some of the evils which exist under our more perfect Government. There must, therefore, have been some advantages in the system to counterbalance its obvious defects, and most of them appear to me to have originated in one fact, that the Government, although it did little to obtain justice for the people, left them the means of procuring it for themselves. The advantage of this was particularly felt among the lower orders, who are most out of reach of their rulers, and most apt to be neglected under all Governments. By means of the Panchayat, they were enabled to effect a tolerable dispensation of justice among themselves; and it happens that most of the objections above stated to that institution do not apply in their case. . . .

"I propose, therefore, that the native system should still be preserved, and means taken to remove its abuses and revive its energy. Such a course will be more welcome to the natives than any entire change, and if it should fail entirely, it is never too late to introduce the Adalat. . . .

"Our principal instrument must continue to be the Panchayat, and that must continue to be exempt from all new forms, interference, and regulation on our part."

We have given these long extracts as they contain the most valuable testimony regarding the institutions of the country in pre-British days and furnish incontestable material for comparison.

But even Elphinstone was unable to override or depose the greed of his masters, the Directors of the East India Company. In reviewing the settlement assessments of the territories under his Governorship he had on several occasions expressed his concern at the rapid growth of revenue, and the only thing he could do was to approve of Mr. Chaplin's decision to fix it at *one-third the gross product.*

We have a piece of valuable evidence on the aspects of this system of taxation left on record by the distinguished English divine, Bishop Heber, who toured India, 1824-26. In his letter to the Right Honourable Charles Williams Wynn, dated Karnatic, March, 1826, he said:

"Neither Native nor European agriculturist, I think, can thrive at the present rate of taxation. Half the gross produce of the soil is demanded by Government, and this, which is nearly the average rate wherever there is not a Permanent Settlement, is sadly too much to leave an adequate provision for the present, even with the usual frugal habits of the Indians, and the very inartificial and cheap manner in which they cultivate the land. Still more is it an effective bar to anything like improvement; it keeps the people, even in favourable years, in a state of abject penury; and when the crop fails in even a slight degree, it involves a necessity on the part of the Government of enormous outlays in the way of remission and distribution, which, after all, do not prevent men, women, and children dying in the streets in droves, and the roads being strewed with carcasses. In Bengal, where, independent of its exuberant fertility, there is a Permanent Assessment, famine is unknown. In Hindustan (Northern India) on the other hand, I found a general feeling among the King's officers, and I myself was led from some circumstances to agree with them, that *the peasantry in the Company's Provinces are, on the whole, worse off, poorer, and more dispirited, than the subjects of the Native Princes;* and here in Madras, where the soil is, generally speaking, poor, the difference is said to be still more marked. The fact is, no Native Prince demands the rent which we do, and making every allowance for the superior regularity of our system, etc., *I met with very few men who will not, in confidence, own their belief that the people are over-taxed, and that the country is in a gradual state of impoverishment.* The Collectors do not like to make this avowal officially. Indeed, now and then, a very able Collector succeeds in lowering the rate to the people, while by diligence he increases it to the State. But, in general, all gloomy pictures are avoided by them as reflecting on themselves, and drawing on them censure from the Secretaries at Madras or Calcutta, while these, in their turn, plead the earnestness with which the Directors at home press for more money.

"I am convinced that it is only necessary to draw less money from the peasants, and to spend more of what is drawn within the country, to open some door to Indian industry in Europe, and to admit the natives to some greater share in the magistracy of their own people, to make the Empire as durable as it would be happy."[27]

With this might be read the following answers given by Mr. Robert Richards, a retired Anglo-Indian officer, to the questions put to him by the Committee of the House of Commons in an enquiry on the subject.

"Where the revenue is collected, as it is in India, on the principle of the Government being entitled to one-half of the gross produce of the soil, and vast numbers of officers, whose acts it is impossible to control, are also employed in the realisation of this revenue, it is a moral impossibility for any people whatever to live or prosper so as to admit of a very extensive commercial intercourse being carried on with them. . . .

"It may be done (i.e. manufacture of articles for foreign exportation) in lands not subject to the aforementioned exorbitant tax. It may also be the case in Bengal, where the Permanent Settlement has been enforced for many years, and where its original ruinous pressure is no longer so severely felt; but it would be quite impossible in lands, for example, subject to the Ryotwari Tax, or from lands where from 45 per cent. to 50 per cent. of the gross produce is actually levied as revenue.

"I am personally acquainted with instances where the revenue assessed upon certain lands has actually

[27] Bishop Heber's "Memoirs and Correspondence," by his Widow, London, 1830, Vol. II, p. 413. The italics are our own.

exceeded the gross produce. I have also known other lands in India where a revenue has been assessed as being specifically derivable from rice lands, plantations of fruit trees, pepper, vines, and other articles, and each portion particularly described; but on comparing the assessment with the lands in question, those very lands have been found to have been nothing but jungle within the memory of man."

The whole subject has been exhaustively discussed by Lieutenant-Colonel Briggs in a book of 500 pages called "The Present Land Tax in India" (London, 1838), in which he points out that among ancient nations — the Greeks, the Romans, the Persians and the Chinese, the right of the State consisted in levying a tax of a tenth of the produce. Among the Hindus the right of the King was to a levy of one-eighth, one-sixth, or one-twelfth of the produce according to the nature of the soil and the expense of cultivation. We make no apology for making the following quotation from page 108 of his book:

"The flourishing condition of the country under the Moghal Emperors is recorded by all European travellers who have visited the East within the last three centuries; and the wealth, the population, and the national prosperity of India, far surpassing what they had seen in Europe, filled them with astonishment. That the condition of the people and the country under our Government presents no such spectacle, is every day proclaimed by ourselves, and we may therefore assume it to be true. . . .

"If I have proved that we have departed from the practice of our predecessors, that we have established a system far exceeding theirs in rigour, even in the worst of their regular governments, then indeed there is some reason to call for a reform, and to hope at least for investigation. . . .

"I conscientiously believe that under no Government whatever, Hindu or Mohommedan, professing to be actuated by law, was any system so subversive of the prosperity of the people at large as that which has marked our administration. . . .

"Although we have everywhere confessed that the heavy pressure of taxation was the most cruel injury they sustained, we have in no instance alleviated that pressure. So far from it, we have applied a false measure for fixing the impost, that of money instead of produce; we have pretended to abolish minor taxes on other classes, but we have laid the amount on the landholder; and by minute scrutiny into every individual's concerns, have, under the plea of justice to ourselves, in many instances deprived the cultivators of the means they enjoyed of paying the heavy taxes from which they sought relief under us, till by rigid exactions we have increased our own revenue and reduced the people to the condition of mere labourers. This is the professed maxim of our rule, the certain and inevitable result of taking the whole surplus profit of land. . . .

"Having assumed that the Government is the sole landlord, it (the present Government), considers the land to be the most profitable source of all revenue; it employs a host of public servants to superintend the cultivator; and it professes to take all the profit. A Land-Tax like that which now exists in India, professing to absorb the whole of the landlord's rent, was never known under any Government in Europe or Asia."

The results of the settlements in the Bombay Presidency in 1824–28 are thus stated in the official language of the Bombay Administration Report of 1872–73 (page 41).

"From the outset it was found impossible to collect anything approaching to the full revenue. In some districts not one-half could be realised. Things now went rapidly from bad to worse. Every year brought its addition to the accumulated arrears of revenue, and the necessity for remission or modification of rates. . . . Every effort, lawful and unlawful, was made to get the utmost out of the wretched peasantry, who were subjected to torture, in some instances, cruel and revolting beyond all description, if they would not or could not yield what was demanded. Numbers abandoned their homes, and fled into the neighbouring Native States. Large tracts of land were thrown out of cultivation, and in some districts no more than a third of the cultivable area remained in occupation."

It is no wonder that the system had to be abandoned and was replaced by another inaugurated by the joint report of Messrs. Goldsmid, Wingate and Davidson in 1847, which established the principle of the separate assessment of each field as distinguished from a holding or a village, for a fixed term of 30 years on the basis of the estimated value of lands. The Bombay settlements are now made on these principles.

The Punjab. The Punjab, which is said to be the granary of India, was annexed to the British dominions, part by Lord Hardinge in 1846 and the rest of it by Lord Dalhousie in 1849.

How the British came into conflict with the Sikhs in the Punjab, after the strong hand of Maharajah Ranjit Singh was removed from the control of its affairs by his death in 1839; how bravely the Sikhs fought; how they were betrayed by the treachery of their own leaders and how Lord Hardinge decided to annex a part of the province, leaving the rest under the sovereignty of the minor son of Ranjit Singh, to be administered during his minority by a council of regency appointed by him and under the guidance of a British Resident with practically unlimited powers, are matters which belong to the domain of political history and are outside the scope of this book. So are all the subsequent events which led to the second Sikh War and the annexation of the Punjab by Lord Dalhousie, in spite of the protests made by Henry Lawrence, the British resident at the Court of the minor Maharaja of the Punjab and many others, who argued that having assumed the guardianship of the person and the property of the minor Maharaja by a treaty solemnly entered into between the British Government and the three guardians of the Maharaja in 1846, the British Government could not by any rule of law, or of justice, equity and good conscience, deprive the Maharaja of his dominions, simply because the Sikh army or some of the subordinate leaders of the Punjab had revolted against the authority of the British. Lord Dalhousie knew of no law but that of Empire-making. The map of British India was incomplete without the Punjab, so he annexed the province and his masters in England approved his decision. There is an authentic official record of the condition of the Punjab, at the time of the annexation, in the first administrative report of the province, compiled by Mr. (afterwards Sir) Richard Temple, under the instructions of the Lawrence brothers, afterwards known as Sir Henry and Lord John Lawrence.

This report shows that the Sikh rule fully recognised private property in land and although the taxation was heavy yet "in some respects the Government gave back with one hand what it had taken with the other." We are told that the land tax under Mahajara Ranjit Singh was in theory assumed to be one-half of the gross produce, but in practice "may be said to have varied from two-fifths to one-third of the gross produce." It was raised not in money but in kind and it was therefore, says R. C. Dutt, proportionate to the produce of the fields in good years as well as in bad years. Under such a system cultivators were not called upon to pay a fixed and immutable sum when their harvest had failed; nor were they required in years of low prices to pay a revenue, calculated on the basis of high prices.[28]

John Lawrence, the first Chief Commissioner of the Punjab after annexation, was a kind-hearted ruler, sympathetic to the people, and his instructions were contained in the following sentence which occurs in one of his letters to Nicholson: "Assess low, leaving fair and liberal margin to the occupiers of the soil and they will increase their cultivation and put the revenue almost beyond the reach of bad seasons." But the actual assessments were not low. Mr. S. S. Thorburn, ex-commissioner in the Punjab, has said that the first effect of the British occupation of the Punjab was over-assessment (Digby's "Prosperous British India," footnote on p. 91). In 1847–48 the Land Revenue of the Punjab was £820,000. Within three years of

[28] Much light has been thrown on Ranjit Singh's Land assessments and his anxiety for the welfare of his subjects by recent researches made by a Punjabi Hindu scholar of the name of Sita Ram, a graduate of the Punjab University, Lahore.

the British annexation it went up to £1,060,000.[29] "There has been a general demand," says the Punjab report for 1852, "among the agriculturists for a return to grain payments,— to a division or appraisement of the crops every season." The figures for 1856–57 and 1857–58 show a considerable increase in revenue as compared with the figures for 1852.

	Demanded	*Collections*
1856–57	£1,485,000	£1,452,000
1857–58	£1,465,000	£1,452,000

In the regular settlements started in 1860, one-sixth of the produce was demanded as the land revenue, but by later rules framed under the Land Revenue Act of 1871 the Government limited its demand to one-half of the actual rents paid by ordinary tenants-at-will in average years, in accordance with the policy determined upon in connection with the then North-western Provinces. In theory, that is the principle on which the land tax is assessed in the Punjab now. Additions to it have been made in the shape of water-rates and various cesses for roads, police, education, etc., etc. The story of these cesses has been very effectively told by Mr. Thorburn, I. C. S. (a retired Financial Commissioner of the Punjab) in his book called "The Punjab in Peace and War," London, 1904. When the Government decided to establish a Famine Insurance Fund every province was required to contribute. Mr. Thorburn gives a picture of how the Punjab quota was raised. Says he: "In the eyes of the Punjab Government, the peasantry were the class to be squeezed, they being 'prosperous,' lightly

[29] Dutt; "India in the Victorian Age" (1906), p. 90.

assessed, accustomed to bear burdens without murmuring and prospectively the chief beneficiaries from the tax. The sum wanted was £120,000 each year. To enhance the land revenue *pro tanto* would have been simple but illegal." So "the legal difficulty was surmounted by calling the enhancements a 'cess.' Accordingly an additional local rate cess of 6 per cent. on the land revenue was legalised and levied." (Page 236.)

Central Provinces. The story of the development of the land tax in the Central Provinces is very similar to that of the other provinces. Immediately after the annexation of the different parts, enormous increases in the land tax were the features of the British assessment. For example, in the Hoshangabad and Leonee districts "the assessment fixed by Major Macpherson in 1821 was £10,359 from an area which had been assessed by the Mahratta Government at £2,277 only." In 1825 it was still further increased to £13,877. This enormous demand could not be realised and remissions had to be made,[30] which "were not sufficient and very strenuous efforts were made to collect the revenue by any means, so that to this day, a most lively recollection of the tortures and cruelties then suffered lives in the minds of the Zemindars." (Settlement Report of Hoshangabad, 1855, by Charles Elliot, paragraph 50.) At last in 1836 a twenty-year settlement was made at a reduced assessment of £6,192.

In the settlement of the Sagor by Col. Maclean (1867) we find the following remarks: "The Government demands press so heavily upon the people that all

[30] R. C. Dutt, "India in the Victorian Age" (1904), p. 292.

enterprise has been crushed, and there is not the slightest attempt at improvement. I have personally satisfied myself that in many instances the Government demand exceeds the gross rental assets of some villages.

"The people have lost heart to that extent that in some instances the rightful owners of hereditary descent refused on any terms to accept the proprietary rights of villages.

"The impressions conveyed to me on inspecting these tracts was that the people were dead, so vast was the desolation, and so scarce the signs of life or of human beings." (Settlement report of Sagar, by Colonel Maclean in 1867.) It is needless to add that this state of things was strongly condemned by the Government of India and new settlements were made in 1863–67. The principle of one-half of the rental of states as government revenue, was adopted, but the actual results in some cases exceeded that proportion (see a table given by Mr. R. C. Dutt on page 30 of his book called "India in the Victorian Age," which he takes from a letter of the Chief Commissioner to the Governor-General of India, No. 1862 of April 11, 1901).

The Present Policy as to the Land Tax. The more recent history of the question and the controversy on the subject have been summed up by Mr. R. C. Dutt in a chapter headed "The Land Resolutions of Lords Ripon and Curzon," in his book "India in the Victorian Age." This chapter is a fair summary of the case on both sides and gives ample quotations from the originals. The general principle is that the Government demand is fixed at 50 per cent. of the rental and the settlement is made for twenty to thirty years. For the effect of this policy on the economic condition of the population of India depending on agriculture and comprising nine-tenths of the whole, the reader is referred to the next chapter.

The general Government position on the subject has been given by us in the earlier part of this chapter from the Blue Book for 1913–14, viz., the statement showing the moral and material progress of India.

A Summary of Land Revenue Receipts from 1861 to 1913–14.

	Land Revenue Receipts, excluding receipts due to irrigation *Land Revenue Receipts* £
1881–1885 (5 years' average)	13,287,000
1866–70 "	13,227,000
1871–75 "	13,977,000
1876–1880 (includes the great famine of South India)	14,076,000
1881–1885 (5 years' average)	14,748,000
1886–1890 "	15,448,000
1891–1895 "	16,522,000
1895–96 "	17,467,000
1896–97 (Famine Year)	15,983,000
1897–98	17,123,000
1898–99	18,307,000
1899–1900 (Famine Year)	17,205,000
1900–1901	17,503,000
1900–1905 (Five years' average)	18,493,000
1906–11 "	20,096,000
1911–12 (Single year)	20,765,000
1912–13	21,282,000
1913–14	21,392,000

"The total increase in the gross land revenue during the past fifty years," says the writer of the Government memorandum (1909) "has been sixty per cent.

measured in rupees; though as the gold value of the rupee has fallen from 24d. to 16d. the increase, if measured in gold, has been less than 6 per cent."

PART FOUR

Even as we look on, India is becoming feebler and feebler. The very life-blood of the great multitude under our rule is slowly, yet ever faster, ebbing away.

—H. M. HYNDMAN,

In "Bankruptcy of India," page 152.

CHAPTER IX

ECONOMIC CONDITION OF THE PEOPLE

"THERE is one fact of all supreme importance — the extreme poverty of the Indian cultivator, and, indeed, of the whole Indian population. Poverty in England or America or Germany is a question of the distribution of wealth. In India it is a question of production." A. Loveday, in "The History and Economies of Indian Famines," p. 5. London (1914).

The Poverty of the Masses. The real answer to the question propounded in the concluding lines of the last chapter, is to be found in the economic conditions of the country and the general poverty of the masses. Here again, the official and non-official versions differ widely. Below is an official expression, culled from a memorandum presented to Parliament in 1909 under the title

SOME RESULTS OF THE INDIAN ADMINISTRATION DURING THE PAST FIFTY YEARS

"In any comparison between the condition of the people of India and those of Europe, it must be remembered that in India, every one marries and marries early; that the population tends to increase at a rate varying from ½ per cent. per annum on the upper Ganges plain, to 4 per cent. per annum in Burma; that there is no poor law or system of poor relief, but everywhere widespread and openhanded charity, so that the infirm, the old, the sick, the cripple, the priest besides many who prefer a mendicant's life, are in ordinary years supported by the alms of their neighbours. Further, it must be remembered that in rural India, from the nature of the climate, and immemorial custom, the poorer classes have fewer garments, and can replenish them more cheaply, than is the case in Europe. Clothes, warmth, shelter, furniture, cost very little for the rural Indian family; the bulk of the population are satisfied with two meals a day, of millet cakes or porridge, some pulse or green vegetable, salt and oil. In coast districts of southern India, and in Moslem families, a little salt fish or meat is added to the *daily* (?) meal."

" General:

" So far as ordinary tests can be applied, the average Indian landholder, trader, ryot and handicraftsman, is better off than he was fifty years ago. He consumes more salt, more tobacco and more imported luxuries and conveniences than he did a generation back. Where house to house inquiries have been made, it has been found that *the average villager eats more food and has a better house than his father; that brass or copper vessels have taken the place of the coarse earthenware of earlier times; and that his family possess more clothes than formerly.* There are exceptional districts, like North Behar, where the rural population is extraordinarily dense, or parts of the Deccan where the soil is extremely poor, and the rainfall precarious; in such tracts, the condition of the landless labourer is still deplorably bad. There are other exceptional tracts, such as lower Burma, Assam, Malabar, Canara, the Himalayan districts, and a great part of Eastern Bengal, where the population is sparse, or not too dense, the soil is rich, the rainfall always abundant, and good markets are at hand; in such tracts, wages are high, work and food are abundant, there is a comparatively high grade of living, and there is little or no *real* poverty. The greater part of India lies between these exceptional extremes, and on the whole, the standard of comfort in an average Indian village household is better than it was fifty years ago. It is quite certain that the population of India absorbs and hoards more of the precious metals than it did formerly, for during the past fifty years, India's net absorption from outside, of gold and silver, has amounted to the equivalent of 6303 millions of rupees, or an increase of 126 millions a year, while during the 22 years ending with 1857, India's net absorption of the precious metals averaged only thirty-two millions a year.

"Conditions of different classes; 1. The Landholding Class. 2. The Trading Class. 3. The Professional Class. 4. The Tenant or Ryot Class. 5. The Labouring Class." (We omit the paragraphs relating to the first three classes.)

"The tenant or ryot class in all provinces, enjoy some share, in some districts a considerable share, in the increased profits of agriculture. In Eastern and Central Bengal, the ryots are well off. In the Central Provinces, where tenant's right is exceptionally strong, the ryots are mostly in good circumstance. But in Behar, in most of the Agra Province and in Oude, the tenant ryot is weak, or has been but recently placed on a firm footing; the population is dense, holdings are small, and many of the ryots are in poor circumstances. They and their families earn something in good years by labour outside their holdings, and when the season is favourable, they live fairly well. A ryot with a tenant right under the land, can generally get credit in a year of short harvest but in a famine year, many of the ryots in the last-named tracts must and do break down.

"The labouring classes, who have no beneficial interest in the land, are in India a smaller section of the people than in England. Still, out of the total Indian population of 294 millions, there are a vast number of labourers, and their condition is most important to the condition of the country . . . the wages . . . have greatly increased. . . . The landless labourer in the thickly populated rural tracts, remote from railways or new industries, lives poorly now, as in generations past, and their wages or earnings, are in some districts, still very small."

The statements contained in the memorandum are very greatly exaggerated, one-sided and incomplete. The writer of the report speaks of the rise in wages, but he does not mention the rise in prices and gives no data on which to base the generalities indulged in by him. A rise in wages is valueless if the rise in prices be proportionately higher. Add to it the fact that the value of the Indian rupee has steadily gone down. It was 2s. in the fifties, about 1s. 10d. in the seventies, 1s. 4d. in the nineties, where it stands now. The statement that "the average villager eats more food" is absurdly false. The argument based on population will be noticed in the chapter on famines, and that on the absorption of precious metals at the end of this book. The picture drawn in this memorandum is wholly incompatible with the fact that the average income of an Indian is £2, or $10.00 a year. In the meantime, we will let eminent Englishmen speak on the poverty of the masses, and the reader may be left to draw his own conclusions. With reference to the statement of the strength of the labouring class the census report of 1911 fixes the number of farm servants and field labourers alone at forty-one millions.

Testimony of English Public Men. Sir William Hunter, one of the most candid writers and a distinguished historian of India, director-general of Indian statistics for many years, declared that 40,000,000 of the people of India were seldom or never able to satisfy their hunger.

Says Mr. J. S. Cotton in his book, "Colonies and Dependencies," p. 68 (1883): "If the security of British rule has allowed the people to increase it does not follow that it has promoted the general prosperity. That could only be done in one of two ways — either by producing a distinct rise in the standard of living among the lowest classes or by diverting a considerable section of the people from the sole occupation of agriculture. . . . Neither of these things has been done. Competent authorities indeed are of opinion that the condition of the lowest classes has become worse under the British rule."

Mr. A. O. Hume, Secretary to the Government of India in the Agricultural Department, wrote in 1880: "Except in very good seasons, multitudes for months every year cannot get sufficient food for themselves and family."

Sir Auckland Colvin, once a Finance Minister in India, describes the tax-paying community as made up in the main of "men whose income at best is barely sufficient to afford them the sustenance necessary to support life, living as they do upon bare necessities."

Sir Charles Elliott, once Chief Commissioner of Assam, wrote in 1888: "I do not hesitate to say that half the agricultural population do not know from one year's end to another, what it is to have a full meal."

The Indian Witness, a Christian paper, once remarked: "It is safe to assume that 100,000,000 of the population of India have an annual income of not more than $5.00 a head."

An American missionary wrote from Southern India in 1902: "The most trying experience I ever had was a three weeks' tour in September of last year (1901). My tent was surrounded day and night, and one sentence dinned perpetually into my ears: 'We are dying for lack of food.' People are living on one meal every two or three days. I once carefully examined the earnings of a congregation of three hundred, and found the average amounted to less than one farthing a head per day. They did not live, they eked out an existence. I have been in huts where the people were living on carrion. Yet in all these cases, there was no *recognised famine!* In Heaven's name, if this is not famine, what is it? The extreme poverty of the poorer classes of India offers conditions altogether extraordinary. Life is the narrowest and hardest conceivable, with no prospect of any improvement. For a family of six persons, many an outfit, including house, utensils, furniture, clothing and all, is worth less than $10.00. The average income for such a family will not exceed fifty cents per head a month, and is frequently little over half that. It may therefore be surmised that not much of this income is spent upon cultivation of the mind, sanitation, or the appearance of the dwelling."[1]

Average Income of the People. According to official estimates, the maximum average annual income per head of the people of India is thirty rupees. Lord

[1] Quoted from William Digby's "Condition of the People of India," 1902, pp. 14–15.

Cromer, then Finance Minister for India, made the first estimate in 1882, placing the average at twenty-seven rupees; Lord Curzon, the late Viceroy, estimated the income of the agricultural population, 85 per cent. of the whole, to be Rs. 30 per year. In his budget speech for 1901, Lord George Hamilton, then Secretary of State for India, said the average income was Rs. 30 (£2); Mr. William Digby, C. I. E., after a full and exhaustive study of the condition of the people, financially and industrially, furnishes overwhelming evidence, as yet unanswered to the contrary, to show that the average annual income of the people of India is not over Rs. 17½ (about six dollars). Considering the value of the rupee, which is equivalent to about thirty-three cents American money, we have the startling condition of millions of people subsisting on from $6.00 to $10.00 per year, or about two cents a day,—this by official estimate.

The Rev. Dr. Sunderland cites these facts and figures, in support of his observations on Indian famines:

"The truth is, the poverty of India is something we can have little conception of, unless we have actually seen it, as alas, I have. . . . Is it any wonder that the Indian peasant can lay up nothing for time of need? . . . The extreme destitution of the people is principally responsible for the devastations of Plague; the loss of life from this terrible scourge is startling. It reached 272,000 in 1901; 500,000 in 1902; 800,000 in 1903; and over 1,000,000 in 1904. It still continues unchecked. The vitality of the people has been reduced by long semi-starvation. So long as the present destitution of India continues, there is small ground for hope that the Plague can be overcome. . . . The real cause of famines in India is not lack of rain; it is not over-population; it is the extreme, the abject, the awful poverty of the people."

The following observation was made in "Moral and Material Progress of India for 1874-75" (Parliamentary Blue Book):

"The Calcutta missionary conference dwelt on the miserable, abject condition of the Bengal ryots, and there is evidence that they suffer many things, and are often in want of absolute necessities. . . . In the Northwestern Provinces, the wages of agricultural labourers have hardly varied at all since the beginning of this century; and after the payment of the rent, the margin left for the cultivator's subsistence is less than the value of the labour he has expended . . . many live on a coarse grain, which is most unwholesome, and produces loin palsy. . . . This extreme poverty among the agricultural population is one of the reasons which makes any improvement in farming and cultivation so difficult."

Says Mr. H. M. Hyndman in "Bankruptcy of India," page 74 (1886 A.D.).

"That the people of India are growing poorer and poorer, that taxation is not only actually, but relatively far heavier; that each successive scarcity widens the area of impoverishment; that famines are more frequent; that most of the trade is but an index to the poverty and crushing over-taxation of the people; that a highly-organised foreign rule constitutes by itself a most terrible drain upon the country."

Said Sir William Hunter, former member of the Viceroy's Council, in a speech in 1875:

"The Government assessment does not leave enough

food to the cultivator to support himself and family throughout the year."

The Pioneer, the semi-official paper of the British-Indian Government, wrote in an article in 1877:

"Worried by the revenue survey, for heavily enhanced public payments . . . the Deccan ryot accepted, for a third of a century *the yoke of British mismanagement* . . . Report upon report has been written upon him; shelf upon shelf in the public offices groaned under the story of his wrongs. If any one doubts the naked accuracy of these words, let him dip into the pages of Appendix A. (Papers on the Indebtedness of the Agricultural Classes in Bombay.) *A more damning indictment was never recorded against a civilised government.*"

Mr. Wilfrid Scawen Blunt, in his "India Under Ripon," pages 236–238, observes:

"No one accustomed to Eastern travel can fail to see how poor the Indian peasant is. Travelling by either of the great lines of railways which bisect the Continent, one need hardly leave one's carriage to be aware of this. . . . In every village which I visited I heard of complaints . . . of over-taxation of the country, of increase and inequalities of assessment . . . complaints of the forest laws, of the decrease of the stock of working cattle, of their deterioration through the price of salt, of universal debt to the users. . . .

Says the same writer, earlier in his work, page 232:

"India's famines have been severer and frequent; its agricultural poverty has deepened, its rural population has become more hopelessly in debt, their despair more desperate. The system of constantly enhancing the land-values has not been altered. The salt tax though slightly lowered, still robs the very poor. Hunger, and those pestilences which are the result of hunger, are spread over an increasing, not diminishing area. The Deccan ryot is still the poorest peasant in the world. Nothing of the system of finance is changed, nothing in the economy which favours English trade and English speculation at the expense of India's native industries. *What was bad twenty-five years ago, is worse now.* At any rate, there is the same drain of India's food to alien mouths. Endemic famines and endemic plagues are facts no official statistics can explain away." (The italics are mine.)

In 1888 a confidential enquiry into the economic condition of the people of India was made by Lord Dufferin. The results of the enquiry have never been made public, but extracts from the reports of the United Provinces of Agra and Oude, and the Punjab, have been published by Mr. Digby in his monumental work. These reports are well worth the attention of the student of economic conditions in India. We can only refer to them briefly. One of the most interesting documents is the report of Mr. A. H. Harrington, Commissioner, of April 4, 1888. Mr. Harrington quotes Mr. Bennett, the compiler of the Oude *Gazeteer,* an officer whom he calls "wholly free from pessimism," as to the condition of the lowest castes of Oude:

"The lowest depths of misery and degradation are reached by the Koris and Chamars," whom he describes as "always on the verge of starvation." These represent from 10 to 11 per cent. of the population of Oude. Mr. Harrington then quotes from papers he himself contributed to *The Pioneer* in 1876, under the heading, "Oude Affairs":

"It has been calculated that about 60 per cent. of the entire native population . . . are sunk in such abject poverty that unless the small earnings of child labour are added to the scanty stock by which the family is kept alive, some members would starve."

Whether the impression that the greater number of the people of India suffer from a daily insufficiency of food is true or untrue, he adds:

"My own belief, after a great deal of study of the *closely connected questions of agricultural indebtedness, is that the impression is perfectly true as regards a varying but always considerable number throughout the greater part of India.*"

Mr. A. J. Lawrence, then Commissioner, Allahabad Division, who retired in 1891, reports:

"I believe there is very little between poorer classes of the people and semi-starvation, but where is the remedy?"

Of Shahjehanpur, another district of the United Provinces, it is stated: "The landless labourer's condition is by no means all that could be desired. The combined earnings of a man, his wife and two children cannot be put at more than Rs. 3 a month. [Less than a dollar of American money.] *When prices of food grains are low or moderate, work regular and the health of the household good, this income will enable the family to have one fairly good meal a day, to keep a thatched roof over their heads, to buy cheap clothing and occasionally a thin blanket.* Cold and rain undoubtedly entail considerable suffering, as the people are insufficiently clothed, and cannot afford fires. A few twigs or dried sticks constitute the height of their ambition, and these, owing to the increased value and scarcity of wood, are more and more difficult for the poor man to obtain." (The italics are in the original.)

Mr. White, Collector of Banda, states:

"A large number of the lower classes clearly demonstrate by their physique, either that they are habitually starved, or have been exposed in early years to the severity of famines; if any young creature be starved while growing, no amount of subsequent fattening will make up for the injury sustained."

Mr. Rose, Collector of Ghazipur, says:

"Where the holding is of average size, and the tenant unencumbered with debt, when his rent is not excessive and there is an average out turn of produce; when in fact, conditions are favourable, the position of the agriculturist is, on the whole, fairly comfortable. But unfortunately, these conditions do not always exist. As a rule, a very large proportion are in debt."

Of the Jhansi Division, Mr. Ward, Commissioner, says:

"A very small proportion in this division are habitually underfed."

Mr. Bays, officiating Commissioner for Sitapur Division, records particulars obtained from twenty families taken at random:

"Nineteen shillings, twopence or less than five dollars per annum for each adult.

"Nine shillings, sixpence, or less than two and a half dollars per annum for each child."

He is of the opinion that this is sufficient to keep them in good health, and adds: "For some reasons, it is not desirable at present that the standard of comfort should be very materially raised."

Mr. Irwin, Deputy Commissioner of Rae Barali, says:

"The mass of the agricultural population, in ordinary times, and the elite always, get enough to eat; but there is a considerable minority in bad seasons who feel the pinch of hunger, and a small minority . . . suffer from chronic hunger, except just at harvest time when grain is plentiful, and easily to be had. I do not understand that the indigent town population are intended to be included in this enquiry. There can be no doubt that they suffer much more than the agricultural classes for want of food, especially the unfortunate *purdah-nashin* women, and indeed, men too, of good and impoverished families, who have sunk in the world, who are ashamed to beg, and live on the remnants of their property and whom every rise in prices hits cruelly hard. For such people dear grain means starvation, while to the producer, it of course means increased value of the produce."

Mr. G. Toynbee, C. S. L., former Member of the Viceroy's Council and Senior Member of the Board of Revenue, said:

"The conclusion to be drawn is that of the agricultural population, 40 per cent. are insufficiently fed, to say nothing of clothing and housing. They have enough food to support life and enable them to work, but they have to undergo long fasts, having for a considerable part of the year to satisfy themselves with one full meal a day."

Grierson's statistics, summed up in *The Pioneer,* in 1893, state:

"Briefly, it is that all persons of the labouring classes, and ten per cent. of the cultivating and artisan classes, *or 45 per cent. of the total population* are insufficiently fed, or housed, or both. It follows that nearly one hundred millions of people in British India are living in extreme poverty."

The Punjab is supposed to be one of the most prosperous provinces of India. Mr. Thorburn, Member of the Punjab Commission, one-time Financial Commissioner, says of the agriculturists of that province in his book entitled, "The Punjab in Peace and War":

"It is worthy of note that the whole revenue of the Punjab, from the largest item, land revenue, to the smallest stamps, £10,000, are practically drawn from the producing masses, whilst the literate and commercial classes, whom the new régime was to benefit at the expense of those masses, escape almost untaxed. (Page 175.)

"Since the mutiny, there have been in all, seven years of famine, viz.: 1860–1, 1876–8, 1896–7, 1899–1901; in addition, scarcities from short droughts in semi-dependent tracts, have been frequent. During the earlier famines, four years in all, out of the annual land revenue demand, apart from water rates or canal irrigated lands, *hardly 2 per cent. were suspended, and the fraction ultimately remitted, or written off as irrecoverable, was infinitesimal. Since 1896, the destitution of a large part of the cultivators having been officially proved, the Government has been less niggardly in granting suspensions and remissions.*

[Italics are mine.] Unfortunately, the relief given coming too late, fails to reach the classes who most require it — the poorest of the peasant proprietary — and only saves the pockets of the capitalist mortgagees and purchasers of holdings. (Page 242.)

"If it be remembered that the average daily income per head of the Indian population is less than three halfpence, and that fully 25 per cent. of that population never attain that average, the hand to mouth existence of the Punjab peasantry, even in normal years, will be realised. If so, their general inability to pay, without borrowing, the land revenue, or to even avoid death from starvation whenever a scarcity from drought occurs, let alone a famine period, requires no demonstration. (Page 243.)

"The Government pronouncement now was that even if the masses of the old peasantry were sinking, it was too late to change a system which, judged by all the criteria applied to European countries, cultivated area, production, revenue under all heads, consumption of spirits and drugs, all showing steady progress except during and immediately after famines. Were the Punjab a single estate, and all the cultivators tenants at will with only one landlord, these criteria would doubtless indicate prosperity. But seeing that its lands are, or were, owned until some thirty years ago by a round million of peasant proprietary families, their prosperity cannot be measured by the gross volume of production and consumption, but depends on the due diffusion amongst the producing masses of the profits of their labours. Statistically, the Punjab might be the richest country, yet its people the poorest, in India, if they were the rack-rented tenants of capitalists. That is the condition towards which our 'system' until 1900 was reducing the 'finest peasantry in India.'" (Page 254.)

Among the latest opinions on this subject, we have

that of Mr. C. J. O'Donnell, retired member of the Indian Civil Service, as expressed in his book entitled: "The Failure of Lord Curzon":

"India is rapidly becoming a land steeped in perennial poverty, and unless some strong and early steps are taken, the English people will find itself face to face with annual famines, due chiefly to the exactions of the State, to the oppression of the poor by the 'Imperialist Empire Builder.'"

As an independent observer, Mr. J. Ramsay Macdonald, M.P., the Labour leader of Great Britain, may be quoted here. In his book, "The Awakening of India," published in 1910, he remarks:

"Sir William Hunter said that 40,000,000 Indians go through life with insufficient food; Sir Charles Elliott estimated that one-half of the agricultural population never satisfied hunger from one year's end to the other; from thirty to fifty million families live in India on an income which does not exceed threepence per day. *The poverty of India is not an opinion,—it is a fact.*"

For independent estimates of the existing conditions of life in the Bombay and Madras Presidencies see the Appendices for extracts from recent articles. We give the rates of wages also in an appendix. Some more opinions are given in other parts of the book (see the Preface and the Conclusion).

PART FIVE

"The test of a people's prosperity is not the extension of exports, the multiplication of manufactures, or other industries, the construction of cities. No. A prosperous country is one in which the great mass of the inhabitants are able to procure with moderate toil, what is necessary for living *human* lives, lives of frugal and assured comfort. Judged by this criterion, can India be called prosperous?

"Comfort of course is a relative term. In a tropical country like India, the standard is very low. Little clothing is required,— simple diet suffices. An unfailing well full of water, a plot of land and a bit of orchard — these will satisfy his heart's desire, if needed, you add the cattle needful to him. Such is the ryot's ideal — very few realise it. Millions of peasants in India are struggling to live on half an acre. Their existence is a constant struggle with starvation, ending too often in defeat. Their difficulty is not to live human lives,— lives up to the level of their poor standard of comfort,— but to live at all, and not die. We may well say that in India, except in the irrigated tracts, famine is chronic — endemic."

—"India and Its Problems," by W. S. Lily, pp. 284–85.

CHAPTER X

FAMINES AND THEIR CAUSES

Famines in the Past. "The famines of India are among the most startling phenomena of our time. They seem to be steadily increasing both in frequency and severity. During the last forty years of the nineteenth century,— from 1860–1900,— India was smitten by not less than ten famines of great magnitude, causing a loss of life that has been conservatively estimated at 15,000,000. These figures are appalling. Such a condition of things naturally awakens the sympathy of the whole world."

Statements like this made by the Rev. Dr. Sunderland of New York, have forced British Imperialists to extenuate their position in the eyes of the nations, by citing the frequency of famines in India in pre-British days, and by the fact that under the old economic order, famines were not unknown in England and France. Sir Theodore Morison, Member of the Council of the Secretary of State for India, opens his chapter on famines in his book called "The Economic Transition in India," by the remark that "dearth or famine, at irregular intervals, was inseparably connected with conditions which determined the old economic order" (page 92). He then proceeds with an account of the English famine of 1586, and the French famines of 1675 and 1699,— following with a description of the Indian famines of pre-British days. Four pages have been devoted to extracts from the diary of "the blunt English sailor, Peter Lundy," about the famine of 1630; four more to extracts from British documents about famines in Madras from 1709 to 1752; thereafter proceeding with extreme brevity to describe the terrible famines of 1770, 1783, 1790–92, and 1837, during the British occupation. Famines during the latter part of the century are described in a page and a half of generalities, although the greatest famines of the century occurred during its latter half. The chapter concludes with a discussion of the nature of Indian famines and what has been done by the British Government to prevent them.

In a paper entitled "Some Plain Facts About Famines in India," read before, and published by the East India Association of London,— Hindu legends, and the great epics, the Mahabbarata and the Ramayana were requisitioned to prove that "severe famines occurred between 1107 and 1143 A. D." A southern tradition was vaguely quoted to establish the fact of a "twelve years' famine," time and place not stated. To these statistics is appended a list of famines during the Mogul dynasty, 1596–1792, itemised as follows:

Sixteenth century, two famines.
Seventeenth century, two famines.
Eighteenth century, four famines (two of which fell within the time of British occupation).

Mr. Digby's Table. The following list of Indian famines of the past, made by Mr. William Digby, is however, more accurate and includes every famine known to Indian history.

11th century.........Two famines, both local
13th century.........One famine around Delhi, local
14th century.........Three famines, all local
15th century.........Two famines, both local
16th century.........Three famines, all local
17th century.........Three famines, area not defined
18th century (to 1745) Four famines, all local

The last thirty years of the 18th century.

1769–1800...........Four famines, Bengal, Madras, Bombay and southern India.

Famines of the 19th century and loss of life thereby; divided into four periods of 25 years:

1800–1825, five famines....Approx. 1,000,000 deaths
1826–1850 two famines.... " 500,000 "
1851–1875, six famines....Recorded 5,000,000 "
1876–1900, EIGHTEEN FAMINES, Estimated 26,000,000 deaths.

"The foregoing official figures show over one million deaths per annum during the last ten years, or two British-Indian subjects passed away from starvation, or starvation-induced diseases, every minute of every day and night, from Jan. 1, 1889, to Sept. 30, 1901! Nevertheless, only a few persons in the United Kingdom are doing aught to prevent the continuance of such an awful state of things, and the Secretary of State for India 'stands amazed at the prosperity' of the region he is governing."[1]

Digby's "Prosperous British India."

The author of "Prosperous British India" then adds (pages 137–139):

[1] A fuller and more accurate list is given by Mr. A. Loveday in his "Indian Famines," London, G. Bell & Sons, 1914, Appendix A. His remarks as to the relief measures taken by Native Administrators before the British are specially valuable. See pp. 102 and 103.

"Are Indian famines more destructive to human life now than in ancient days? Yes — they were more destructive within the famine areas until '76–78; since then, the Famine Code, when acted upon, as it mercifully was in 1901, checks mortality. The extent of the relief administered may be judged when, in the district of Raipur, forty inhabitants out of every hundred were on relief. As much time and energy given to devising means of prevention as have been devoted to relief measures, would ere this have stopped famines. There are districts in Bombay, in which, despite the Famine Code, people died like flies. Meanwhile, the Census Returns have been published:

1891 Total population of India	287,223,431
1901 Gov't estimate of normal increase as it should be	330,306,945
1901 Population as it actually was	294,000,000

"The Indian special correspondent of the *Lancet*, writing to that journal May 16, 1901, put the loss of life at 19,000,000 people. To quote:

"'During the last decade, it is estimated that the total population of India has only increased by 2,800,-000 (?) a rate considerably less than that of the previous decade. Two causes only can affect the numbers of people; a diminished birth-rate — at the outside, 20 per cent. could be put down to this cause. An enhanced mortality must be the chief factor. It is estimated there were 20,000,000 more deaths than there should have been, and if we put 1,000,000 deaths down to plague, there remain 19,000,000 that can be attributed either to actual starvation or diseases therefrom.'

"This statement by what is probably the foremost medical journal in the world, means that the loss of life thus recorded represented 'the disappearance' of fully one-half a population as large as that of the United Kingdom."

Famines in the Twentieth Century.

1901—General famine year, direct expenditure on relief, £556,000.

1902—"Considerable distress" in Central Provinces; relief expenditure, £315,500.

1903—Failure of crops in parts of upper Burma.

1904—Bengal, "bad;" Punjab, "unfavourable;" Central Provinces, "deficient;" Madras, "rice-crop failed, considerable deficiency;" Bombay, "poor;" Gujrat, "famine but not acute;" United Provinces, "fat ;" Bundelkhand, "famine;" Agra, "agriculture disorganised."

1905—Bengal, "partially bad;" United Provinces, "scarcity and famine;" Punjab, distress, relief works in Delhi; N.W. Frontier, "poor;" Central Prov. & Barar, "rice-crop failed," "relief works;" Madras, "unfavourable;" Bombay, "famine conditions in Deccan," etc.

1906—Bengal, "partly fair, rest poor;" East Bengal and Assam, distress of last year continued to this; United Prov., ditto.

1907—A year of general famine.

1908—Famine continued, severe distress in Orissa; disaster in Behar.

"In 1907–8 a widespread failure of the autumn harvest, and serious reductions in the area and out turn of the spring crop forced large numbers to resort to Government Relief. The executive was faced with the necessity of providing direct measures of famine relief in an area of 66,000 square miles with a population of 30,000,000. Gratuitous relief continued till the end of August."

Thus the general famine of 1907 persisted in large districts until 1909. Bengal, Behar, Central Provinces with Berar, Assam and Bombay, all felt the effects and suffered acutely, most of them having relief works and gratuitous relief grants until 1909.

In 1911 the rainfall failed over a considerable area in Gujrat in the Bombay Presidency and also in 1912 in the Ahmednagar District of the Bombay Deccan. Again rains failed over large areas in the United Provinces in 1913-14. This famine affected 17,000 square miles with a population of five and a quarter millions while distress was grave in 30,000 square miles with a population of fourteen millions. There was acute distress in parts of Bengal in 1914-15, yet the export of grain from India was never stopped.

Famines During the British Period. Critics of British rule in India argue:

1. That famines have been more frequent under British domination.
2. That there have been a larger number of "general" famines, during British rule, than were ever known before in Indian history.
3. That though Indian famines are primarily due sometimes to failure of monsoons, and at other times to floods and other causes beyond the control of man, yet the widespread distress and huge mortalities that have followed the failure of monsoons during British occupation are to a great extent due to the economic effects of Great Britain's fiscal policy in India, which annihilated indigenous industries, exacted exorbitant land revenues and impoverished the people.
4. That the development of railway systems with an eye to furthering British trade, has been pushed to the detriment of canal construction and other methods of irrigation.
5. That the widespread mortality and woful destitu-

tion of the people during famine periods are preventable.

6. That famine conditions are now chronic in India.
7. That the Indian famines of modern times are not famines of foodstuffs, but of money — there being at all times sufficient food in the country to feed the entire population, had the people the wherewithal to buy it at the prices demanded by export-merchants and dealers.

The facts for the famines of the decade 1900 to 1910 are taken from the government Blue Books. In the majority of the reports the mortality is neither given nor estimated. The facts, however, speak for themselves; famine or scarcity over all, or a large part of India, every year, from 1901 to 1910. To a people ravaged by starvation and disease, the decrease in powers of resistance necessarily increases mortality lists. In the year 1899-1900, one of the greatest famine years of the century, more than a million persons died in British India alone. Preceded by the "exceeding great" famine of 1895-97, it proved, in Lord Curzon's words, to be the "most terrible famine in Indian history." Crops, and incidental losses were estimated to be not less than £150,000,000;[2] the total admitted loss of life in forty-seven years, from 1854 to 1901, was 28,825,000 persons!

Causes of Famines. The British Imperialist ascribes Indian famines to the following causes:

(1) Shortage of rainfall and other natural causes. (2) Overpopulation. (3) Lack of thrift by the In-

[2] Sir T. W. Holderness estimated it at £80,000,000, quoted by Loveday, p. 124.

dian ryot in years of prosperity, particularly on the occasions of marriages and funerals.

All of these ostensible causes have been examined from time to time, by honest and disinterested Britishers, actuated by humane motives. Most prominent and often most outspoken among them have been those who served their Government in India in various capacities. Their observations are based, not on casual trips of a few days or months, but on periods of service extending over twenty-five and thirty years, or longer. Various Americans have examined the facts about Indian famines, and pronounced themselves in agreement with these British humanitarians, as to their real cause.

Shortage of Rainfall. On page 140 of his book, "Prosperous British India," Mr. Digby propounds the question:

"Why is it India is more liable to devastation by famine than are other countries? Answer: Not because rains fail and moisture is denied; always in the worst of years there is water enough poured from the skies on Indian soil, to germinate and ripen the grain,—but because India is steadily growing poorer."

For detailed information on this point, and an analysis of rain registers for nearly ninety years, Mr. Digby refers the reader to a chapter in the life of Sir Arthur Cotton (Hodder & Stoughton, London) entitled, "Is famine in India due to an insufficiency of Land?"

Says the Rev. Dr. Sunderland, of New York:

"It is generally supposed that famines in India are always in years of very light rainfall; this is a great mistake — they are often years of very heavy rainfall. The only trouble is, the rain comes too early, too late, or too much at a time, *and is not stored.* The water is allowed to go to waste for lack of storage, hence there is disaster. The year of the great Madras famine of 1877 was one with the enormous rainfall of sixty-six inches. In the year of the Orissa famine, 1865-66, the rainfall was sixty inches. In the Bombay famine of 1876 the rainfall of the year was fifty inches. In the famine of 1896-97 in the Central Provinces, the record of the two years was fifty-two and forty-two inches. In the great famine year, 1900, the average rainfall where the famine was most severe was, (I omit fractions) Northwestern Provinces, thirty-two inches; Punjab, eighteen inches; Central Provinces, fifty-two inches; Central India, thirty-six inches; Rajputana, twenty inches; Berar, thirty-one inches; Bombay, forty inches. Thus we see, in most instances, the real lack is not *rain,* it is *storage.* Says Major Philip B. Phipson, and few persons can speak with more authority: 'The water supply of India is ample for all requirements; it only requires to be diverted from her rivers, stored up from her rainfall, and distributed over her fields, to secure such an abundance as shall leave no single human being wanting it.' "[3]

Are the Famines of India Due to Over-Population? This question also may best be answered in the language of Dr. Sunderland:

"Very little study of the facts furnishes an answer to this question. The population of India is not so dense as in a number of the European States, which are prosperous, which have no difficulty in supporting their people, and in which famines are never dreamed of. Nor is the birthrate high in India. It is less than in England, and much less than in Germany and other Continental countries. India is not overpopu-

[3] "Indian Poverty and Indian Famines," p. 52, published from the *Asiatic Quarterly Review,* by Wm. Hutchinson, D.D., London, 1903.

lated.[4] Even under present conditions, she produces more than enough food for all her people. Were her agricultural possibilities properly developed, she could easily support a greatly increased population. There are enormous areas of waste land that should be brought under cultivation.[5] The Hon. D. M. Hamilton, in his speech in the Viceroy's Council on the Indian Budget for 1904, declared that there are a hundred million acres of cultivable land still available in India. In these very large reclaimable areas, and in the opportunities for the extension of irrigation already referred to, we have ample provision for increase in India's population.

"But beyond these is another resource still greater. Long ago, Sir James Caird urged upon the Indian Government the necessity for better agricultural methods, calling attention to the fact that a single additional bushel per acre raised by the ryot would mean food for another 22,000,000 people. But the addition of a bushel per acre is only a beginning of what might be done. Here is a resource practically inexhaustible, which, added to the others, makes the suggestion that population outstrips agricultural possibilities, and that therefore, famines are inevitable, positively ludicrous."

The following figures support Mr. Sunderland's conclusion:

		Average Increase of Population per year per million
Germany, 1837 31,589,547	Germany, 1911 64,925,993	14,528
Belgium, 1866 4,827,833	Belgium, 1912 7,571,387	11,919
England, 1871 21,495,131	England, 1911 31,045,270	11,726
Japan, 1908 49,588,804	Japan, 1914 53,696,888	10,270

[4] Mr. Loveday remarks: "It is difficult to find evidence to prove that over-population in India is a reality" (p. 99).

[5] Of late something has been done in this direction with beneficial results.

		Average Increase of Population per year per million
Hungary, 1880 15,737,259	Hungary, 1910 20,886,487	11,443
India, 1861 215,798,302	India, 1911 302,494,794	8,636
British India, 1901 231,610,000	British India, 1911 244,270,000	5,623
Native States, 1901 62,755,116	Native States, 1911 70,888,854	13,085

The following table (Hazells "Annual" for 1917) supports Dr. Sunderland's statement:

Increase of Population

	1881–1891	*1891–1901*	*1901–1911*	*Total*
England and Wales	11.7	12.2	10.9	34.8
Australian Commonwealth	41.1	18.9	18.1	78.1
German Empire	9.3	14.0	15.2	38.5
Hungary	11.0	10.3	8.5	29.8
Netherlands	12.4	13.1	14.8	40.3
United States	25.5	20.7	21.0	67.2
India	13.2	2.5	7.1	22.8

The population of Russia is said to be increasing at the rate of 2,500,000 a year. The total population, in 1916, was 182,182,600. Comparing the pressure of population per square mile we find that while the United Kingdom has a population of 374 per square mile; Austria 222; Belgium 658; Denmark 280; France 193; German Empire 311; Hungary 270; Italy 315; Japan 356; Netherlands 607; Switzerland 236; India has only 158. Then Japan with a density of population twice as great as that of India and only one-sixth of her area arable does not suffer from famines.

Should the reader enquire at this point, why Indian agriculture is still primitive, the reply is,—want of capital.[6]

[6] Mr. A. Loveday, in his book on "The History and Eco-

Are Famines Due to Scarcity of Food? Says Dr. Sunderland: "But even under present conditions, with irrigation as imperfectly developed as now, and so large a part of the rainfall wasted, India is one of the greatest food-producing lands. No matter how severe the drought may be in some parts, there is never a time when India as a whole does not produce food enough for all her people. Indeed, in her worst famine years, she exports food. In her worst famine years there is plenty of food to be obtained, and in the famine areas themselves, for those who have money to buy with. This the Famine Commissioners themselves have told us.

Says Mr. J. Ramsay MacDonald, M.P., in "The Awakening of India," page 163: "In studying famines, one must begin by grasping what it is and how it presents itself. Even in the worst times there is no scarcity of grain in the famine stricken districts. At the very worst time in the Gujerat famine of 1900, it was shown by the official returns that there was 'sufficient grain to last for a couple of years in the hands of the grain dealers of the district. It is, therefore, not a scarcity of grain that causes famines.' In recent times, famine has been caused by a destruction of capital and the consequent cessation of the demand for labour.

nomics of Indian Famines," (London, 1914) discusses the question at some length. He acquits the Indian agriculturist of all charges of "laziness or inefficiency" and adds that "all experts praise him." In his opinion, supported by that of Dr. Voelker (expressed in his report on "Improvement of Indian Agriculture, 1893), "it is not the lack of skill on the part of the cultivator but the smallness of his holding, the scarcity of capital and the decay of domestic industries and his incapacity to withstand the strain of famine" that is responsible for the intense distress caused by famines.

High prices coincide with low wages, and unemployment, and the people starve in the midst of plenty."

Is the Distress Due to the Extravagance of the Ryot on Occasions of Marriages and Funerals? The reports of the government enquiry in 1887–88 repudiate this theory. Says Mr. Digby:

"Taking the first twenty cases exactly as they appear in the record of the Government enquiry in which reference is made to indebtedness, they do not sustain the assertion of the Lieutenant-Governor. In only two of these cases are marriage and family expenses put down as the occasion of indebtedness. In one case, the amount was the trifle of Rs. 10, half already repaid in monthly instalments of one rupee. That is to say, 10 per cent. of borrowings only, are specifically for marriage purposes. In the Punjab, Mr. Thorburn's particulars compare not unfavourably: 'Of seven hundred and forty-two families, only in three cases was marriage extravagance the cause of their serious indebtedness.' The common idea about the extravagance of marriage is not supported by evidence. Unnecessary marriage expenses show a tendency year by year to decrease. This is susceptible of statistical proof:

	Full Indebtedness	*Marriage Expenses*	*Percentage*
Circle I.	Rs. 142,737	Rs. 9,491	6½
Circle II.	" 179,853	" 12,418	7
Circle III.	" 88,234	" 9,687	11
Circle IV.	" 188,145	" 15,161	8
	Average: less than 8%		

Mr. Loveday has also incidentally spoken of the extravagance of the Indian ryot. Examining into the causes of the ryot's indebtedness he says: "Temptations to unnecessary extravagance have been accompanied in some instances by a growing pressure from above for rent, by an inelastic demand for land revenue and to a less degree in the more distant parts, by an insecurity from enhanced assessments (page 131).

The True Cause. We have laboured in vain if the reader is not in a position, after these citations, to judge for himself. The question: what causes Indian famines? is best answered in the language of the American gentleman quoted above. Says Dr. Sunderland:

"What then is the cause of the famines in India? The real cause is the extreme poverty of the people. It is a poverty so severe, that it keeps a majority of all on the verge of suffering even in years of plenty, and prevents them from laying up anything to tide them over in years of scarcity. If their conditions were such that in good seasons they could get a little ahead, in the bad years they could draw upon that as a resource. This would not save them from hardship, but it would from starvation. But as things are, the vast majority have no such resource."

"If the poor sufferers are so fortunate as to be received by the government at the famine relief works, where, in return for exacting labour in breaking stone, or similar work, they are supplied with sufficient means to buy food to sustain life, then the hardiest of them survive until the rains come, when, with depleted strength they go back to their stripped homes, and barehanded, begin as best they can to raise a new crop and support such members of their family as may be left. Here we have the real cause of the famines in India."

FAMINE RELIEF

As to famine relief, the work of the English deserves ungrudging praise.[7] They have reduced it to a science. One is sorry the brain, the energy, the talent, the zeal employed in saving life and ameliorating distress, should not have been spent in preventing famines, instead of in systematising relief. The demoralising effect of such relief cannot be sufficiently appreciated by the foreigner. India has perhaps the largest number of professional beggars in the world, yet the average Indian, be he Hindu or Mohammedan, hates nothing so much as accepting charity. The middle class Hindu would rather die than let his wants be known and relieved by a stranger. This systematic relief of the British is undermining the innate fineness of feeling and converting the people into a horde of "shameless beggars" (according to English interpretation). It is true the money spent in famine relief comes from the pockets of Indians, it is all money that has been wrung from the people at one time or another, in various ingenious ways. But all the masses feel and know is that they receive charity in small doles; it is that consciousness that demoralises them. Says Mr. J. Ramsay MacDonald, M.P., in his "Awakening of India":

"In their strenuous efforts to provide relief when famine is upon the land, our officers are above praise. The story of famine relief in India will shine with a bright glow, after many other achievements of ours

[7] For the famine relief measures of native governments in pre-British days, see A. Loveday's work on "The History and Economics of Indian Famines," pp. 102 and 103.

have ceased to emit a beam of light. . . . Yet this relief work, so unlike the charity which India has been accustomed to dispense, has had a solvent effect on Indian social organisation. It tends to pauperise the people, to make them lose their self-respect; it damaged the status of some; it destroyed the morals of others. Indeed the coarsening and degrading effects which come from relief works are the same in India as they are at home."

The present writer has had personal experience in famine relief, having organised private relief works for orphans and other famine stricken people, during three of the most disastrous of these periods that occurred within the last twenty-five years: the famines of 1897, 1899 and 1907–98. He travelled widely over famine-stricken areas in the superintendence of relief, and can assert from personal experience that the "coarsening and degrading," and the utter demoralisation that results from the British system of famine relief, beggars description. Mr. MacDonald adds:

"Over and over again, Government has been warned that its duty is not to relieve, but to prevent, and the only way to prevent is to strengthen the economic position of the cultivator, mainly by extricating him from the financial meshes in which he lives, and to give support, as far as possible, to the old economy by encouraging its methods of mutual helpfulness."

Let us examine what has been, or is being done, by way of prevention.

Building of Railways. "In one way," says Mr. MacDonald, "railways have added to the difficulty and have widened the apparent famine area. In the first place, they are the means by which the export of Indian grain is carried on. No one who has not been in India and seen the workings of the system, from the great granaries at Karachee to the agencies in every little village having a surplus of anything to be sent away,[8] can grasp the colossal nature of the export organisation. One firm alone saps the blood of Indian life like a tropical sun, leaving dust and barrenness (it might be added, destitution) behind.

"A week or two after harvest, India's surplus (?) wheat and rice have passed into the hands of dealers, and when the monsoon fails, she starves. The cultivator used to have reserves. He has practically none now. He has a little money, but not much, and it is just this turning everything into cash which is the source of so much of his trouble.[9] When famine overtook India in olden times, if the famine stricken tract was in distress, neighbouring tracts were little affected, owing to lack of communication, thus preventing famine influences from affecting neighbouring markets. The means which relieve famine widen its influence, because scarcity in one part immediately puts up prices in another, and deepens poverty everywhere. The

[8] The qualification is superfluous, since agencies are established in villages which produce large quantities of grain, irrespective of whether they have a surplus to be sent away. Crops are sometimes sold before they ripen. As a rule, they are purchased when the harvest is in.

[9] But this turning of resources into cash helps the British manufacturer and enables the British report writer to talk of the prosperity of the cultivator, shown by his consumption of British goods. The money left over from indebtedness, if there be any, is spent in buying clothes, cigarettes, wine, etc., all British importations, and within a few weeks after the harvest, the cultivator wakes to find himself on the verge of starvation. As to the effect of railways on the destruction of the native industries and the concentration of labour on agriculture, see Loveday, p. 107.

poison which used to be virulent but local, is now milder but carried further through the system."

Says Sir B. Fuller in "The Empire of India" (London, 1913), "Railways blunt the edge of famine but by equalizing prices cause general distress" (p. 67). He also remarks that during an Indian famine two-thirds of the Indian population lose their means of livelihood. See also A. Loveday, p. 107.

Building of Canals and Irrigation Works. The famine commission of 1878 recommended the building of canal and irrigation works as the most important step. This work was neglected, comparatively speaking, for a considerable period, and has only within this century received some attention. The figures of profits made by these canals tell their own astounding tale; the prices which the Government charges to reap such profits, can only be exorbitant. Mr. Thorburn, the retired Financial Commissioner of the Punjab, states in his book, "The Punjab in Peace and War," written in 1904:

"The annual net return on the outlay on canals now averages 11 per cent. and in another decade may rise to 18 per cent. The Chenab Canal already gives this rate of interest." (Page 275.)

The eastern Jumna Canal has been yielding a net revenue of from 20 to 25 per cent. throughout the decade 1901–11. The lower Chenab Canal yielded a net revenue of 34.06 per cent. on the capital investment in 1911–12. These figures show how relentlessly the water rates are assessed. In canal-irrigated areas, the cultivator has to pay three taxes: (a) Ordinary land revenue. (b) A water rate graded on the increase in price and productivity of the land caused by its inclusion in a canal zone,—called in Hindusthani, "*Khush haisiyyati*" or "water-advantages." (c) The price of the water actually used.

Pressure on Land. Mr. Gait, I. C. S., admits frankly in his report on the census of 1911 that "there seems to be no doubt that the number of persons who live by cultivation is increasing at a relatively rapid rate." Reviewing the increase or decrease of persons employed in industries he notices a fall of 6.1 per cent. in the number of persons supported by textile industries only during the decade 1901–11. There has been a similar decrease in the hides and skin industry and in workers in metals.

In 1911 there were 7113 factories in British India employing 2.1 million persons out of a total population of 244 millions, or 9 per mille. Of these, two-fifths of the total number were employed in growing special products, 558,000 in textile industries, 224,000 in mines, 125,000 in transport, 74,000 in food industries, 71,000 in metal industries, 49,000 in glass and earthenware industries, the same number in industries connected with chemical products, and 45,000 in industries of luxury.

The Opening of Agricultural Banks. This step was advocated as far back as 1884, and was promptly rejected by the Secretary of State. After a good deal of delay, cogitation and discussion, village co-operative societies were started in 1904. These are now to be found in every province "in a state of more or less vigour." In 1914 there were 14,566 Co-operative Credit Societies in India, of which 13,715 had been started to provide agricultural credit. In an article contributed to the *Calcutta Review* Sir D. Hamilton states the total membership of the Co-operative Credit Societies as 750,000 with a capital of £5,000,000. Very properly he calls it a "mere drop in the ocean."

Special Agrarian Legislation. As a palliative for the heavy indebtedness of the agriculturist, the result of a too-rigorous revenue system, a land-alienation act has been passed in the Punjab, prohibiting alienation of land by members of agricultural tribes, specially notified by the local government,—except to members of the same or other tribes so notified. This measure is of extremely doubtful utility. It has been denounced by British officers as unsound and mischievous, in its likelihood to absorb the holdings of many small peasant-proprietors into those of a few big landlords. There is a keen controversy over it, in the Punjab, but there is not space enough to include the arguments for or against it here. As a measure of famine prevention, it is useless.

The official reports give frequent expression to the growing prosperity of India, which are apt to mislead those who do not bear in mind real conditions of acute distress. The Blue Book for 1904–05 says of the districts of Agra and Oude: "THE YEAR ENDING SEPT. 30, 1904, WAS THE LAST OF A SERIES OF FAT YEARS!" These provinces had several famines in 1896–97–99 and 1900–01. This reduces the "series" to two or three years. Such general statements of prosperity made in official reports should be read with a great deal of discrimination, if not with actual distrust.

CHAPTER XI

RAILWAYS AND IRRIGATION

The Government Policy. The railway policy of the Government of India has been a subject of controversy between Indian and British publicists as well as among the latter *inter se.* The Indian publicists are almost unanimous that the railways in India built and constructed with foreign capital and managed by foreign agents, have been economically ruinous to India, and the British publicists are divided into two classes: those who condemn the railway policy of the Government of India and those who point out in figures of traffic and the growth of foreign trade conclusive facts showing the success of railways there. But before we state the case for both sides we want to say once for all, that although there is no doubt in our judgment that the railway policy of the Government of India has been the source of indescribable misery to the people of India, economically and financially the railways have largely contributed to the unifying of India, and to the growth of national consciousness; they have broken down social barriers; they have facilitated travel and thereby helped social reform and in the broadening of the Indian people's outlook. Unfortunately the price we have paid for these benefits has been too heavy for a poor people like those of India. With these preliminary remarks we will proceed first to give some outstanding facts about Indian railways and then discuss their bearing on Indian economics.

The length of railway lines open on March 31, 1915, was 35,285; the mileage under construction at the end of 1914–15 was 437. The number of passengers carried in 1914–15 was 451 millions and the tonnage of goods 81 millions.

The following tables compiled by Mr. Dora Swami, an Indian publicist, and verified by us will be found useful. (Vide *Hindusthan Review*, Allahabad, January, 1916.)

Comparative Table of Figures of Foreign Trade.

		Total Millions	Imports Millions	Exports Millions
1913	United States of America	862	362	500
1913	United Kingdom	1403	769	634
1911	Germany	942	510	432
1911	France	712	392	320
1913	India	290	127.5	162.5
1911	Russia	270	114	156

Comparative Table of Traffic.

		Passengers Carried	Goods Carried
1910	United Kingdom	1240 millions	489 millions tons
1910	United States of America	971 "	1849 " "
1910	Germany	1541 "	576 " "
1910	France	509 "	173 " "
1910	Austria-Hungary	409 "	217 " "
1916	India	451 "	81 " "

Comparative Table Showing Mileage of Railways, National Wealth and National Income of Different Countries.

	Railways Miles	Wealth Millions of £	Income Millions of £
United States of America	252,000	39,124	5000
Germany	39,500	20,000	2000

	Railways Miles	*Wealth Millions of £*	*Income Millions of £*
Russia	50,000	13,000	1000
India	35,300	3,500	600
France	32,000	11,675	1460
Canada	29,300	2,072	259
The United Kingdom	23,400	16,500	2140
Austria Hungary	29,200	12,500	1400
Australia	20,000	1,312	164
Italy	11,100	8,000	800
New Zealand		320	40

Per Capita Wealth and Income.

	Wealth in Pounds	*Income in Pounds*
The United States of America	391	50
Germany	366	47
The United Kingdom	320	40
New Zealand	294	38
France	292	33
Australia	262	32
Canada	259	29
Austria Hungary	240	27
Italy	228	23
Russia	76	9
India	11	1.9 or say 2

These figures tell their own tale — while in the matter of national wealth and national income, India is at the bottom of the list, in the matter of railway mileage she is fourth.

The Beginning of Railway Policy. We have not the space to give even a brief history of the railway policy of the Government of India and of the history of railway progress in that country. The subject may well be studied in Mr. Horace Bell's book on "Railway Policy in India" (Revington, Perceval & Co., London, 1894) as also in Thornton's "Public Works."

In the former "the author has designedly abstained from criticism and from the assertion of his own views," though reading between the lines one can, in places, guess the author's opinion. For example, on the very first page discussing the beginning of the railway policy in 1843–44, the author remarks:

"Thus apart from the comparative novelty of railways even in Europe and in face of much more serious and urgent matters, it would not have been surprising if the 'Honourable Board' in Leadenhall Street, had regarded the proposals as untimely or premature. This, however, does not appear to have been the view taken at any time either at home or in India, and notwithstanding that much more weighty business was in hand, the railway promoter found himself in favour and a desire shown to help rather than retard the progress of the scheme."

The first guaranteed Indian railway was formed in 1849–50 and "during the next thirty years the sum of over £99,000,000 was raised in the English market under the security of the Indian Government's guarantee of 5 per cent. As up to the year 1877 the net earnings of these railways were not sufficient to pay the guaranteed interest, the State had to advance the sum required out of the ordinary budget. These accumulated arrears of interest amounted in 1881 to the enormous sum of £28,425,119."

All authorities, Indian and Anglo-Indian, are agreed that the first period of railway construction from 1849–50 to about 1873 was characterised by gross extravagance and other abuses which were fully exposed before the Finance Committees of 1871, 1872, 1873 and 1874. It was then resolved that the State should undertake construction with borrowed capital.

In 1873 an official chronicler predicted "the cessation of heavy outlay on construction." In 1878 Sir Arthur Cotton recommended "the summary and indefinite suspension of nearly all railway schemes and works." In 1880 the Famine Commission pleaded for larger outlay on works of irrigation as compared with railways. But all these predictions and hopes and recommendations came to nothing, because the interests of the British merchant and manufacturer demanded the extension of railways, and after all they are the men whose opinions count in England. The progress in railway construction may be judged from the fact that while up to 1880 only 9,310 miles of railway had been constructed, by 1900 the mileage had risen to about 25,000 miles. In March, 1915, it stood at 35,285. In the twenty years from 1880 to 1900 more than 15,000 miles of railway was constructed as against less than 10,000 in the preceding thirty years, and in the next fifteen years more than 10,000 miles more were added. Writing of the railway policy of the Government of India, the Honourable Mr. D. E. Wacha, the ablest Indian authority on finances, said:

"At the very outset we cannot help remarking that the breathless pace at which capital, like water, has been expended during the last few years, at the behest of the interested Chambers of Commerce, is not only inordinate but most improvident. The entire railway policy of the Government, specially in its financial aspect, demands the most searching investigation by an impartial tribunal of experts wholly independent of influence at Calcutta and Whitehall. We are confident it would reveal facts which would certainly not redound to the credit of the Government. Indeed, even on the recorded evidence taken by the East India

Finance Committee of 1871–74, better known as the Fawcett Committee, there is ample material to condemn the policy of the State. Huge blunders were made entailing colossal expenditure on the tax-payer which were held to be culpable. The student of railway finance has to dive deep into those old but most important records to corroborate the statement we make here.

"The worst and most inexcusable feature of Indian railway policy is the supreme indifference and neglect of the authorities to the crying wants and wishes of the Indian public — those vast millions of the population who travel about 36 miles in a year and who now contribute the largest portion of the coaching traffic amounting to 13 crore[1] rupees per annum. *The interests of the European mercantile community are deemed of paramount importance while those of the Indian population at large have been uniformly held of secondary importance, if at all.* At the beck and nod of the former, with their screaming organs of opinion behind, the Government readily spend millions like water on railways without an ultimate thought of the tax-payers and the return such capital would give. It is the greatest blot on Indian railway administration that it ignores the interests of the permanent population and is eager to satisfy first the cry of the interested and migratory European merchant. No private railway enterprise would spend such enormous sums of money and no proprietary body, however rich and influential, would tolerate in any part of the civilised world, the loans after loans, ranging from 15 to 20 crores, which are annually borrowed and expended without let or hindrance, save for a kind of official control, which is no control at all . . . It is a dismal tale, the history of Indian railway finance from first to last. As a matter of fact it is recorded in

[1] A Crore is ten millions and a Rupee is valued roughly at 33 cents of American money.

black and white in one of the important appendices to the report of the Royal Commission on Indian expenditure (1896–97), generally called the Welby Commission, that from 1848 to 1895, the whole system of Indian railways cost to the State, that is the tax-payer, fully 55 crore rupees; and though since that date there have been gains, still, in the railway ledger of the Government of India there is a debit balance against railways of as many as 40 crore rupees.

"It is since 1899–1900 that Indian railways have turned the corner and earned something for the tax-payer on his colossal capital recorded in the Administration Report for 1910 at 430 crore rupees! The average gain since 1904–05 has come to 3 crore rupees per annum. There are no doubt paying railways; but there are also losing ones and these 3 crores are the net balance of gain after writing out the losses. The large gains of the earning railways are absorbed by the losing ones, as could be easily discovered on a reference to appendix 9 of the annual administration report which gives the financial operations of each system of railways.

"Meanwhile, let us mark the progress of this Railway rake during the decade. Perhaps the best way would be to exhibit the most salient features worth knowing and weighing in the following table:

		1901	*1910*
Capital outlay, crores of	Rs.	339.17	439.04
Gross earnings, crores of	"	33.60	45.76
Working expenses, crores of	"	15.75	25.16
Percentage of working expenses to gross earnings, crores of ...	"	46.79	53.10
Net earnings, crores of	"	17.88	20.60
Percentage of net earnings on capital outlay		5.27	5.46
Net gain to the State, that is to the general tax-payer *after* deducting interest on loans borrowed for capital and other indirect charges, crores of	"	1.27	2.75

		1901	1910
Percentage of net gain on total capital outlay, that is to say, the rate of dividend earned by the State or the tax-payer on the total capital		0.38	0.62
No. of miles open		25,370	36,064
No. of passengers carried		19.47	37.15
Passenger earnings, crores of.....	Rs.	10.07	17.12
Goods traffic, crores of tons		4.34	6.50
Goods earnings, crores of	"	21.24	30.43
No. of European employees		5,493	7,411
No. of Eurasian employees		8,175	9,583
No. of Indian employees		353,278	526,499

"The first fact that strikes one is the increase in capital outlay. Capital was increased in 10 years from 339 to 439 crore rupees, that is by 100 crores, equivalent to 30 per cent. Next, while the gross earnings increased by 12.16 crore rupees or 36.20 per cent., the gross working charges increased by 60 per cent.! That is to say, the working charges progressed at almost double the ratio of gross earnings! But how stand the *net* earnings, that is, gross earnings *minus* gross working charges? The increase amounted to 2.72 crore rupees in 10 years equivalent to 15.30 per cent., say 1.5 per cent., per annum. Can it be said that this growth of net earnings at the rate of 1.5 per cent. per annum is commensurate with the growth of capital outlay at 3 per cent.? It should take away the breath of any railway capitalist with an economic conscience. Here practically may be seen the economic phenomenon which in agricultural industry is called the law of diminishing returns. Increased outlay does not mean proportional increase of income. Moreover, with a larger growth of capital, even that income must later on diminish! This evidently will be the financial result if capital is added to capital blindly like Ossa on Pelion from year to year. It should be remembered that these net earnings do not take into account the enormous interest which has to be annually paid on the borrowed railway capital.

When that interest and other indirect charges are deducted as any banker, merchant or man engaged in business should do, the net gain, the *true* net gain or dividend to the shareholder, who is in reality the taxpayer as represented by the State, was only 1.27 crore rupees in 1901 and 2.75 crore rupees in 1910. Or, to put it in another way, the percentage in the former year was only 0.38 per cent. and in the latter 0.62 per cent. on the respective colossal capital. Let the reader just imagine a paltry percentage, a little over ½ per cent., and a little under ¾ per cent.! Here may then be discerned the *final financial result* to the taxpayer. How miserable compared to even 2½ and 3 per cent. of railways by private enterprise elsewhere. In the case of private enterprise there are a number of joint proprietors of a railway. In the case of the State, which represents the tax-payer, there is only *one* proprietor. Beyond that there is no difference. But when the joint stock railway company, after providing for all charges and interest on borrowed monies, divides among its proprietors in the United Kingdom and elsewhere a dividend on its share of capital, say 2½ to 3 per cent. at the lowest, here in India, the dividend goes a little beyond *half a per cent.!* Thus though Indian railways show progress generally, the ultimate financial progress is indeed most disappointing. The only satisfactory feature is the growth of coaching and goods traffic. The number of passengers increased by fully 17.68 crores in 10 years, say, at the rate of 1.76 crore per annum. The growth is equal to 90 per cent. in the decade, while the percentage of increase shown in coaching receipts came to 70. Goods traffic showed an increase in receipts of 9.19 crore rupees, equivalent to 43.26 per cent. Of course, it goes without saying that with 10,691 more miles of new railways open or under construction, the number of all classes of employés should increase. The total increase was 176,577, say at the rate of 17,657 per year. The European employés increased by 35, the Eurasians by 17, and the Indians by 50 per cent. *But the railway authorities have for years deliberately suppressed the salaries and wages annually earned by each class of employés.*"

While the railway administration reports and the government blue books repeat every year the number of Europeans and Indians employed on Indian railways they have persistently omitted to state the amount paid to the classes in salaries. According to the parliamentary return of salaries of May 17, 1892, there were, in all, 2,448 Europeans earning salaries of 1,000 rupees (333 dollars) and upwards per annum in the civil and military employ of the Government of India. Their total salaries came to R. 8,062,840. There were, however, only 895 natives who earned salaries of R. 1,000 or upwards per annum and the total of these salaries amounted to R. 1,367,350. It will be very interesting to have similar information about railway employés. In discussing the blessings conferred on India by the railway system, the Anglo-Indian imperialist is apt to point out:

(a) The huge growth of the foreign trade of the country.
(b) The number to whom the railways give employment.
(c) The help which, in years of scarcity, the railways afford in carrying the surplus produce of one province to another.

Whether (a) is a blessing or not depends on who profits by the foreign trade. We have already shown that the foreign trade is in the hands of the Europeans, and while they purchase Indian produce on their own terms, they convert it into manufactures and resell the same to India, also on their own terms, pocketing all the profits which accrue from manufacture, carriage, insurance, brokerage, etc. As to (b), the number of natives employed by the Indian railways cannot be by any means larger than what were employed in the transportation business on land and waterways before the railways. The railways have practically displaced both. As to (c), in this respect the railways have been more of a curse than a blessing. They have helped in the export of grain more than the needs of the Indian population warrant. Sir W. W. Hunter has left it on record that if every Indian were to have two full meals every day there would be left much less to export than is at present exported. The export of food stuffs has raised prices, without raising the wages of labourers to the same extent. The rise in prices has been one of the potent causes of the increase in land revenue, which in its turn compels the peasant to sell his crops at the price offered by the exporter. All this adds to the income of the railways. Writes Mr. A. K. Connell:[2]

"To sum up, the joint results of railways and free trade may be briefly stated in this way: India used to clothe itself, now England sends clothes, and Indian weavers have lost an enormous source of income, with the gain to the country of the difference in price between English and Indian goods. But to pay for these goods India has to export vast quantities of food and those who sell this food make larger profits than before. Therefore a certain portion of the community

[2] "The Economic Revolution of India and the Public Works Policy," p. 53.

gain by cheaper cotton goods and higher prices for grain. But in order to attain this result they have had to pay the sums before mentioned to build the railways. Besides that, they have to support in years of scarcity a gigantic system of outdoor relief. Is it not obvious that, taking the economic changes as a whole, the country has lost an enormous source of wealth? If the import of cotton to India and the export of grain from India ceased to-morrow, the Indian people would be the gainers, though the Indian Government would be at its wit's end. In fact, the interests of the two are not identical. The Indian Government is now doing its best to stimulate the export of wheat in order to lessen its 'loss by exchange'; but this will only result in higher food prices in India. We now see the explanation of Mr. Hunter's assertion that two-fifths of the people of British India enjoy a prosperity unknown under native rule; other two-fifths earn a fair, but diminishing, subsistence; but the remaining fifth, or forty millions, go through life on insufficient food. And in ten years, according to Mr. Caird, there will be twenty millions more people to feed. Can it, then, be maintained that the material condition of India has been improved by the enormous outlay on railways?

"But you forget, replies the opponent of these heretical views, that in time of famine the railway brings food to starving districts. What would have become of the people of Madras, Bombay, and the North-West Province during the last famine if it had not been for the railways? My reply is: What did become of them? It is true, the railways brought grain; yet they had previously taken it away, and they brought it back at a quadrupled price, and the Government had to spend millions of pounds to enable the peasants to buy it, and even then could not prevent frightful mortality. What has been the native's custom from time immemorial of providing against bad years? Why, the simple method of Joseph in Egypt—that of storing grain. This is what the official report on the Mysore famine tells us:

"'The country had suffered in former years from deficient rainfall, but actual famine had been staved off by the consumption of the surplus ragi, a coarse millet, stored in underground pits, from which it is withdrawn in times of scarcity, as the grain will keep sound and good for forty and fifty years.' Only two of the Famine Commissioners, Messrs. Caird and Sullivan, seem to have recognised the importance of this custom. In the above-quoted very interesting appendix to the first part of the report, they write on the subject of grain storage as follows: 'The food of the people is of the simplest kind, grain, salt, and a few condiments for a relish. The grain is easy to handle, bears storage in pits for many years, and the people themselves grind it as they require it. The pits are made in the ground, in a manner with which the natives are familiar, and cost nothing beyond the encircling ring of baked clay and labour in construction.' It is this storage of grain, the easiest kind of Famine Insurance Fund, that the teachings of plain experience have forced the native to adopt throughout the length and breadth of India, though the amount of stores varies according to the necessities of each district.

"Since the introduction of railways there is reason to believe that the ryot, tempted by immediate gain, or forced by taxation to sell his grain, is beginning to store rupees instead of food; but, as he cannot eat his rupees or jewelry, and cannot buy fuel so as to keep the manure for the land, and has, according to the Famine Commissioners, to give in famine times a quadrupled price for his food, it is very doubtful whether he gains in the long run. Anyhow, the landless labourer, who has no produce to exchange for rupees, finds the market price in time of scarcity utterly beyond his means. Then the Government comes to the rescue with relief works, the railways make roaring profits — in fact, famine and war, both exhausting for the country, are perfect godsends to the foreign investor — and the Indian Government complacently holds up its Public Works policy to an admiring and interested English public. It wholly omits to mention that in time past nearly £30,000,000 of taxation have been squeezed out of the country to pay interest charges, and that, if that sum had been left in the agriculturist's pockets, he might himself have been better able to face bad times, and have helped the labourer to do the same. But Sir John Strachey utterly ignores this aspect of the question; he is quite content with pointing to the relief works, and then insists on the necessity of constructing more railways to meet the next famine cycle. One would suppose that railways proceeded as a free gift out of the benevolent bosoms of British capitalists, instead of being paid for out of the hungry bellies of the Hindoo ryot. The sum of £30,-000,000 represents the amount which India has had to pay out of taxation to get its railways built, and then it has paid £15,000,000 (part of which went to the railway shareholders) to keep the people alive, and after all has lost about five millions of human beings."

This was written in 1883. Since then the evil has grown enormously out of proportion to the so called advantages. For fuller information and discussion of the subject we may refer the reader to Mr. A. K. Connell's book, to Mr. A. J. Wilson's "An Empire in Pawn," to Mr. Digby's "Prosperous British India," to the statements made by Messrs. Naoroji, Wacha, Gokhale and others before the Royal Commissioners on Indian Expenditure in 1896, and to the evidence given before the Famine Commissioners of 1880 and 1897–98. We have no space left to discuss the policy underlying railway rates and railway fares in India.

The Indian Chamber of Commerce and the British Indian Association of Calcutta both have voiced the feelings of the Indian community as to the unfairness of the discrimination that is made in favour of foreign trade, to the neglect and cost of inland trade and Indian industries.

Benefits of Capital Investment. There remains one more point to be noticed. It is often said that the foreign capital invested in Indian railways must have benefited the country a great deal by affording "increased profitable occupation to the people of the country." The statement was examined by Mr. Connell (page 31 of his book, 1883) and his reply was:

"The truth about the capital expenditure is as follows: Of the Guaranteed Railways capital of £96,794,226, spent up to the end of 1880–81, £46,918,177 were withdrawn in England and £49,876,049 in India, while the charge for interest, amounting, as shown above, to about £28,000,000, was almost entirely remitted to England. Thus of the sum total of capital required for the construction of these railways only £21,000,000 were actually spent in India, and as the sum remitted by the railway companies themselves up to 1881 reached the amount of over £29,000,000, there was no balance at all remaining in the country. Indeed, there was a deficit on the whole transaction of £8,000,000. So far, then, from this investment of foreign capital leading to an 'outlay of a larger sum than the interest sent away,' it actually led to the outlay of a smaller sum than would have been spent in the country if no guaranteed railways had ever been built.

"Of the £32,000,000 odd raised for State railways, twenty-four millions have been appropriated in India, and seven and a half millions in England, while the charge for interest, between two and three millions to be added to the capital account, has also gone to England."

Irrigation. The total outlay on irrigation works up to the end of the year 1914–15 was as follows:

Productive major works	£33,780,252
Protective major works	4,364,073
Minor works	4,525,445
Total....	£42,669,770
The total area irrigated was	25,600,000 acres.

The net receipts on capital outlay for the three classes of irrigation works were:—8.97; 0.59, and 4.52 per cent. respectively. Of the permanent debt £41,122,020 was on account of irrigation out of a total debt for public works (railways and irrigation) of £275,245,288 on the last day of March, 1915.[3] It must be freely acknowledged that the twentieth century has seen a very wise change in the policy of the Government of India in the matter of irrigation works to bring large tracts of waste lands under cultivation. The way in which this last is being done is open to several objections but the work itself is highly commendable and beneficent.

[3] The latest facts and figures are taken from the "Material and Moral Progress" report for 1914–15, issued under orders of Parliament.

CHAPTER XII

EDUCATION AND LITERACY

Early Conditions. It is a mere truism that education and literacy are not the same thing. One may be well-educated without being literate, and vice versa. Old Hindu India was universally educated as well as literate. During Moslem domination, India was only partly educated and partly literate. In this connection the reader should remember the remarks of Elphinstone and others about education in pre-British days quoted in the chapter dealing with agriculture. Education and literacy in mediæval India were in no way less than the same in mediæval Europe. Towards the end of the eighteenth century, India had as much education and literacy as Europe. The nineteenth century, however, has brought almost a complete revolution. It is an age of universal literacy. Under modern conditions, literacy is the necessary road to economic efficiency, and that is denied to India. If education makes a man gentle, kind, God-fearing, considerate, temperate and sober, India has enough of it. Even her masses have sufficient background of character and intelligence. They are quick to understand and ready to assimilate. But this is an era of scientific knowledge. For that, literacy and formal instruction are necessary steps. In that India is lagging behind other nations. The Government has made no provision for the instruction of the masses.

Eighty-two of every hundred boys of school age, and ninety-five of every hundred girls, receive no instruction. Education in India is neither universal, nor compulsory, nor free. The kind of education provided for in Indian schools is in its nature antiquated; it does not fit its recipients for the battle of life, according to modern conditions. The expenditure on education is trifling when compared with other countries. The neglect of every kind of vocational training is most palpable. There is no provision for training skilled labour, nor any worth the name for teaching modern languages and modern commerce. The following facts taken from the last quinquennial report of the Government of India, published in 1912, speak for themselves.

Facts and Figures about Education

Total population of India	315,156,386
Population of British India	244,267,542
School enrolment for 1912....................	6,781,000

The population of India of school age has been calculated as 15 per cent. of the total. The actual time spent under primary instruction is three to eight years. This period, however, cannot be taken as sufficient to obtain permanent results. The primary course ordinarily occupies from five to six years; the average age of school life is from the completion of the fifth to the end of the eleventh or twelfth year. These ages include 13.7 per cent. of the population, if we reckon to the end of the eleventh year, and just below 16 per cent. if we reckon to the end of the twelfth year. On the assumption of 15 per cent. of the population being counted as of school age, only 17.7 per cent. of that number are now at school (i.e., at the end of 1912.)

Total expenditure on education in 1912	£5,239,507
Amount expended on education from *public* funds just one-half the total	£2,700,000

The average cost of education of a pupil in India is twelve shillings and ten pence, or about $3.10; of this amount, the share defrayed by the Government from public funds is a little more than one-half, or six shillings and eight pence,—$1.60.

Number of universities in India in 1912	5
Two have been added since that time, making a total of	7
Number of colleges affiliated to the universities	179
From 1907 to 1912 there was an increase of	3
Number of students in colleges	36,533
[1] Expenditure on university education (p. 43)	£90,000

One hundred and twenty-three of the hundred and seventy-nine colleges in India are those in which purely arts courses are given; the number of students registered for arts courses, 28,196. The number has risen by 10,000 in the *quinquennium.*

Law. There are twenty-five law colleges where courses in law and jurisprudence may be pursued. The number of students registered was 3,046.

Medicine. Of medical colleges there are five, with a total enrolment of 1,822 students.

[1] The total expenditure on colleges for general liberal education is given as 4,726,000 Rs. or about $1,600,000 (p. 61). This includes income from fees and private benefactors.

Engineering. Engineering is taught in four colleges and three schools, with a few miscellaneous classes given in private and other institutions. Madras has one college of engineering, with provision for an elementary study of the subject in three technical schools. Bombay boasts of one college and three small aided engineering classes. In Bengal there are one college and two technical schools. The United Provinces have one engineering college among them. In the Punjab there are one school and one class held in a private college. Burma has one school where engineering is taught. The number of pupils availing themselves of these courses is not shown in the Government report on technical institutions, but the following figures were obtained from the tables given in the second volume:

Total number of students in Governmental Schools and Colleges of Engineering 1,607
Total cost to Government of enrolled students in Engineering Rs. 799,388 or $267,000.

Agriculture. There are three government institutions where agriculture is taught, with a total enrolment of 267 students. Cost to Government: Rs. 170,-353, or $56,784. These figures, taken from page 258, table 139 of the report, do not tally with those given in vol. i, ch. 1, dealing with the subject of agriculture. It would appear from this account that there are seven agricultural colleges in India:

I. At Pusa, opened in 1908 as a post-graduate school. Nineteen pupils were registered, but by 1912 their number fell off to seven. Short courses were given in such subjects as management of cattle, poultry, fruit-growing, lac and silk production. From 1908 to 1912 students enrolled in special courses were 2; 45; 59; 33 respectively.

II. Poona College, in 1908 made a separate institution; in 1912, 104 students were enrolled, of whom 15 took short courses.

III. Coimbatore College, opened 1909; students enrolled in 1912, 50.

IV. Behar and Orissa College opened 1910; in 1911–12 students numbered 18.

V. Cawnpore College and Research Laboratories; projected 1907–8, formal opening 1911, with enrolment of 122.

VI. Nagpur College, with 58 students; time of opening not stated.

VII. Lyalpore College, opened 1909; in 1912 enrolled 49 students.

In addition to these there are four veterinary colleges and one school, with a total attendance of 458 students.

Technical and Industrial Education. There are three classes of technical and industrial educational schools: 1. Technological institutions for instruction in principles of science as applied to industrial arts, with the intention of producing masters and managers of industry, and scientific advisors;

2. Technical intermediate schools for the training of foremen and others who require some knowledge of scientific principles and machinery;

3. Trade or craft schools intended to train artisans to follow their calling with dexterity and intelligence.

"In 1907," we are told (page 176), "there were no institutions of class 1 in India, though education of an advanced type was given in mechanical and electrical engineering at the professional colleges. In place of such institutions, scholarships tenable abroad were offered Indian students, that they might benefit by the facilities available in England and elsewhere. *The scholarships were first started in* 1908 *and have been given on an average of about nine a year"* (that is to say, three for every 100,000,000 people.) [Italics are ours.]

During the quinquennium, an institute was opened at Bangalore, Mysore, for which a sum of more than a million dollars was donated by a private individual, the late Mr. J. N. Tata of Bombay. It took the Government about ten years to formulate its policy in connection with the gift. Eventually, in 1911, the institute was opened. Seventeen students entered, and, in the language of the report, "it is too early to judge the results." Besides the endowment fund, the Tata family have given land in Bombay which yields an annual income of Rs. 125,000 or about $41,666; the native State of Mysore has contributed a sum of Rs. 500,000, or $166,666; the Government of India contributed one-half that amount towards the initial expenses, and adds the magnificent sum of $29,000 a year towards upkeep and expenses. The institution, which originally owed its existence to private munificence, is hampered on every side by government interference and restrictions. Public opinion holds that the teaching is incompetent, and that no education worthy the name is being imparted.

In 1911–12 there were altogether two hundred and forty-two technical and industrial schools of the second and third class, out of which but twenty-five are maintained by the Government. At the close of 1912, there were 12,064 pupils in these schools, out of which number only 1,365 were in government schools; the latter are very poor institutions, from the point of view of both teaching and equipment. In the year just cited, the total amount of money spent on the upkeep and expenses of these government schools was Rs. 525,506 or about $175,000,—provincial revenues, local and city funds included.

Thus, out of a population of 315,000,000, only 12,-064 pupils are receiving technical and industrial training, and this mostly of an elementary kind. A comparison of government expenditure for technical education, in India and in America, would be an interesting study in extremes.

Commercial Schools. At the close of 1912, there were twenty-eight commercial schools, with 1,543 students enrolled. Six of these schools are maintained by the Government. The total expenditure for the year was Rs. 28,888, or less than $10,000, provincial and local funds included.

Art Schools. Of these there are four throughout the length and breadth of India, with a total enrolment of 1,234, or about four art students in a million. The total expenditure incurred by the Government for this branch of education is Rs. 164,049, or $54,683.

Education of Europeans. The Europeans in India, British and native States included, number about 301,-433. The report shows that of these 36,000 are at school; it adds that practically all those of an age to receive education are getting it. The cost of educating these 36,000 children is Rs. 6,524,645 annually, out of which sum Rs. 2,124,554 are derived from public revenues. The compiler of the report points out with care that the annual tuition fee for a pupil in an European institution averages Rs. 38, while for a pupil in an institution for Indians it averages Rs. 2. Let it be remembered, as the report itself points out, "that the majority of European pupils are educated in secondary schools," while the majority of Indian pupils are educated, when at all, in elementary schools; thus the comparison loses all its force. The average cost of education for an Indian pupil is estimated at $3.00 a year (Rs. 9–4–11–); the average cost of education for a European student is Rs. 181, or $60.00 a year. Towards the expense of the Indian's education, the Government contributes $1.50 a year, while its expenditure for the European student is $20.00 a year. This vast difference in favour of the European student is specially significant when viewed in the light of the fact that the bulk of the revenues spent on all education in India comes, of course, from the pockets of the tax-paying natives.

Education of Girls. There are only 952,911 girls at school in the whole country, which constitutes 5.1 per cent. of the girls of school age. The following figures are taken from page 215 of the quinquennial report:

	Colleges	*High Schools*	*Middle English Schools*	*Middle Vernacular Schools*
Institutions ...	12	135	193	168
Pupils	173	15,269	15,033	13,804

Primary Schools
12,866 with 446,225 pupils.

Total number institutions	13,394
Total number pupils	490,504

It is said that these latter figures represent only "those in schools especially established for girls."

The average cost of educating an Indian girl is Rs. 4.6 per annum, i.e., slightly less than $1.50. The cost to public funds is about half of that amount, Rs. 2.5 per annum.

The total amount spent for the education of girls is Rs. 6,075,045 or a little more than $2,000,000. Less than half is defrayed from public funds.

CHAPTER XIII

CERTAIN FALLACIES ABOUT THE "PROSPERITY OF INDIA" EXAMINED

THERE are certain outstanding fallacies about the "prosperity of India," which form the stock in trade of British imperialists in all discussions relating to India. We will examine them briefly.

(a) The first and foremost of them is the argument that is based on the absorption of precious metals by India during the last seventy years. In a paper bearing the date August, 1911, in the collection of the East India Association papers, it is said that within the seventy years preceding, India absorbed gold of the value of £240,000,000, out of which no less than £82,000,000 worth was imported in the first decade of the twentieth century, leaving a balance of £158,000,000 for the preceding sixty years.

Taking the figures from the statistical abstracts of 1901–02 to 1910–11, the total of net imports of gold comes to a little over £75,000,000 only.

The writer of the East India paper also gives the figures of silver imports. He says that within the seventy years India absorbed 2,250,000,000 ounces of silver, out of which 720,000,000 ounces were imported in the decade immediately preceding, valuing it at £88,000,000.

To the quantity of gold thus imported he adds another £35,000,000 as likely to have been in India in 1840 and this brings the grand total to £275,000,000 for the total stock of gold in India in 1911. Similarly he values the total stock of silver in India, at the end of 1910, as worth £250,000,000. On the basis of these figures he remarks, "with such figures before them, how can people say that India is being drained of her material wealth?"

Mr. Digby's masterly reply to this argument is contained in Chapter V of his monumental work. We can only notice the argument very briefly.

First as regards the total value of gold and silver imported into India, Mr. Digby's figures for the sixty-five years from 1835 to 1900 come to £377,853,857. From this figure Mr. Digby deducts the following:

The British Indian Mints coined in sixty-five years from silver supplied by Government ..	£34,570,665
The Feudatory States have minted, say	13,000,000
Total	£47,570,665
To this must be added, to replace wear and tear, estimated before a Committee of the House of Commons at £666,666 a year	£43,333,290

as also £65,000,000 on account of wastage in the trinkets and ornaments of the population at the rate of one penny per head per annum. This account gives a balance of £221,949,902 to the credit of the people of India in sixty-five years. Dividing the balance on the average population of 180,000,000 during the period, Mr. Digby concludes that in the sixty-five years concerned, the treasure imported into India would amount to £1 4s. 1¼d. per head or to 4¼d. per head per annum.

Taking the figures of the writer of the East India paper, the total value of the imports of gold and silver into India in ten years from 1900 to 1910 would be £170,000,000 or say an average of £70,000,000 per annum. Divided on 315,000,000 it results in about 4s. 5d. per head per annum (110 cents). This average is struck without making any deductions for coinage, for government reserves and for "the hoards" of the feudatory States.

In the statement of moral and material progress of India for 1911–12 "the total importation of gold sovereigns for the decade" is given as £57,000,000, out of which about £18,000,000 were imported in 1911–12 alone. Of this, nine millions were held in government treasuries, and forty-eight millions were either in circulation or held by the people.

The total net addition to the silver currency during the decade was about sixty-eight crores of rupees valued at £45,300,000. This sum includes only rupees and half rupees.

On March 31, 1912, the Government reserve consisted of

Gold	£21,259,400
Silver Coin	£10,328,100
Bullion	£ 52,500

It would be thus seen that after proper deductions the net treasure *really* absorbed by the people and princes of India considerably dwindles.

At this stage it would be well to remember that the native States of India take a great deal of precious metals in return for the goods which they supply.

Their import of merchandise per head is considerably less than in British India and they get the price of their exports mostly in bullion.

The fact is that when making pleas like this the British Imperialists forget the huge population with which they are dealing and fail to make the necessary deductions. Besides, they ignore that India is a heavy borrower. Debts raised in England must be sent to India in the shape of gold and silver.

No one contends that there are no rich people in India. Some of the rulers of the native States may have amassed big treasures. Besides, the Government contractor, the banker, the lawyer and the stock exchange dealer have all made some money. In every country, however poor generally, there must be a certain section of the population who are rich. Their existence, though, does not prove that the people are prosperous. The fact remains that in spite of these imports of gold and silver the average income of an Indian has been officially estimated to be not more than $10 a year [1] and the average wealth per capita in India is £11. We have given the comparative tables in another chapter.

(b) The trade figures are also cited as proof of India's prosperity. We have already shown who profits by this trade. If we divide the total foreign trade on 315 millions of Indians it comes to much less than £1 per head.

(c) The same may be said about the figures relating to railways. See the chapter on railways.

[1] At which figure it has stood for the last thirty years (see Appendix).

As to the poverty of the masses and the general lack of money in India, we may in conclusion quote from an article by Sir D. Hamilton in the July, 1916, number of the *Calcutta Review.*

Says Sir D. Hamilton:

"We have given India peace; but we have not given her power—the power to rise in the human scale. India is four-fifths of the Empire but has not one-fifth of her strength . . . Weak in education, weak in medicine, weak in sanitation, weak in political power, and weak in all that is due to weakness in finance more than anything else."

Again:

"Money is power, and modern money is Credit, of which India has little or none; and a people without Credit are a people without a present or a future."

"How is it," asks he, "that in the year of our Lord 1916, after a hundred years of British rule and under a Government the most humane in the world, India is so bare of Credit and Cash." His answer is: "Mainly because the Government has overlooked the first principles of political economy. . . . The first object of its political economy has been to square its own budget rather than to enable the people to square theirs. It has enabled the people to provide a plentiful revenue not for themselves but for others."

"The national purse is empty for peace as for war and will remain empty until the purses of the people are first filled in accordance with the first principles of political economy."

"Russia understands this."

Sir D. Hamilton then makes some quotations from a recent speech of the Russian Finance Minister and finally winds up this part of his paper by remarking,

"While Russia plans and prospers, is India 'to wait and see'?"

In another part of the same paper he observes, "Financially the people stand where they did at the commencement of British rule."

The Indian Nationalists, however, think that the people are financially worse off than they were at the commencement of British rule.

How the recent "gift" of $500,000,000 by the Government of India to the Imperial Government will affect the financial resources of India remains to be seen.

CHAPTER XIV

TAXES AND EXPENDITURE

Abstract of Revenue and Expenditure. The preceding chapters of the book give some idea of the principal sources of government revenue and also what proportion of them is spent in England.

In this chapter I propose, for facility of reference and comparison, to give a summary of government revenue and expenditure. The statistical abstract available to me is that of 1913–14, and I take my figures from it.

Gross Revenue for 1913–14	£85,207,175
Expenditure charged to Revenue in India	62,583,079
Expenditure charged to Revenue in England	20,311,673
Surplus	2,312,423

PRINCIPAL HEADS OF REVENUE

Land Revenue	£21,391,575
Opium	1,624,878
Salt	3,445,305
Stamps	5,318,293
Excise	8,894,300
Customs	7,558,220
Assessed Taxes	1,950,250
Forest	2,229,872
Registration	518,962
Tributes from Native States	616,881
Provincial Rates	180,210
Total	£53,728,746

Net receipts from Railways	£17,625,634
Irrigation	4,713,159
Military Receipts	1,369,652

Interest	£1,352,119
Post Office	2,410,210
Telegraph	1,188,309
Mint	339,841
Receipts by Civil Departments such as Courts of Law, Jails, &c.	1,408,286
Miscellaneous Receipts	772,579
Total Revenue ..	£85,207,175

Expenditure

Charges in respect of Collections, Refunds, Drawbacks, Assignments and Compensation	£9,274,597
Interest on ordinary Debts and ordinary obligations	1,515,653
Post Office	2,092,019
Telegraph	1,180,965
Mint	132,630
Salaries and Expenses if Civil Departments	17,934,199
Miscellaneous Civil Charges	5,403,804
Famine Relief and Insurance	1,000,000
Railway Revenue Account including interest on debt	12,836,101
Irrigation	3,531,867
Other Public Works	7,010,038
Military Services	21,265,765
Total Expenditures	£83,177,688
Deducting two minor sums about provincial allotments not spent the total expenditure chargeable to Revenue remains	£82,894,752
Expenditure not charged to Revenue for Railways, Irrigation works and the construction of new Delhi	12,212,596
Total Charges	£95,107,348

Ingenious Way of Calculating the Burden of Taxation. In the statistical abstract a very ingenious method is adopted to show the burden of taxation.

(a) The heads of Taxation are reduced to Salt, Stamps, Excise, Provincial Rates, Customs, Assessed Taxes and Registration. All other

> sources of income are omitted. The figure realised from these sources is thus reduced from over 85 millions to 27,278,680. This figure divided over the estimated population of British India brings the payment per head to 2 shillings and 2-4 pence.

It is however added that "if Land Revenue [which is not properly taxation] be added the payment per head comes to 3 shillings and 10-4 pence."

It may be noted that receipts from opium, courts of justice, jails, railways, post office, telegraphs, canals, forests and public works are all excluded, omitting other minor heads of income.

The Growth of Army Expenditure. In 1884-85 the total army expenditure was 170 million rupees, i.e., a little less than 57 million dollars.

In 1899-1900 it was 264 millions of rupees = 88 million dollars.

In 1909-1910 it rose to 286 millions of rupees = 95⅓ million dollars.[1]

In 1914-15 it was about 306.5 millions of rupees = over 102 million dollars (£20,434,915).

In the budget of 1916-17 22 million pounds or 330 millions of rupees or 110 millions of dollars were provided for.

As to the percentages of military expenditures to the total budgets of the different parts of the British Empire, see an article in *The Nineteenth Century and After* for February, 1917, by Yusaf Ali from which extracts are given in appendix (A).

[1] Figures are taken from the Honourable Mr. D. E. Wacha's pamphlet on "Indian Military Expenditure." This year's budget exceeds 26 millions sterling.

The army alone absorbs the total revenue from land and more.

The Growth of Expenditure on Education. To a total of £6,696,587 spent on education from all sources including fees and private munificence in 1913–14, the provincial funds contributed £2,436,900 (see the statistical abstract).

According to the Year Book (1915) issued by *The Times of India* Office, Bombay, the Government of India spent on education 2,610,000 in 1912–13. In the year 1913–14 they made a provision of 4,078,000 in the original budget, but in the revised one the figure was reduced to 3,242,000. In the budget for 1914–15 a provision of 4,000,000 was made, but in the financial statement made by the finance-member in March, 1916, it was explained that the total sanctioned was not spent and in the estimate presented by him for the next year the figure available for education was actually reduced.

It was my intention to show how much of the expenditure on the civil departments consisted of salaries paid to Europeans in India, but the latest figures available to me are those given in the Material and Moral Progress Statement for 1911–12 and they are not complete. It is stated in that report that out of the aggregate salaries of officers drawing twenty-five dollars a month (£5) or over

Europeans received	........R.	3,590,000
Eurasians "	....	844,000
Indians "	....	2,457,000

Of posts carrying salaries of R. 1000 a month (333⅓ dollars or £66⅔) 1721 were held by Europeans and 161 by Indians. For a comparison of the salaries enjoyed by Europeans in the service of the Government of India with corresponding officers in the United States, see appendix.

CHAPTER XV

SUMMARY AND CONCLUSION

THE British conquest of India has no parallel in history. It is the most romantic and the most subtle of all political revolutions that have taken place in the world. It was never formally planned; it was never authoritatively resolved upon. Yet, paradoxical as it may seem, we cannot believe it was the blind accident that Professor Seeley characterises it. In the preface to the second volume of Sir William Hunter's "History of British India," the editor has said:

"As early as 1687 the Court of Directors hoped to lay the foundations of a large, well-founded, sure English dominion in India for all time to come."

He inclines to think the British aimed at a commercial rather than a political supremacy, but the history of British acquisition in India conclusively proves that successful commercial ascendency is but the sure and inevitable prelude to political domination.

Of all forms of conquest, that which proceeds under the guise of commerce is most insidious, most prolonged and most devastating to the conquered. A military invasion, undertaken from frankly political motives, at least does not take the people unawares. The wars of olden times were short and swift, and their results certain. A change of despotisms mattered little to the people of East or West; in the long run, they adapted themselves to the change. The swift horrors of warfare, with its decisiveness of action and certainty of outcome, are inconceivably preferable to the slow tortures of a military invasion that comes cloaked under the guise of commercial enterprise. Had the British Government, in 1757, invaded India by force of arms and subjugated the country on the open field of battle, a century of incessant warfare, no less agonising because of its protracted nature, might have been spared her. But behind military and commercial exploitation skulked the lust for political dominion. Most of the misfortunes of India, from 1757 to 1857, are due to the manner in which she was subjugated. 'To the victor belong the spoils' is a universal law of warfare, but martial law cannot last forever, and a more stable government under politicians and statesmen inevitably reasserts itself. But who is to call a halt on the plundering of commercial adventurers? Where is the limit to their greed and rapacity?

India was never conquered by the English sword—not by military valour, but by a subtle and cunning diplomacy. To have used more direct means, based upon an avowed determination to subdue the country by force of arms, would have roused the warring chiefs to a sense of mutual danger, and united them against the common enemy. When Clive, in 1765, offered to conquer Hindustan for Great Britain, Pitt refused, saying it was beyond the resources of the government. The conquest of India was accomplished in the only way England could afford to do it, at India's expense. Lulled by professions of a purely commercial interest, the native chieftains vied with one another in extending opportunities of trade to the British, in return for military services rendered by these armed merchants in subduing local rivals. Too late they found that the mailed fist which encompassed the ruin of their enemies was turned with equal effectiveness against themselves!

The English policy was simple and consistent — to create schisms in the camps of the Nabobs and Rajahs, using one side against the other, for the furtherance of their own interest. Could the Nabob of Bengal have seen the finger of fate in the concessions to build forts and factories on his eastern coast, which he granted to the East Indian traders; could the Vizier of Oude have foreseen that the power whose help he invoked to ruin Benares and extirpate the Rohillas would in less than a century pension off his descendants as helpless parasites on its mercy and magnanimity; could the Grand Mogul have realised the significance of his grant of Dewani to Clive; had the Nabob of Karnatic had prophetic eyes to read the future ruin of his house when he obtained aid from the English to overcome the Mahrattas; if the Nabob of Surat and the Rajah of Tanjore might have read their twin fates in the stars — this petty warfare would have coalesced into a united stand against this alien foe, and cast him out of India. But what Indian prince could doubt the treaties of "eternal friendship" sworn to by these British traders,— or their solemn abjurations of all thoughts of territorial aggrandisement? A house divided against itself cannot stand, and betrayed by their own rivalry.

they sold their country to a foreign power, whose servants, urged on by private greed and patriotic zeal, bought their undisputed sway over a continent.

Philip Francis, in an epigrammatic speech delivered on Indian affairs in 1787, describes the process thus:

> "From factories to forts, from forts to fortifications, from fortifications to garrisons, from garrisons to armies, and from armies to conquests, the gradations were natural, and the results inevitable; where we could not find a danger we were determined to find a quarrel."

The directors of the East India Company wanted money. That was the burden of their communications to Warren Hastings and his successors in the Presidency of Bengal. But their agents in India also wanted money for themselves. It was well said by one of them that when "more money could not be had by legitimate means, they took to the road." Trade, external and internal, afforded too restricted and slow accumulations of wealth; political intrigues, backed up by military force, could alone secure desired results. The examples of Clive, Governor Vansittart, and Warren Hastings offered too strong an inducement of success to be resisted by men of human passions and human weaknesses undeterred by any check upon their fears. Governors and members of council, not to mention generals and commanders, all had their fixed share in the booty which every military exploit brought. In addition to the ordinary loot, secured in the sacking of towns after military conquests, every treaty entered into with a native prince was ratified by large grants of money made by the latter "to the officers concerned in settling the treaty."[1]

Every interest, private and public, personal and patriotic, drove the representatives of the East India Company to seek opportunities of exploitation through military operations and political intrigues. Most of the proceeds of prize money, booty and presents were appropriated by the company's servants, the charges of administration and the maintenance of the army being met by the revenues proper. From time to time, the directors reiterated in solemn terms their freedom from territorial designs, but where treaties had been made, and lands acquired, they quietly confirmed the former and accepted the latter, often conferring signal honours on those instrumental in securing them.

India's misfortunes were thus enhanced by the vacillating policies of the merchant masters of the company, whom Chatham once described as "the lofty Asiatic plunderers of Leadenhall Street."

The traders of Leadenhall were not conquerors. They did not care for an empire. What they wanted was money, and they were quite happy when the military and political operations of their servants brought them substantial gains. But when the reverse was the

[1] One such item is £300,000 mentioned by Malcolm in connection with the treaty which was made with Tipu. Another by Torrens: "when the prize money came to be decided upon, after the campaign of 1799, £100,000 which, *according to rule* would have fallen to the share of the Governor General, Marquis of Wellesley, the latter waived in favour of the troops." (Malcolm, Vol. I, Ch. 5, note,—Torrens, "Empire in Asia," pp. 230, 248.) Another mention of prize-money in connection with Lord Wellesley is made in reference to the war with Scindhia.

case, they were equally ready to condemn and repudiate.[2]

Between these conflicting policies, the Indian people were ground into the dust. The security of the native rulers was practically gone from the moment Warren Hastings confiscated the territories of the Rajah of Benares and assisted the Vizier of Oude to exterminate the Rohillas. Thus their own chiefs could not protect them from new ones whose wars of exploitation soon developed into wars of annexation. It was the Marquis of Wellesley who first saw the monstrosity of the dual system, and who determined by hook or crook to put an end to native rule. With the total lack of scruple characterising most empire builders, he pursued a policy of deception, telling deliberate lies in his public despatches, while availing himself of every pretence to make wars and snatch territories.[3]

Justice, honesty, fair play, and the wishes of the

[2] Sheridan described their attitude when he said that "there was something in their operations which combined the meanness of a pedlar with the profligacy of a pirate. Alike in military and political manœuvres could be observed auctioneering ambassadors and political traders, and thus we saw a revolution brought about by affidavits, an army employed in executing an arrest, a town besieged on a note of hand, a prince dethroned for a balance of account. Thus it was they united the mock-majesty of a bloody sceptre and the little traffic of a merchant's counting house, wielding a truncheon with one hand, and picking a pocket with the other." (Speech, Feb. 7, 1787, Parl. Hist., Vol. XXV, Col. 287.)

[3] The Rajah of Benares lost his territory for refusing to make an exorbitant contribution towards defraying the expenses of the Company's wars in the South, for which he recognised no obligation. The Rohillas were extirpated because the Nabob of Oude required it in compensation for large sums he was forced to pay to the English.

Torrens, p. 221, for quotations of Marquis of Wellesley's despatches, Vol. I, and certain correspondence between the Governor General and Mr. Dundas.

people never entered into the programme of Wellesley and his lieutenants, who entered wholeheartedly into his schemes. The only reeinerion was the chance of success for their enterprises. Arguing against immediate further conquest, the Marquis wrote to Munro:

"I agree with you that we ought to settle the Mahratta business and the Malabar Rajahs, but I am afraid that to extend ourselves will rather tend to delay settlement . . . *as for the wishes of the people, I put them out of the question.*"[4] The italics are ours.

Munro was for out and out conquest, though he cautiously added, "we should not all at once attempt to extend ourselves so far, for it is beyond our power, but we should keep the object in view, though the accomplishment might require a long series of years. The dissensions and revolutions of the native governments will point out the time when it is proper for us to become actors."[5]

Thus spoke the company's representatives in India, the while they openly opposed territorial expansion and signed treaties sworn to endure till the sun and moon failed in their course. Native dissensions and revolutions not coming with sufficient speed, the servants of the company used every available means to hasten them, for the furtherance of their designs. Alliances were made, and broken; subsidies were demanded and exacted, and residents placed in native courts to sow the seeds of internal dissension and domestic revolution. Says Torrens:

"Lord Wellesley's purpose in persuading the Native

[4] Gleig's "Life of Munro," Vol. I, p. 266.
[5] *Ibid.*, Vol. I, p. 123.

Governments to maintain within their confines bodies of English troops, instead of Native corps officered by Frenchmen, was too obvious to be misconceived. . . . It was obviously meant and felt, if not declared, to be a guarantee against the development of schemes hostile to English interests and the growth of English ascendency. . . . It was the glove of mail courteously but undisguisedly laid upon the shoulder of Native rule, with an irresistible but patronising air, felt to be a little heavy and hard at first, but soon destined to become habitual.

"Its financial scope was conceived and executed with the same pitiless and inexorable purpose. The permanent appropriation of revenue for the maintenance of the subsidiary force was calculated mainly with the inability of the State to bear it. . . . The opening of a running account of deficiencies, arrears, balance cleared off from time to time by new concessions, became inevitable. Arriving at ultimate supremacy, the means taken were called by the subject race, perfidiously wicked,—by the conquering race, profoundly wise."[6]

Besides bodies of English troops stationed at native courts, there were the active efforts of the Residents, "everywhere feared and hated as the symbol of humiliation," employed in corrupting ministries, spying on chiefs, and seeking provocation to disrupt and disorganise the government in which they played the rôle of dictator.[7]

Glimpses of these Machiavellian policies may be found in the contemporary records of the great actors

[6] Torrens, "Empire in Asia," pp. 233-34-35.

[7] See Garwood, Wellesley Correspondence; also "Papers and Correspondence of Lord Metcalfe," regarding the policy of Sir Thomas Barlow; also the Private Journal of Lord Moira, Vol. I, p. 44, quoted in Torrens, Chapter XIX.

themselves, a glance at which will amply repay the reader who desires first hand knowledge. Enough has been said to illustrate the point taken, that the British subjugation of India was a long process of military and economic exhaustion, a sort of killing by inches, which took a century to complete. Many a noble-minded Englishman tried, as best he could, to alleviate the sufferings of the people of India. Some of these attempted to persuade their masters at home to adopt a more humane policy towards the country which they were exploiting to its ultimate ruin. But they failed. There were periods of comparative peace, when some constructive upbuilding was attempted, but on the whole, the century was one of destruction and exploitation. People died by millions: the country was drained of wealth; fields were devastated and manufactures ruined; the seal of poverty, hopeless, unmitigated, unredeemed, was set upon the land once fabled for its riches.

Lord Dalhousie, so lauded by English historians for his high-minded justice, may be regarded most charitably as the unintentional and involuntary instrument of Providence which brought India's long agony of civil strife and bloodshed to a close. His unjustifiable and piratical acts exasperated both people and princes, and drove them to open rebellion. The British were now determined to make an empire from East to West, and as early as 1816 had decided to "annihilate all powerful native Governments."[8] So the criminal breaches of trust and acts of high-handedness in regard to the Punjab, Oude, Jhansi, Nagpur, Satara and

[8] Metcalfe, in "Kaye's Life," p. 432.

Scinde but hastened the annexation which at best could only have been deferred a few years longer. Up to 1858, India was British by courtesy only. After the mutiny, the British Government took over the direct administration of its affairs. Queen Victoria started the new régime auspiciously with a proclamation guaranteeing equal treatment of natives and English,—promises so far honoured more in the breach than in fulfilment. The reason is obvious. Under the Crown, as under the Company, there is the same clash of interests between Indian democracy and British plutocracy — under the new system, as under the old, England still battens on India's wealth, which is drained off in a golden stream, bearing her life blood with it. During the last fifty-seven years, the fiscal policy in regard to the Great Dependency was laid down in Whitehall, and no English Cabinet dared to sacrifice the interests of the British merchant class for a mere consideration of Indian well-being.

As the prosperity of Britain is grounded on manufactures and trade, British interests demand that India live, toil and have her being to the end of British prosperity, by sending grist to the mill and buying the flour. Hers is the double roie of supplying the raw material and purchasing the finished product. A self-governing India would never submit to play this part, hence she remains a dependency under pressure.

A distinguished Indian economist said recently: "India's misfortunes are due to the fact that she is economically passive; what she needs is to be economically active."

It is futile for Indians or English to talk of India's

economic development until she is free to lay down her own fiscal policy in her own interests. This can never be until the Indian Government is so transformed as to make it responsible, not to the India Office in London, but to the people of India themselves. The present Administration has neglected everything upon which her prosperity as a nation could be built. There is virtually no provision there for producing skilled labour of the higher order; education, both general and technical, is shockingly neglected. In all the length and breadth of India, there is but one technological institute, and this owes its existence to private munificence. Even now its usefulness in promoting the development of Indian industries is virtually nil, so hedged about with restrictions is its management.

The principal industry of India is agriculture, yet before 1907 there was not a single agricultural college in the whole country. A privately-endowed commercial college has been opened recently in Bombay, but even this institution rests under the suspicion of being a reserve for third-class men from England.

For a number of years, Indians have been crying for a definite Government policy towards native industries. This agitation reached its climax during the present war. The successful entry of Japan as a competitor has forced the hand of the Administration, and a commission has been appointed to inquire and report upon the industrial situation. The questions of tariff and fiscal policy are declared to be outside its scope, and already the independent Indian mind suspects the appointment of this body a mere sop to public opinion. The Hon. D. E. Wacha, Member of the Supreme

Legislative Council, a recognised authority on Indian finance, declared he had no reason to think this Commission likely to be different from others of which we have had such bitter experience in the past. "In the long run," he says, "their recommendations are akin to a change from Tweedledum to Tweedledee."

The economic situation of India to-day was very tersely summed up by the able young publicist, the Hon. C. Y. Chintamani, in his address to the Provincial Conference at Jhansi, Oct. 8, 1916:

"The mass of the population is poor, very poor. A state of destitution, accompanied by disease and debt, is the normal condition of the bulk of the people. A comparative study of the aggregate annual national income, expenditure and savings of the peoples of different countries, would reveal a painful state of things in India. John Bright said that if a country possessing a most fertile soil and capable of bearing every variety of production, found the people in an extreme state of suffering and destitution, there was some fundamental error in the government. The observation was made of India. The Duke of Argyll, Secretary of State for India under Gladstone, recorded his opinion, 'of chronic poverty and permanent reduction to the lowest level of subsistence such as prevail among the vast population of rural India, we have no example in the Western world.' In a paper on the wealth of the Empire, read before the British Association in 1903, the aggregate annual income of the United Kingdom (whose population is less than our United Provinces) was put at 1,750,000,000 pounds and that of India at 600,000,000 pounds, roughly, 30 rupees per head per annum. The general survey of the Empire led Sir Robert Giffen to consider 'how vast must be the economic gulf separating the people of the United Kingdom from India when we find that 42,000,000 of people in the United Kingdom consume in food and drink alone an amount equal to the whole income of 300,000,000 Indians. Unless relieved from their state of semi-starvation, the Indian problem and difficulty remain untouched.' He further pointed out the anomaly of Britain requiring of India and India alone, a substantial military expenditure, though the wealth of the self-governing colonies is so enormously greater than that of India. This though the Indian army is freely used for imperial and general purposes, and is not employed exclusively for local defence.

"Agriculture is our one national industry, but it is in a depressed state. We are told that the increased cultivation of exportable crops such as jute, cotton and oil seeds, and the higher level of prices have brought greater prosperity to India — but all things considered, their state is hardly better than before, and the oft-recurring famines, each one meaning, besides intense suffering, enormous loss of wealth; the growing pressure of the revenue demand; and the higher cost of living have made their condition worse. The output per acre is smaller in India than elsewhere, because the cultivator cannot afford to adopt costlier methods. The magnitude of agricultural indebtedness is appalling, nor is it due to the extravagance of the ryots. The land revenue system has an intimate bearing on the condition of the agricultural population, and Mr. J. E. O'Connor recommended a general reduction of 33 per cent. in the Government demand, a plea as ineffectual as the repeated resolutions of the Indian National Congress and the efforts of Mr. R. C. Dutt have been.

"Manufacturing industries are a second source of national wealth. India was not a stranger to them in the past, but what was euphemistically described as 'the tide of circumstance' deprived her of them. Mr. Justice Ranade's impressive description of our industrial helplessness is not out of date: 'The country is fed, clothed, warmed, washed, lighted, helped and comforted generally by a thousand arts and industries in the manipulation of which its sons have every day a decreasing share. This dependency has come to be regarded as a plantation, growing raw products to be shipped by British agents in British ships, to be worked into fabrics by British skill and capital, and to be re-exported to India by British merchants to their British shops there and elsewhere. Stagnation and dependence, depression and poverty — these are written in broad characters on the face of the land and its people.' The recent Government efforts at industrial development hardly touch the fringe of the problem.

"A third source of wealth,— foreign trade, does not contribute to the prosperity of Indians, being mainly in the hands of Europeans whose home is away from India, besides the drain of wealth due to political causes."

Indian public opinion is thus practically unanimous on the following points:

(a) British policy in India is responsible for the destruction of Indian industries.

(b) The British Government in India has so far failed in a duty which is recognised by all national governments to revive indigenous industries and establish new ones.

(c) The fiscal policy of the Indian Government has been dictated from Whitehall mainly in the interest of British trade, in opposition to, and often in defiance of the best Anglo-Indian administrators.

(d) India has suffered from a constant drain of her national wealth, which has enriched England to India's cost.

(e) While free trade has been profitable to England, it has been ruinous to India, with its doctrine of *laissez-faire*.

(f) Railway construction, by means of foreign loans, interest on which was guaranteed by the Government to be paid from Indian revenues, has been ruinous to Indian finance. Up to 1899–1900 it brought no return to the tax-payer.

(g) The railways discriminate against Indian industries and internal trade in their freight rates.[9]

(h) The governmental neglect of education, general, commercial and technical, retards the growth of modern industries in India, as it results in lack of skilled labour.

(i) In view of India's impoverished condition, there can be no justification for the system of costly administration in force for the past 150 years, as it is maintained at the expense of native economic, industrial and educational development. Far too much money has been spent on the military.

(j) India's resources have been squandered in military expeditions in which she had no interest. A policy of Imperial expansion has been followed at the cost of India.

(k) The only effective remedy for these crying evils is "self-government," with "fiscal autonomy."

In the language of one of our most conservative leaders of public thought, the Hon. Mr. D. E. Wacha, already quoted above:

"If Indian poverty is to be reasonably reduced, if the standard of living of the teeming masses is to be

[9] The Chairman of the Indian Merchant's Chamber and Bureau of Commerce stated in his last annual report: "The indigenous Industries Committee appointed by the Bombay Government found that over and above the difficulties of lack of expert advice, and *of adverse railway rates*, in some cases, these industries suffered from under-capitalisation." Italics are mine. The British Indian Association of Calcutta, a body of Bengal Zemindars, have recently made the same representation on railway discrimination, to the Government.

satisfactorily raised; if education and sanitation are to be greatly accelerated, the first and fundamental assumption is a well-devised scheme of fiscal autonomy. Unless the people are allowed full freedom to work out their own economic destiny, it is hopeless to foresee a prosperous India."

Thus we see that not only the left wing of Indian Nationalists, but conservative native opinion as well, sees in self-government the only potent remedy for the Indian Problem.

English opinion on the subject is widely divided. The number willing to concede India her rights is painfully limited. A few intellectuals favour the idea, as well as a scattering of radical thinkers, writers and Members of Parliament. Those statesmen who are at the helm preserve an ominous silence. In the meantime, the proposal to make the colonies partners in the Empire has created consternation in India. Indian opinion on the point was correctly voiced by the Hon. C. Y. Chintamani when he remarked: —

"Brother-delegates, the war has brought the supreme question of India's political status to the front. What is to be her future position in the Empire, and what the system of internal government? The fervid utterances of British statesmen, the even warmer utterances of politicians and the British press, during the early months of the war, must be still fresh in your minds. England went to war for the practical assertion of the rights of nations to freedom, and India was not to be denied. The British Empire, of which India comprises the largest single whole, was to be a really free empire. India was not for long to remain a mere dependency,— she was to be recognised as a partner. Imperialism was no longer to stand for the aggrandisement of the white peoples at the expense of the coloured races, so-termed. Indians were no longer to be mere subjects of exploitation for the benefit of His Majesty's colourless subjects. Even the colonists of the self-governing dominions seemed to be thinking kindly of us. We have always asserted our indefeasible right to absolute equality of status, and these first signs of recognition gave us fresh hope to claim what we have always been entitled to as our just right, and not a favour. The Prime Minister and other eminent British statesmen have made repeated public declarations that the constitution of the Empire will undergo a change upon the war's termination. But in the whole of the discussions very little reference to India is found. The Secretary of State, our 'Grand Mogul at Westminster,' has had scarcely a cheering word to utter. He has found time to put through Parliament two such uncalled-for and retrograde measures as the Indian Civil Service Act and the Government of India Act — the Prime Minister has spared parliamentary time for their passage through both houses; but the annual debate on Indian affairs has been suspended during the last three years, and there has been no authoritative statement on the policy of His Majesty's Government in relation to India. In India itself, the 'new angle of vision' has manifested itself in the form of internments and prohibitions under the 'Defence of India' Act; a too free employment of the arbitrary 'Press Act,' with controversial legislation, increased police expenditure (particularly the C. I. D. branch) and a reduced outlay on education.

"But a far worse menace confronts us. It has been given out that the present self-governing dominions are to be admitted into partnership with England in governance of the Empire; the Crown Colonies, India among them, will be subjected to a further degradation of their already low political status, subject to the politicians of Canada, South Africa, Australia and New Zealand. Why should any one think of inflicting such a grievous wrong upon India? What are these colonies of yesterday by the side of this hallowed land of ours, which stretches in its sublime past to the beginnings of humanity, with a culture and a civilisation which will for all time shed lustre on the human race; with qualities of heart and head in respect to which her children need fear no comparison with any people in any country; and looking forward with confidence, to a future not unworthy of her ancient past? Why should they be our rulers,—why should we suffer them to be? We mean to insist with greater determination that there shall be no governing caste in India,—no rulers and ruled, but equal subjects with common rights and obligations, living on terms of manly comradeship. How galling to contemplate subjection to the colonies whose superior title in any respect we see no reason to acknowledge. It is our imperative duty to make it known to all concerned that India's position in the Empire shall, in all respects, be identical with that of the present self-governing dominions. To compromise is to commit political suicide as a nation and a race."[10]

English opinion on the economic effects of British rule in India may be divided into three classes:

First: Men such as Hyndman, Digby, Martin, Wilson and others, who frankly admit the economic harm done to India by British rule, and express their regret therefor.

Second: Men who do not admit the economic exploitation of India by England, but maintain that England's management has made India more prosperous than ever before in her history. To this class belong men of the Strachey school.

Third: Men who honestly admit the fact of In-

[10] Since the above was in type a reassuring statement on the subject has been made by the Secretary of State for India.

dia's exploitation for England's profit, but who justify it by the right of conquest. They maintain, and rightly, that India was acquired for the purpose of commercial gain, and should be administered on that basis. This is the *Morning Post* school, and thoroughly to be commended for the absence of hypocrisy, which governs the utterances of diplomats and political apologists. Grandiloquent bursts of rhetoric are inconsistent with British bluntness and do no credit to her national candour. If Englishmen have exploited India, it can be justified on the only tenable ground of India's having allowed herself to be so exploited. One nation does not conquer another out of philanthropy, and at its best, the rule of one people over another can be but "benevolent despotism." Domination is always dictated by self-interest, justified by the right of might. The crime of India was her weakness, and she expiates it under the heel of Imperialism. Let her grow strong or perish — the world gives no place to senility.

Such is the creed of the twentieth century, worked out in the bloody struggles of the past, and in the law of the survival of the fittest. But in expounding the law, let us not prate of ethics. Exploitation and conquest may have peculiar ethical value in the vast economy of Nature, but for that, credit and a sanctimonious justification is not given to the exploiter and the conqueror. Let me not rob a weaker brother, and cry "holier than thou" as an added claim to his possessions. It profanes the might of right.

It lies within the reader's judgment, based on the facts here stated, to decide how benevolent is England's despotism in India. British rule in India has its brighter side. Young India has drunk deep from the springs of liberty and the rights of man, as embodied in English history and literature; it has imbibed the spirit of modern civilisation, epitomised in the activity and energy of the West; it is learning that fundamental law of nations, "self-preservation is the law of life." From her own standpoint, England has not been an unmixed blessing to India, and from ours, she has not proved an unmixed curse. She has taught us the blessings of the wealth she has deprived us of; she has awakened the need for the education she has not given; she has proven the value of the power she dares not bestow. The West has not knocked at the door of the East without response,—we are learning to answer it in kind. Patriotism, Nationalism, Human Brotherhood and the Rights of Man echo around the world to-day, but before these sacred sentiments become truths no less sacred, they must be won, it seems, by right of might.

England says that she had ruled India to India's own best interests, and that we should never have been so prosperous or happy as a nation, as under British rule. Imperial Britain would imply that Englishmen are angels, dwelling in an Utopian dream. Where is the human being above self-interest and greed? Where is the man who will not wield his power to his own ends? One may meet such individuals, though they are rare; but to seek for a nation so disinterested as to rule another in the best interests of the latter, is futile. It is time England, as well as India, faced the situation squarely and accepted it for what it is, or make a better one.[11] There has never been sincerity in the relationship of foreign ruler and native ruled. The farce of paternalistic dominance must end, and some clear adjudication be made of respective rights and obligations, else a grim tragedy will be enacted Under the existing system, a thin stratum of government officials. drawing princely salaries,— lawyers, bankers, constructors and stock-exchange traders,— may ignore the humiliation of their position, and consider themselves benefited by British rule. But the majority of them are sullen and discontented, feeling themselves for what they are — parasites, battening on the vitals of their motherland. The masses, whether traders, agriculturists or labourers, are being crushed beneath the weight of this pitiless Western Juggernaut. From one-third to one-fifth are insufficiently fed, housed and clothed; ninety per cent. are illiterate; truly, if "to be weak is miserable," their helplessness makes them most wretched. The very efforts of Englishmen themselves to succour them have failed, under the present inexorable régime.[12] The

[11] "The connection between England and India is a political anomaly that has no parallel in history. Calling the Indians 'our fellow subjects' is misleading." ("Colonies and Dependencies," Macmillan & Co., 1883.)

[12] Says Mr. Thorburn, late Financial Commissioner of the Punjab (p. 349): "Looking back for twenty-five years, remembering the causes of the Afghan War of 1878–80, the straining of our relation with the Amir, 1890–93, the subsequent thrusting of 'friendly relations' and a protectorate upon the independent tribes beyond our frontier, the enforced delimitations of some of their hinterlands, the futile consequential wars of 1897–98; unprejudiced minds must recognise that the tax-paying masses of India have received scant consideration, and that some of the heads of Government and subordinate officers answerable for the blunders and wastage of different periods, should have been discredited, instead of

attempt of Lord Crewe to carry his India Council Reform Bill of 1914; the attempt to obtain an Executive Council for the United Provinces under the Government of Lord Hardinge; the effort to repeal the countervailing excise duties on Indian cotton goods, all ended in failure, and demonstrate the hopelessness of ameliorating the system. There is but one panacea for Indian ills; the road may lie rough before us, the march long and dangerous, but the goal lies clear ahead as the *summum bonum* of our national existence: Home Rule, Self Government, Autonomy. This is the end for which we must live, putting our soul's salvation upon the attainment of Liberty, the spiritual heritage of man. Woe to us if we fail! Eternal glory if we succeed!

rewarded. So long as the Government of India is practically an irresponsible despotism, and the Indian public merely a powerless mass of uninformed and inarticulate taxpayers, muddling misrepresentation and waste in the conduct of Indian foreign affairs will not cease, and high-placed blunderers in authority will never be called to account. Until some force in India arises with the power, the will and ability necessary for securing a commonsense management of affairs, business-like prudence will not always be practised.

"Present methods suit a bureaucracy: unless forced from the outside, reforms from inside are hopeless. Without the certainty that the truth will come out, and be intelligently examined and judged, no government will proclaim its mistakes, or alter its ways." ("Punjab in Peace and War," p. 349.)

APPENDIX A

Extract from an article by A. Yusaf Ali, a retired Indian Civil Servant, published in *The Nineteenth Century and After* for February, 1917:

"The Indian Income Tax brings within its net only 332,000 persons out of a population of 244 millions in British India, the exemption limit being as low as 66 pounds (that is $330). Only 13,000 persons have an income of 666 pounds ($3,330) or over in British India."

The following remarks are made in regard to the Government policy of control of the price of wheat during the war:

"Government policy in the matter was directed towards two objects: (1) to divorce India prices, which by themselves would have been lower, from the world prices. (2) To secure the surplus of India's bumper wheat production last year for lowering the prices of wheat in the United Kingdom. In 1915 the prices broke famine records and went as high as six seers for one rupee in a year when the wheat crops had been splendid and the prices would, in normal times, have been very low."

Mr. Yusaf Ali gives the following figures about the military expenditure of the different parts of the British Empire and its proportion to the total Budget of Revenue:

Military Budget for 1913–1914

	Millions of Pounds	*Percentage to total Budget of Revenue*
Great Britain	28.2	14.5
India	18	22
Australia	2.5	10
Canada	1.5	5
South Africa	1.15	7.7

This is exclusive of the cost of the Imperial Service troops maintained by the Indian Princes at their own cost and used by the British for Imperial purposes.

APPENDIX B

Extracts from an article by Mr. Manohar Lal, B. A. (Cantab), late Minto Professor of Economics in the University of Calcutta, published in the *Indian Journal of Economics* for July, 1916:

"The average income per head has remained the same (that is $10 a year) during the last thirty years and more. . . . It is a fact that deserves careful study at the hands of all students that with signs of growing prosperity everywhere, with an undoubted advance in the whole apparatus of industrial life, the average Indian income has remained stationary. How far this fact involves that a vast proportion of our population can have taken no share in the general urban rise in India, and in view of the undeniable fact of large increases in prices how far it probably has entailed some depression in the economic status of her masses—these are enquiries that must present themselves to every student of economics in the country, and thoughtful Indians have not been able to interpret their bearing in a sense favourable to the country's prosperity.

. . . .

"Poverty, grinding poverty, is a tremendous fact of our economic, and therefore national, position, and it is to the mind of the present writer an immeasurably more potent fact than even the ignorance and illiteracy that prevails among our masses. This poverty exposes us to the havoc of disease and pestilence, famine and plague and it makes advance at every step difficult."

Mr. Monohar Lal then compares the food budget of an English workingman's family, that of a railway carriage washer with that of an Indian field labourer as given by Mr. Keating, an Englishman, in his very careful work on rural economy in the *Deccan* and observes:

"It is a picture of literal starvation mentally, and all but so physically; it can represent the life of no unit of civilised humanity."

Further on, summarising the present situation, he remarks:

"Indian population grows, her earning power per head is stationary, such increase in her industries as has taken place is nothing compared to the growth of her population. The inference is irresistible; life in India continues on the lowest plane, untouched by all the movements and progress that is in the air."

APPENDIX C

How the Villagers Live in the Madras Presidency—An Article from the Tribune of Lahore of January 19, 1917.

In England and other European countries the study of the condition of the working classes has led to their improvement. A similar study of the condition of the Indian people is necessary to devise measures for their economic improvement. The Government were asked several times to hold such enquiries in villages exposed to frequent famines. But they thought that it would serve no useful purpose to do so. In England private individuals and public associations have aroused sympathy for the working classes and Government have readily adopted necessary reforms. It would be useful if similar work was undertaken by individuals and associations in India. A good example has been set in this direction by Mr. S. P. Patro, who read an interesting paper at the Madras Economic Association on the 11th instant. His Excellency the Governor presided. The enquiries were held in 15 villages of the Ganjam District and the places selected were those in which the conditions were alike as far as possible. The people living in the villages were asked certain questions regarding their income and expenditure as also their debts. And care was taken to prevent exaggerated or incorrect answers by verifications of facts supplied by others. After going through the details of assessment, population, number of agriculturists, the income of a typical family, the food consumed, etc., Mr. Patro found that in a particular village the budget of the ryot showed a deficit of Rs. 22–9–0 every year and it was not possible to obtain a full meal every day. Dealing similarly with a typical village in the Chicacolo division, Mr. Patro found that the annual income of a family of a typical zamindar, who had wet and dry lands, was Rs. 129–8–0, and that the expenditure, including cost of rice, oil, clothing, etc., was Rs. 181–8–0, leaving a deficit of Rs. 52 a year. For marriage and litigation the head of the family raised a loan of Rs. 380 in 1907 and discharged the same in 1913 by sale of rice and by living on inferior corn and the profits of rice-pounding. The family had full meals only from January to the month of May according to the statement of the ryot. In a zamindari village the annual income of a typical family was Rs. 316 and the expenditure Rs. 321–6–0 and there was a debt outstanding against the family. In another zamindari village, the income of a typical family was Rs. 786 and the expenditure Rs. 698–4, leaving a balance of Rs. 68 to the credit of the family whose affairs were conducted in a most economic way. That was not a profit, but it represented the wages which the members of the family earned for their personal labour on the land at Rs. 14 a head per year. On these facts Mr. Patro made the following remarks:

"I tried to place before you actual conditions observed in my investigation into some of the villages in the Ganjam district. The investigation commenced more than a year ago, and I do not attempt to discuss the many problems to which the studies give rise. Others will have to draw conclusions and advocate remedies. From the sketches it will be seen how the population is increasing and the actual cultivating owners are decreasing; how the holdings are split up, and the landless labourers are growing, how little improvement is made in agricultural methods and how little possibility there is for improving agricultural methods owing to the growing poverty, physical deterioration and indebtedness of the agriculturist; how the cultivation of the present holdings can never pay and the ryots are sinking lower and lower. The rations available for the agriculturist in some cases are poorer than the diet given to the prisoners in jails. That large number of agriculturists and labourers emigrated to Calcutta, Burma, Straits Settlements and other places is a common factor in all these villages. In the last named village about one hundred out of a population of about 878 have gone out in search of better wages and to work in non-agricultural work. There is therefore pressing need for full enquiry into the economic conditions of the agricultural population in this Province."

These enquiries are very interesting and show the desirability of conducting similar enquiries in other provinces and districts. Punjab is not much different from Madras in regard to the land tenure and general conditions of the agricultural population. We think that the enquiries made by Mr. Patro are of particular interest to us and the fact that the people are sinking lower and lower in poverty is particularly distressing. That some of them receive poorer diet than the jail population is a statement which should suggest the adoption of urgent remedies. Mr. Patro, it will be seen, does not want Government to accept his conclusions but invites further enquiries of the kind. Throughout India educated people are pressing for the reform of land laws so as to improve the condition of the masses, and experienced men have shown how deeply the ryots are sunk in poverty and indebtedness. Mr. Patro's enquiries go to confirm these opinions and to contradict the official theory about the prosperity of the peasantry. In the typical village homes whose family budgets were examined the people had an annual deficit in three out of four cases — a fact which cannot but show the pitiable condition of the agriculturists. His Excellency the Governor expressed his appreciation of the enquiries made by Mr. Patro and admitted that the facts ascertained must be fairly accurate, though no general conclusion could be drawn from them alone.

APPENDIX D

WAGES IN INDIA

The reports and publications of the Government of India do not give sufficient data to enable one to fix the exact position of the wage earner in the national economy. In the latest report on prices and wages the only retail prices given are those of food grains, only one kind of *dal* (pulse) and salt. The report gives wholesale prices of staple articles of export and import, but they are of no help in fixing the wage earner's budget. As regards wages there is also a great deal of confusion. For some districts the wages are given up to 1906, for others up to 1907, 1909, and 1912. In some cases the wages given are monthly ones; in others weekly or daily, rendering it impossible to make comparisons. However, some approximate idea of wages can be gathered from the following tables compiled from the above mentioned report. The Indian currency unit is a rupee. This is divided into 16 annas. Roughly three rupees are equal to an American dollar and an anna is equal to two cents. We give the approximate equation in dollars of the Indian rupee in the table. The wages are given for the various towns mentioned in the report, omitting all reference to Burma.

Bengal.	*Weekly wage of an able bodied agricultural labourer*	*Weekly wage of a mason, carpenter, or blacksmith*
Rangpur	$1.00 (1910)	$1.66 (1910)
Backerganje	$ .82 to $1.00 (1910)	$1.30 to $1.66 (1910)
Calcutta	$1.33 (1917)	....
Patna	$ .49 (1907)	$1.00 (1907)
United Provinces of Agra and Oude.		
Cawnpore 1906	$ .33 to $ .49	$1.66
Fyzabad 1906	$ .16 to $ .33	$ .49 to $ .66
Meerut 1906	$ .35	$ .82
Punjab.		
Delhi 1909	$ .82	$1.66
Ameitsar 1909	$ .79	$2.50
Rawalpindi ...1909	$ .82	$2.33
Sindh.		
Karachi 1912	$1.08 to $1.33	$2.08 to $3.33
Bombay.		
Belgaum 1908	$ .50	$1.16 to $1.33
Ahmadnagar .1914	$ .82	$1.33 to $2.00
Bombay 1912	$1.33	$2.33 to $3.50
Ahmadahad ..1912	$ .66	About $2.00
Central Provinces.		
Jubbulpur 1908	$ .50	$2.50
Nagpur 1908	$ .66	$2.00 to $2.50
Raepur 1908	$ .50	$1.33
Madras.		
Bellary 1907	$ .50	Less than $1.50
Madras 1907	$ .50	" " "
Salem 1907	$ .35	" " "

Postal Runners. Only in one division, that of Sindh, do the postal runners in the service of the Government get one dollar a week. In others they ordinarily get two-thirds of that amount. In some places they receive even less than that. These are the figures for 1914.

Postmen. Postmen, who are also in the employ of the Government and are supposed to be literate, get salaries ranging in amount from \$.90 to \$1.33 per week (1914).

Railroads. In the railroad service (1914) we find the following figures:

Mirzapur-East Indian Railroad.

	Skilled labour	*Unskilled labour*
Carpenter	\$1.00 to \$1.66	\$ .50
Blacksmith	\$1.66	
Permanent Inspector..	\$2.00	

Cawnpore.

Skilled ....\$ .50 Unskilled...Less than \$ .50

Delhi.

Skilled labour from \$1.66 to \$2.30 Unskilled....about \$ .66

Lahore Railway Work Shops.

Skilled Fitters ....\$1.66 Unskilled ....\$ .70
Skilled Carpenters.....\$1.75

Average daily wages paid on canal work, foundries, and workshops:

Skilled labour.................from 7¢ to 16¢
Unskilled labour..........ordinarily below 7¢

Weekly wage paid in a *paper mill in Bengal, 1914:*

Skilled labour: Blacksmiths and Machine men......\$2.50

Skilled	*Unskilled coolies*
Bricklayers, Carpenters, Engine men..from \$1.30 to \$1.50	Men...............\$1.00
	Women.............\$ .60

Weekly wages in a brewery in the Punjab:

Skilled labour from \$1.66 to \$2.30 Unskilled....about \$.66

Weekly wages paid in an army boot factory at Cawnpore:

Foreman	\$2.50
Saddlers	2.08
Machine operators...............	1.70
Fitters	1.40

Carpenters	$1.40
Cutters	.82
Saddler's assistants	1.00
Tanners	.66
Messengers and storemen	.58
Beltmakers	.72
Work distributors	.72

Average weekly wages in a cotton mill in Northern India, 1914:

Men	from $.66 to $.80
Women	.35
Children	$.35 to $.43

Average weekly wages in a cotton mill, Bombay:

Scratcher	$1.00
Grinder	1.30
Card tender	.85
Lap carrier	.92
Fly carrier	.66
Reeler	1.26 to 1.66
Presser	1.50
Binder	1.50 to 3.00
Drawer	1.16 to 2.16
Doffer	.84
Doff carrier	1.00
Spare hands	.84 to 1.00
Warper	2.14 to about 3.00

In the sizing department the wages range from $.84 to $4.00 a week, the sizer and the weaver getting from $1.33 to about $4.00, all the other hands getting about one-half that amount.

Average weekly wages paid in a woollen mill in Northern India, 1914:

Unskilled labour	$ .66
Skilled labour:	

Card room:

Card mistri	$3.33
Feeder	.89
Card cleaner	1.33
Spare hands	.80
Mixer	.80

Mule room:

Head mistri	$4.16
Minder	1.33
Piecer	.66
Spare hands	.84

Finishing department:

Washing and bleaching	$1.50
Dyeing	1.60
Dyer	.84

Weaving department:

Mistry	a little over $2.00
Healder	a little over .84
Weaver	a little over 1.10

Engineering department:

Boiler mistri	$1.35
Engine man	.70
Oil man	.70
Head carpenter	3.30
Turner	a little less than 2.00
Boiler man	.80
Fitter	1.52
Blacksmith	2.00
Carpenter	1.33
Tinsmith	1.25
Leather man	.75

Average weekly wage in a jute mill in Bengal, 1914:

Carding	$ .66
Spinner	1.16
Minder	1.20
Beawer	1.40
Weaver	a little less than 2.00
Coolies	less than .16 per day
Mistries	about .35 per day

Weekly wage in a Cawnpore Saddlery Establishment, 1913–14:

Sirdars	$1.00 or less
Lascars	.50 or .60
Carpenters, workmen	1.00
Painter mistries	1.00
Painter workmen	.83
Tanner mistries	.28
Bullock drivers, Sweepers	.50 or less
Water carriers	.50 or less

There has been no increase in these wages since 1879 in the case of some of these workmen, and none since 1889 in that of others.

WAGES IN GOVERNMENT ESTABLISHMENTS

In *government offices* most of the menials, ushers, and orderlies are paid from $.50 to $1.00 a week.

A *Police Constable* in 1914, got from $.66 to about $1.00 a week. An officer in the *Police Department* started with a weekly salary of about $1.00.

Primary School Teachers in some cases start with a salary of $.66; in others they get from $.82 to $1.00 per week.

Clerks in *Government Offices* start with $1.33 a week.

The disparity between the salaries of the lowest servants and those higher up, and between Indian and European governmental employés may better be studied from the figures given in the next appendix.

APPENDIX E

THE COST OF ADMINISTRATION IN INDIA, JAPAN, AND THE UNITED STATES OF AMERICA

The President of the United States, who ranks with the great royalties of the world in position, gets a salary of $75,000 without any other allowance. The Prime Minister of Japan gets 12,000 yen, or $6,000. The Viceroy and the Governor General of India get 250,000 rupees, or $83,000, besides a very large amount in the shape of various allowances. The cabinet ministers of the United States get a salary of $12,000 each, the Japanese 8,000 yen, or $4,000, and the Members of the Viceroy's Council $26,700 each.

In the whole Federal Government of the United

States there are only three offices which carry a salary of more than $8,000 a year. They are:

The President of the General Navy Board..........	$13,500
Solicitor General..................................	10,000
Assistant Solicitor General...........	9,000

All the other salaries range from $2,100 to $8,000. In the State Department all offices, including those of the secretaries, carry salaries of from $2,100 to $5,000. In the Treasury Department, the Treasurer gets $8,000, three other officers have $6,000 each. All the remaining officials get from $2,500 to $5,000. In the War Department there are only two offices which have a salary of $8,000 attached to them: that of Chief of Staff and that of Quarter Master General. The rest get from $2,000 to $6,000. In the Navy Department besides the President of the General Board mentioned above, the President of the Naval Examination Board gets $8,000 and so does the Commandant of the Marine Corps. All the rest get from $6,000 downwards. In the Department of Agriculture there is only one office carrying a salary of $6,000. All the rest get from $5,000 downwards. The Chief of the Weather Bureau, an expert, gets $6,000. In the Commerce Department four experts get $6,000 each, the rest from $5,000 downwards. These are the annual salaries.

In Japan the officials of the Imperial Household have salaries ranging from $2,750 to $4,000. Officials of the Higher Civil Service get from $1,850 to $2,100 a year; the Vice-Minister of State, $2,500; Chief of the Legislative Bureau, $2,500; the Chief Secretary of the Cabinet, $2,500; and the Inspector General of the Metropolitan Police, $2,500; President of the Administrative Litigation Court, $3,000; President of the Railway Board, $3,750; President of the Privy Council, $3,000; Vice-President of the Privy Council, $2,750, and so on. All these salaries are yearly.

When we come to India we find that the President

of the Railway Board gets from $20,000 to $24,000, and that two other members of the Railway Board get $16,000. Secretaries in the Army, Public Works, and Legislative departments get $14,000. Secretaries in Finance, Foreign, Home, Revenue, Agriculture, Commerce, and Industry departments get $16,000. The Secretary in the Education Department gets $12,000; Joint Secretary, $10,000; Controller and Auditor General, $14,000; Accountant General, from $9,000 to $11,000; Commissioner of Salt Revenue, $10,000; Director of Post and Telegraph from $12,000 to $14,000.

Among the officers directly under the Government of India there are only a few who get salaries below $7,000. Most of the others get from that sum up to $12,000. The fact that the population of the United States consists of people of all races and that there is a constant flow of immigration makes the work of administration very difficult and complex — far more so than the administrative problems in India.

PROVINCIAL ADMINISTRATION

The United States Government has under it 48 States and Territories. Some of them are as large in area, if not even larger than the several provinces of India. The Governors of these States are paid from $2,500 to $12,000 a year. Illinois is the only State paying $12,000; five States, including New York and California, pay $10,000; two, Massachusetts and Indiana, pay $8,000; one pays $7,000, and three pay $6,000. All the rest pay $5,000 or less. There is only one territory under the United States Government, the Philippines, which pays a salary of $20,000 to its Governor General. In India, the Governors of Madras, Bombay, and Bengal each receive $40,000, besides a large amount for allowances. The Lieutenant Governors of the Punjab, the United Provinces, Behar and Burma get $33,000 each besides allowances. The Chief Commissioners receive $11,000 in Behar, $18,700 in Assam, $20,700 in the Central Provinces, and $12,000 in Delhi. The Political Residents in the Native States receive from $11,000 to $16,000, besides allowances. In Japan the Governors of Provinces are paid from $1,850 to $2,250 per year, besides allowances varying from $200 to $300.

The provincial services in India are paid on a far more lavish scale than anywhere else in the world. In Bengal the salaries range from $1,600 for an assistant magistrate and collector to $21,333 to Members of the Council, and this same extravagance is also true of the other provinces.

Coming to the Judiciary, we find that Justices of the Supreme Court of the United States get a salary of $14,500 each, the Chief Justice getting $15,000; the Circuit Judges get a salary of $7,000 each, the District Judges $6,000. In the State of New York the Judges of the Supreme Court belonging to the General Sessions get from $17,500, and those of the Special Sessions from $9,000 to $10,000 each. City Magistrates get from $7,000 to $8,000 each. In India the Chief Justice of Bengal gets $24,000; the Chief Justices of Bombay, Madras, and the United Provinces, $20,000 each. The Chief Judges of the Chief Court of the Punjab and Burma get $16,000 each, and the Puisine Judges of the High Courts the same amount. The Puisine Judges of the Chief Courts receive $14,000. In the Province of Bengal the salaries of the District and Session Judges range from $8,000 to $12,000. District Judges of the other provinces get from about $7,000 to $12,000. The Deputy Commissioners in India get a salary in the different provinces ranging from $6,000 to $9,000 a year. The Commissioners get from $10,000 to $12,000. In Japan, the Appeal Court Judges and Procurators get from $900 to $2,500 a year. Only one officer, the President of the Court of Causation, gets as much as $3,000. The District Court Judges and Procurators are paid at the rate of from $375 to $1,850. It is needless to compare the salaries of minor officials in the three countries. Since the Indian taxpayer has to pay so heavily for the European services engaged in the work of administration, it is necessary that even the Indian officers should be paid on a comparatively high scale, thus raising the cost of administration hugely and affecting most injuriously the condition of the men in the lowest grades of the Government service. The difference between the salaries of the officers and the men forming the rank and file of the Government in the three countries shows clearly how the lowest ranks in India suffer from the fact that the highest governmental officials are paid at such high rates.

THE POLICE

In New York City, the Chief Inspector gets $3,500 a year; Captains, $2,750; Lieutenants, $2,250; Sergeants, $1,750, and Patrolmen, $1,400 each. In Japan the Inspector General of the Metropolitan Police gets $2,500. The figures of the lower officials are not available, but the minimum salary of a constable is $6.50 per month, besides which he gets his equipment, uniform and boots free. In India, the Inspector Generals get from $8,000 to $12,000, Deputy Inspector Generals from $6,000 to $7,200, District Superintendents of Police from $2,666 to $4,800, assistants from $1,200 to $2,000, Inspectors from $600 to $1,000, Sub-Inspectors from $200 to $400, Head Constables from $60 to $80, Constables from $40 to $48 per year. We have taken these figures from the "Indian Year Book" published by the *Times of India,* Bombay. We know as a fact that the Police Constables in the Punjab are paid from $2.67 to $3.33 per month, that is from $32 to $40 per year. The reader should mark the difference between the grades of salaries from the highest to the lowest in India, as compared with the United States and Japan. While in India the lowest officials are frightfully underpaid, the highest grades are paid on a lavish scale. In the other countries of the world this is not the case.

EDUCATIONAL DEPARTMENT

In the United States (we quote the figures of New York City), the lowest school teachers get a salary of $720, rising to $1,500 a year. In the upper grades salaries range from $1,820 to $2,260. Principals of elementary schools receive $3,500, and assistants $2,500. In the High Schools, salaries range from $900 to $3,150, in Training Schools from $1,000 to $3,250. Principals of High Schools and Training Schools receive $5,000 and the same salary is paid to the District Superintendents. The Commissioner of Education in New York gets $7,500. In Japan the Minister of Education, who is a Cabinet Member, gets $4,000, and the lowest salaries paid to teachers range from $8 to $9 per month. In the United States, college professors make from $5,000 to $7,000 per year. In Japan they range from $300 to $2,000. Coming to India, we find that while the administrative officers and even the college professors get fairly high salaries, the teachers in the schools are miserably underpaid.

CONCLUSION

We don't believe there is a single country in the world where the difference between the remuneration allowed to the highest and the lowest officials is so disproportionally marked as in India. Yet we find that there is a tendency still further to increase the salaries of the high officials, European and Indian, while even very slight increase in the salaries of the underpaid lowest servants of the State are most grudgingly given. Moreover, the high officials get allowances almost equal in amount to their salaries. This is not true in the case of the lower officials. The fact is that the British Government in India does not attach enough importance to the common man; his needs are often overlooked in the desire to please the high officials and keep them contented. Considering that every man in India is supposed to have a family, the condition of the lowest officials is most miserable, in some cases almost necessitates corruption. The Government of India must know this, yet they do nothing to remedy the state of affairs. A rise in prices is claimed as a good ground for raising the salaries of the highly paid civilians, but the same weight is not attached to that reason when the question of increasing the salaries of the lower grades arises.

The figures relating to military services in India are not available, but we know that the above remarks and comparisons have as much force in the case of the Military Service as they have in the ones we have cited above.

Note. The Royal Commission on Public Services has actually recommended a substantial increase in the salaries of European officials by the incorporation of what was temporarily allowed to them as exchange compensation allowance, in their salaries as also otherwise.

PROPORTION OF INDIANS IN HIGHER SERVICES — LATEST FIGURES

Total of appointments with a salary of Rs. 200 a month or upward ($66) 11,064. Held by Indians, 42 per cent.

Total of appointments with a salary of Rs. 500 per month ($166) = 4,986. Held by Indians, 19 per cent.

Total of appointments on Rs. 800 per month or above = 2,501. Held by Indians, 10 per cent.

APPENDIX F

FURTHER NOTES

Gold Value of Rupee. Until 1871 the gold value of the rupee except in one year always exceeded 1s. 11d. In 1872–3 it fell to a little over 1s. 10¾d. and thenceforward downward until in 1894–5 it reached 1s. 1d. The difference it made to India may be judged from the fact that the sterling value of the bills paid in England, in 1894–5, was £15,770,533. The rupee equivalent actually paid by the Government of India was 28·9 crores (or 280·9 millions) of rupees while at the rate prevailing in 1872–3 it would have amounted to only 16·6 crores. In this way India suffered a high financial loss. The sterling debt contracted at the time when the value of the rupee was about 2s. was afterwards converted into a rupee debt when the value of the rupee had fallen to 1s. 4d.

Says Mr. A. J. Wilson ("An Empire in Pawn"), p. 26:

"The Indian people pay altogether more now than ever they did. More of the net proceeds of their labour goes every year to pay the foreign debt charges under *one head or another,* because the aggregate of these charges increases."

. . . .

"The official mind has created a cloud-world of its own and looks at all Indian affairs from a point of view so far above everything native, so conventional and entirely bureaucratic, that it is easily able to demonstrate to us *a priori* that Indian populations are happy and flourishing, though millions of them be dead of starvation or to gush about loyalty with a mutiny and massacre hanging on their heads."

(P. 28.) "The Stracheys and men of that official set present only the outside of the sepulchre to view. There is an official India where all is well, an India serenely indifferent to the toiling India, and there is an India composed of nearly 200 millions of toiling and suffering people."

(P. 28.) "The truth of the matter is, that the natives of India are in no sense their own masters in the conduct of their trade any more than in the conduct of their government. Our system of land revenue alone would bring, and does bring them into a state of slavery and abject dependence, almost whether we like it or not."

INDEX

INDEX